"In the city, people of different ranks stand scowling and apart; but when they go to hunt, to fish, or any other sport or occupation in the field, they are fellows. Nature thus makes brotherhood; and if all mankind would study nature, all mankind would be brothers."

Hints to Sportsmen by Dr. E. J. Lewis

"Game is one of the last pure products in the world."

John Bain, Bain of Tarves, Game Suppliers,
Aberdeenshire, Scotland

Contents

Introduction:
The New Game in Town / 1

Ingredients / 7

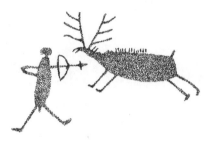

BIRDS / 13

LARGE GAME / 91

SMALL AND EXOTIC GAME / 163

GAME SAUSAGE, PÂTÉ, AND OTHER CHARCUTERIE / 193

GAME PIES AND TURNOVERS / 213

SMOKED GAME / 225

MARINADES AND RUBS / 241

SAUCES / 251

SIDES AND SALADS / 265

American Game Time Line / 288

Supporting America's Native Game / 292

Sharing the Bounty / 293

Mail-Order Sources / 294

Nutritional Data / 297

Bibliography / 299

Acknowledgments / 302

Index / 304

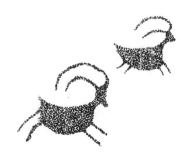

INTRODUCTION
THE NEW GAME
IN TOWN

* * *

Two white-tailed deer

GAME HAS COME a long way since colonial cookbooks listed it between furniture polish and glue.

For the first time since the turn of the century, chefs from Seattle to New York are featuring game dishes on their menus. The old prejudice of game meat being tough as shoe leather is quickly disappearing, since today's game—much of it farm-raised—is tender and flavorful.

While yesterday's lavish restaurants and simple taverns might have offered Chesapeake Bay duck or a saddle of Minnesota venison, much of the game we eat today is not native to America. Game, or "exotics" as some like to call them, has suddenly taken on a whole new meaning—from New Zealand venison to French ducks raised in the San Joaquin Valley. The bison burger served in a roadside New England diner came from a Wyoming ranch. The lean ostrich on the menu in Kansas City was raised in Texas.

Nonetheless, many sportsmen still hunt wild game. Being married to a hunter, I've been cooking wild game for more than thirty years, and eating it for longer than that.

As a child, I loved the plump wild mallards my mother used to roast. But it wasn't until the early years of my marriage that I started cooking game myself. When I was a student, the majority of the meat I ate was the game my husband brought home from fall forays. I learned how to substitute venison in any dish normally made with beef or pork. My husband and I taught ourselves how to smoke game and how to make sausage, proving once again that necessity and hunger are the mothers of invention. From those lean years, we have fond memories of our Saturday night dinners, when we invited other graduate students to our home for a huge pot of savory venison stew and homemade bread. While we no longer depend upon hunting as our only meat source, we still enjoy entertaining family and friends with our game dinners, only these days the menu is likely to include grilled buffalo burgers, ostrich satays, or wild boar chops.

As a longtime game cook, I've watched the recent comeback of game into the culinary limelight with particular interest. Several years ago, a friend told me about a local company that was selling game. Being curious, I called and asked the owner to fax me his mail-order list. I was dumbfounded when four single-spaced typed pages arrived. It included game imported from Scotland and New Zealand, as well as many varieties of game birds and meats raised throughout the United States, including some here in my own state, Oregon.

With my curiosity tweaked, I wanted to know more. What were the differences between wild and farm-raised game? What was Cervena venison? Why is Scottish game so highly regarded? How did we go from a nation of game eaters to a nation of non-game eaters. And finally, why is game making a comeback with chefs and home cooks?

As I began my research, one recent book in particular caught my attention: *Undaunted Courage: Meriwether Lewis, Thomas Jefferson, and the Opening of the American West*, by Stephen E. Ambrose. I was so taken by the author's description of game in the early-nineteenth-century wilderness that I traveled to the prairies and mountain passes that Ambrose so eloquently described in his book. I tried to imagine what it must have been like for the Corps of Discovery in the fall of 1804, as I read how Stephen Ambrose described it:

> The great mammals of the Plains were gathering into herds. Many of them, including elk, pronghorn, and buffalo, began their mass migration to their wintering grounds. Sooner or later on their trek, most of the herds had to cross the river, thereby creating one of nature's greatest scenes. Overhead, Canadian geese, snow geese, brants, swans, mallards, and a variety of other ducks were on the move, honking and quacking as they descended the river. The fowl and mallards were in prime condition, which meant that the buffalo ribs, the venison haunches, the

beaver tails, the mallard breasts all dripped fat into the fire as they were turned on the spit, causing a sizzle and a smell that sharpened already keen appetites.

Seeing the endless prairies and visualizing the infinite number of wild game animals that once roamed the land made it easier to understand how the small group of explorers consumed 9 pounds of meat each day on their trek.

At the famous Buffalo Bill Historical Center, in Cody, Wyoming, I began to understand how the entire culture of the Plains Indians was built around the buffalo. More than one hundred different objects were made for their daily lives from the buffalo: tipis, robes, dresses, shirts, moccasins, leather pouches, medicine bags, shoulder blade hoes, ladles, cups, quivers, saddles, tendons for sewing, bridles of twisted buffalo hair, and so on. In food preparation, as this description written by George Catlin in 1832 explained, the buffalo provided more than just a good piece of meat:

> The dish of "pemican and marrow-fat," of which I spoke, was thus:—The first, an article of food used throughout this country, as familiarly as we use bread in the civilized world. It is made of buffalo meat dried very hard, and afterwards pounded in a large wooden mortar until it is made nearly as fine as sawdust, then packed in this dry state in bladders or sacks of skin, and is easily carried to any part of the world in good order. "Marrow-fat" is collected by the Indians from the buffalo bones which they break to pieces, yielding a prodigious quantity of marrow, which is boiled out and put into buffalo bladders which have been distended; and after it cools, becomes quite hard like tallow, and has the appearance and very nearly the flavour, of the richest yellow butter. At a feast, chunks of this marrow-fat are cut off and placed in a try or bowl, with the pemican, and eaten together. . . . In this dish laid a spoon made of the buffalo's horn, which was black as jet, and beautifully polished.

And equally as important was the spiritual role the buffalo played in their lives. The buffalo was their guardian spirit and lavish ceremonies were held in its honor, including elaborate rites for healing and thanksgiving. Today forty-eight Indian tribes are raising buffalo commercially, an exciting development. The Crow Indian Reservation in Montana's Big Horn Mountains has the largest herd of fifteen hundred head.

In New Mexico, where my daughter and I hiked in the Sangre de Cristo Mountains to learn about the Ancient Ones who subsisted on game, we searched out their petroglyphs of hunting scenes in Sandia Canyon. In Chicago, I discovered that the city's first settler was a trapper, Jean Baptiste Point de Saible. In New York, I was surprised to learn that Brooklyn's Coney Island was named Konijn Eiland (Rabbit Island) by the Dutch, for its large rabbit population.

And in my own backyard I read through the old records of the Hudson Bay Company at Fort Vancouver, Washington, and learned how the fur trade—the search for soft gold—brought the first European settlement to the Northern Territories.

I was starting to fathom the vast numbers of wild game in early America, although it wasn't until I read through old diaries and manuscripts at the Pennsylvania Historical Society that I realized how hunting and eating game were an important status symbol in colonial America to those who had emigrated from Britain where hunting game was limited to royalty and their designees. Shortly after the American Revolution, early lawmakers ruled that the land belonged to all the people, guaranteeing the right and privilege of hunting and fishing to all Americans.

In *Martha Washington's Booke of Cookery,* the journal of recipes passed down to the nation's first First Lady from her mother-in-law, the one recipe that caught my attention was: "Another way to make Beef like Red Deare." After reading other journals from that era, I discovered similar recipes, proving that even though the populations of the burgeoning cities were making the transition to eating domesticated farm animals, game was still highly prized.

Game remained on American restaurant menus until 1918 when the Migratory Bird Act was passed, making market hunting for birds illegal. Americans began to rely on domesticated farm animals for their main source of meat.

Recent years have brought a boom to the farmed game industry. Since fatty diets have been scientifically proven to be unhealthy, consumers are demanding leaner meat. All game, whether wild or farm-raised, is nutritionally impressive—low in fat and cholesterol, yet still high in protein. The savvy game farmers of the '90s do not administer steroids or growth hormones to their animals, making farm-raised game meats a healthy alternative to other meats.

To meet the growing demand for low-fat, naturally raised meat, we have imported a variety of animals from around the world, which have readily adapted to American living. In many states, laws having to do with how animals are raised and slaughtered have been changed to include farmed game, requiring processors to be licensed and pass sanitation inspections before selling their product. All farm-raised game comes under the jurisdiction of the Federal Food and Drug Administration, with voluntary guidelines set by the U.S. Department of Agriculture. The commercial game industry is rapidly expanding, and the market hunters of yesterday—the men who supplied America's restaurants with wild game—are the predecessors of today's astute game farmers and purveyors.

Today's commercial game is raised either on farms or ranches. Farmed game live in controlled environments, which produces animals with a milder taste. Game animals, such as wild Russian boar or axis deer in Texas, are raised "free-range" on ranches. They develop firm muscles and a unique flavor from foraging.

Animals from both farms and ranches are harvested with the same modern processing technology, making them more tender than game harvested by a hunter. And neither will have that "gamy" flavor associated with wild game that has had an adrenaline rush, or has been improperly handled from the field to the kitchen. With the consistently high quality of commercially raised game, it's no surprise that the popularity of game is rebounding.

In addition to the ready availability of locally raised game, modern transportation makes it possible to import top-quality game meat from around the world. In New Zealand, I spent a day riding on a three-wheeler through the lush Canterbury Plains to witness firsthand how deer are farm-raised there. In Scotland, I tagged along with a game buyer, checking the larders of the great hunting estates from which they buy their supplies. In both countries, I was impressed with the high quality of game being shipped throughout the world.

I have learned we can also buy kosher game, Chinese-style ducks (sold with head and feet on) in Asian markets, and wild goat from Australia, imported for our swelling Latino community. The availability of commercial game today is as varied as our population.

When I wasn't traveling, I was home in my kitchen, cooking my way through that extensive list from my local game distributor. For the first time, my husband and I discovered the pleasures of buffalo, guinea hens, muscovy ducks, nilgai antelope, and fresh caribou.

Because of the wide selection of high-quality farm-raised game now on the market, the time is ripe for an updated look at cooking game. Few cooks realize how extensive the supply is and even fewer know how to cook game properly.

Wild About Game is divided into chapters based on the type of game, e.g. birds, large game, and small and exotic game. At the beginning of each chapter is a complete discussion of each type of animal—both wild and farm-raised—including what these animals eat, how and where to buy them, plus how to cook them.

Following these are the recipes—the best part. Some are for farmed game, while others are new twists on wild game dishes that I've cooked for more than thirty years. All the recipes have been tested; I've provided suggestions for non-game substitutions, such as Cornish hens for squab or pork tenderloin for venison, where applicable.

Other chapters include recipes for smoking game, marinades, rubs, stocks, sauces, and accompaniments. In the back of the book is a list of distributors and producers of game meat. Many will ship meat by mail order.

As we reach a new century, game has come full circle. For centuries, it was harvested from the wild as Americans' only source of meat. Over the years, it disappeared from many of our plates. Now it's back—more sophisticated than ever thanks to restaurant chefs' innovations—just when we needed a protein source that is lower in fat and healthier for us.

INGREDIENTS

Nez Perce woman making pemmican, a form of dried meat

⸛ ⸛ ⸛

AMERICAN GAME HAS a natural affinity for many of the indigenous foods of the New World. Wild mushrooms, fresh berries, roasted nuts, and the assertive punch of spicy chiles highlight the unique flavor of game, but there are a variety of other ingredients to consider as well.

A simple guideline to follow is to cook game with white meat with ingredients that will not overpower its delicate flavor; match the more intensely flavored dark game meat with more assertive ingredients. The two exceptions to this rule are rabbit and guinea fowl, which like chicken go with a wide range of flavors.

The seasons help me determine what ingredients to use. In the fall, I pair game with wild mushrooms, fresh chiles, apples, pears, persimmons, huckleberries, and nuts; in the winter, with root vegetables—celeriac, carrots, turnips, and sweet potatoes, as well as potatoes, cabbage, high-quality dried or frozen fruits, and spicy fruit preserves; in the summer, fresh berries and tree fruits—cherries, mangoes, nectarines, and peaches; and in the spring, asparagus and morel mushrooms. I use more spices in the cooler months and more fresh herbs when it is warmer, and I can't emphasize enough the importance of using the freshest of both.

BEANS

Game and dried beans have a mutually beneficial relationship when they are cooked or served together. The beans absorb the rich flavors of the game, while the dense meat is moderated by the soft-textured legumes. There are many varieties to choose from, but a few of my favorites are Great Northerns, pintos, flageolets, cannellini, and black beans. I keep a ready supply in my pantry year-round.

Rinse and sort the beans in a large pot, discarding any that are shriveled or off-colored. Cover 1 pound of beans with 6 to 8 cups of cold water. Soak them overnight, or for the quick-soak method, bring them to a boil and cook for 3 minutes. Turn off the heat and let the beans stand, covered, for 1 hour. Drain and discard the soaking liquid.

To cook the presoaked beans, add 6 cups water or stock, a quartered onion, and a ham hock for flavor, if you wish. Bring to a boil then simmer with the lid tilted until the beans are tender, about 45 minutes to 2 hours, depending on the type of bean.

BUTTER

I use unsalted butter, which is usually fresher than salted butter and allows you to better control the amount of salt in a recipe.

CHILES

The complex flavor of game meat has an affinity for chiles, many of which have berry undertones. A few of my favorites include chipotles—smoked jalapeños—and pasilla, ancho, and the New Mexican red chiles, which I grind and use in rubs.

Dried chiles should always be dry-roasted before they are reconstituted or used in rubs to intensify their flavor. Wear rubber gloves to remove the seeds and membranes. Dry-roast the chiles in a skillet over medium-high heat for 2 to 3 minutes, but do not let them blacken. Cover with boiling water and allow them to soak for 20 minutes. Drain, reserving the soaking liquid, and discard the stem and seeds.

To make a chile puree, puree the pulp of a reconstituted dried chile in a blender or finely chop with a sharp knife. Add a tablespoon or two of the soaking liquid to make a puree about the consistency of tomato paste.

Fresh chiles are also roasted to intensify their flavor, not their hotness, and to remove their skins, which can become tough and difficult to eat when cooked. Grill fresh chiles over high heat until they are completely charred on the outside. Put them in plastic bags to steam for 15 minutes. Pull the charred skin off under running water. Discard the seeds and stems. Cut into long strips.

FRUIT

Fruits and game naturally complement each other, with the sweetness of the fruit counterbalancing the richness of the meat, and vice versa. I use fresh-from-the-tree fruits and berries when they are available. During the off-seasons, I buy high-quality frozen fruits and berries and thaw them in a single layer on a paper towel for 20 minutes. When using fruit in a game dish or accompanying sauce, take care not to overcook them or they will fall apart. Soft berries, like blackberries, raspberries, and black raspberries just need to be warm throughout. Dried fruits, such as dried sweet cherries or figs, can be substituted for fresh in sauces. They do not need to be reconstituted.

HERBS

Fresh herbs are readily available in most supermarkets. They enliven game dishes by adding a layer of intensity and a welcome splash of color when used as garnishes. Substitute one-third of the amount of dried herbs for fresh.

Always buy dried herbs, such as oregano and thyme, whole, when they are available. Crush them in the palm of your hand before adding them to the dish. Whole herbs remain fresh longer than ground herbs.

LENTILS

There are many different types of lentils, but for their flavor and texture, I prefer the small French dark green lentils, sometimes called *Le Puy*. They can be difficult to find. I buy them at my favorite neighborhood delicatessen.

MUSHROOMS

The earthy flavor of mushrooms adds a complexity and richness to all game dishes. Like game, there are a variety of mushrooms available with a wide range of flavors. I use the more delicately flavored mushrooms—commercial mushrooms, crimini, and chanterelles—with mild-flavored game, such as rabbit and pheasant, and stronger-flavored mushrooms—porcini, shiitakes, morels. and portobellos—with heartier-flavored game, such as venison and buffalo.

Buy fresh mushrooms that are heavy, firm, and without cracks or tears. Mushrooms that are open are mature and will have more flavor than button mushrooms. Clean with a brush, damp cloth, or a quick dunk under running water. Trim off the ends (discard the entire tough stem of shiitakes) and cut into $1/8$- to $1/4$-inch slices. Wild mushrooms are expensive, so I often use half wild mushrooms and half domestic mushrooms.

Always brown fresh mushrooms in butter or oil to bring out their natural flavor before adding them to soups or stews.

Dried mushrooms are intensely flavored and are good additions to sauces and stews. Reconstitute them before using by soaking for 15 to 30 minutes in water, wine, or stock. Strain the liquid to get rid of any grit that may have been on the mushrooms and use the soaking liquid when possible.

NUTS

Roasting nuts before they are added to game dishes, salads, and baked goods brings out their flavors. Heat intensifies the flavor of their natural oils, just as lightly browned butter is more flavorful than uncooked butter. In general, most nuts can be roasted at 400°F for 8 minutes, with the exception of dense nuts, such as hazelnuts. Roast hazelnuts at 275°F for 20 to 30 minutes, or until their skins crack. To remove as much of the skins as possible, rub the nuts with a rough dish towel or between your hands.

SALT

I use coarse kosher salt, which is sold in 3-pound boxes in the kosher ingredients section of the grocery store. It is half as salty as regular table salt, but has a pure, clean taste.

SPICES

Dry-roasting whole spices before grinding them intensifies the flavor of their natural oils. I use a 5-inch cast-iron skillet placed over high heat. For instance, put a heaping $1/2$ teaspoon of whole cumin seeds in a small skillet over high heat. Gently shake the pan as they toast. When they start to brown and pop, remove them from the heat. Grind in an electric coffee grinder reserved specifically for this purpose or in a small food processor.

Freshly ground black pepper adds a spicy pungency to game dishes instead of the flat flavor of preground pepper. Buy either Tellicherry or Lampong peppercorns.

Paprika is made from a variety of sweet pimiento peppers that are grown in

Hungary, Spain, California, and South America. Its characteristic flavor ranges from mild to hot and spicy, the color from brilliant red to a dark blood-orange. I prefer mild paprika, commonly sold as "sweet paprika," because it complements game dishes without overpowering them.

Like all spices, paprika should be replaced when it gets old, at least once every 6 to 8 months. I order it from a company in New York (see Mail-Order Sources, page 294, for the address and phone number).

Beware of using too much spice on game. The flavor of venison, for instance, is lost when the meat is coated entirely with a black peppercorn crust. The seasoning on game should enhance the flavor, not overpower it.

STOCK

I use the homemade Chicken Stock (page 264) or Black Chicken Stock (264), but low-sodium canned chicken broth or beef broth can be substituted.

WINES

The best wines to complement the unique flavor of game come from game territory—the Pacific Northwest, California, Australia, New Zealand, and France. Which one to serve depends upon the game you are cooking and how you are preparing it.

I'm not a wine expert, but I am a devoted wine drinker and wouldn't think of eating a game dinner without a nice bottle of wine to enjoy with it. I have concluded, after thirty years of trial and error, that the secret of pairing wine and game, or any food for that matter, is balance. If I simply serve wine with the same flavor intensity as the game I am cooking, I will have made a successful choice.

For example, I pair mild-tasting game, like rabbit and pheasant when they are simply prepared, with a dry pinot gris or medium-bodied pinot noir. If their preparation is spicy, I'd serve a peppery zinfandel, to stand up to the bold flavors. With red meat game I want a more assertive wine. If I grill or roast venison, for example, I like a merlot or cabernet sauvignon, but if I'm serving a savory stew, I pull out the big bullets—hearty pinots, syrahs, and Bordeaux.

When summer heats up, I switch to the cool crispness of full-bodied chardonnays and dry rieslings to serve with grilled game piled high on a heap of salad greens.

In the very simplest of terms, the wine and food must complement one another— you are looking for that perfect balance. If you ask your wine merchant for help, be sure to explain not only what type of game you are cooking, but how it is going to be prepared.

BIRDS

Black Chicken · Dove · Wild Duck · Farm-Raised Duck · Wild Goose

Farm-Raised Goose · Wild Grouse · Farm-Raised Grouse

Farm-Raised Guinea Hen · Wild Partridge · Farm-Raised Chukar Partridge

Wild Pheasant · Farm-Raised Pheasant · Wild Pigeon · Farm-Raised Pigeon

Wild Wood Pigeon · Farm-Raised Poussin · Wild Quail · Farm-Raised Quail

Ratites (Ostrich, Emu, Rhea) · Common Snipe · Wild Turkey

Farm-Raised Wild Turkey · Woodcock

Three men and a dog hunting turkeys

G AME BIRDS ARE one of life's greatest gustatory pleasures. They come in all shapes and sizes with an equally diverse range of flavors, from the delicate white meat of pheasant to the rich dark meat of squab. And because all the birds have their own unique flavor, simple recipes are just as delectable as the most complex, making game birds ideal for beginning game cooks.

Not too long ago a good friend of mine from the Midwest, who had never cooked a game bird before, called me. A hunter had given her two wild ducks and she wanted to know how to cook them. I gave her my standard wild duck recipe, and the next day she reported back the humorous results. As the birds began to roast, they started to emit a strange fishy smell. At first, she lit a few scented candles, then a lot of candles. She was sure the neighbors thought they were having some kind of séance. Next they opened windows, not something normally done in Iowa in January. Finally, when she and her husband just couldn't stand it any longer, she took the ducks out of the oven and set the pan outside her back door in the snow, thinking she would put them in the garbage in the morning. But not everyone thought those birds smelled funny. While closing the kitchen window, she spotted the neighbor's black standard poodle happily gnawing on those odd-smelling birds.

The next day she phoned the hunter to find out where those birds had come from. Sure enough, they were fish-eating ducks. The lesson in this story is that ducks have discriminating palates, too, so it is essential to know not only what type of bird it is, but where it came from.

Knowing where the birds were shot should tell you something about their diet, and whether they are birds you want to eat. Birds that live on the coast and eat a diet of fish, such as mergansers and coot, will have a fishy taste and no amount of marinating will make them palatable. Not all waterfowl, however, is fishy tasting. The flavor of wild duck will vary, depending upon whether its diet consists of marine life (clams, fish, snails) or vegetation (seeds, sprouts, corn), or a combination of both. The birds with the finest flavor, such as mallard or canvasback ducks, are primarily vegetarians, depending on where they find themselves. A widgeon along the coast will have a fishy taste, but if it is shot inland, it will be delicious. And, as we learned from my friend in Iowa, there are inland fish-eating ducks, too.

To avoid an unpleasant mistake, identify the species and its probable diet before you start plucking. Many cookbooks suggest soaking a fish-eating bird in an acidic solution, such as wine or water mixed with lemon juice or vinegar. Although this may help mask the fishy notes, nothing will completely eradicate their characteristic flavor.

For practical purposes, wildfowl are divided into three main classifications: waterfowl, upland, and migratory upland birds. Waterfowl include ducks and geese—those birds associated with wetlands. Upland game birds are birds that are not waterfowl and not associated with wetlands—pheasants, quail, grouse, partridge, and sometimes turkeys (some states consider turkey large game). Migratory upland game birds are non-water birds that migrate from one region to another and include mourning doves, band-tailed pigeons, woodcock, and sandhill cranes.

How the birds are handled from the field to the kitchen is just as important as cooking them properly. Hunters should follow a few basic rules for all fowl. Once the birds have been shot, eviscerate as soon as possible and keep them cool to decrease the chance of spoilage. Any puncturing of the digestive tract by BBs releases the bacteria normally found in the intestine. These bacteria multiply rapidly at warm temperatures and spoil the meat.

Many hunters like to age their upland game birds by hanging the unplucked birds by the neck in a cool place. Hanging serves two purposes: to develop the flavor of the bird and to tenderize the meat. Enzymes in the muscle cells are released when animals are hung or aged that break down the surrounding tissue, making it both more tender and flavorful when it is cooked.

In cold weather, game birds can hang outside for up to 10 days; in damp and warm weather, no more than 3 to 4 days. The aging process is not a rigid procedure but a matter of individual taste. Europeans age their birds longer than Americans and Canadians do, which produces a more intense, "high" flavor. This ancient practice is a virtue that likely evolved out of necessity, a result of tastes becoming accustomed to strong-flavored game before the days of refrigeration.

There are several different methods for removing the feathers. You can pluck birds either dry or moist. Dry plucking is the easiest, but certain fowl with delicate flesh, such as geese, must be dipped in warm sudsy water before plucking. When plucking, pull the feathers in the direction they grow to avoid tearing the skin.

Removing the breasts and legs is preferable for some wild birds, such as pheasant, which have especially delicate skin that tears easily. Pluck a narrow row of feathers the length of the breastbone. Insert the tip of a boning knife flush against the breastbone and cut off the breast meat, pulling as you go. Repeat for the other side and separate the breast meat from the skin and feathers. Cut the legs and thighs off at the joint and trim away the skin. Skinless meat needs to be cooked in a sauce or with butter, oil, or bacon fat to keep it moist.

Once the birds have been drawn, hung, and skinned or plucked, they are ready to be cooked or frozen. Skinned birds should be thoroughly wrapped airtight in plastic wrap, then double-wrapped in freezer paper and frozen at 15°F, or lower. They will keep at this temperature for 1 year before they begin to lose their fine flavor.

Cooking wild birds is always a gamble because determining their age is difficult, with the exception of a few upland game species. Young male pheasants (cocks) have a spur on the back of their legs that is pliable and blunt at the end. Adult cocks have spurs that are firm and pointed at the ends. Both young pheasant and grouse have bills that are more pliable than older birds. If you pick them up by their lower jaws and they break, you will know the birds are young. Young partridges have a breastbone that breaks easily and have yellow rather than blue-gray feet.

In general, wild birds are cooked either hot and fast or slow and low. The breast meat from a wild goose, for instance, should be either quickly sautéed over medium-high heat or slowly braised. Roasting whole wild fowl—instead of breasting the birds—extracts flavor from the carcass, and the carcass helps maintain moisture. If you wish, lay a meaty piece of bacon or two across the birds' breasts. This technique, called barding, adds flavor and helps to keep the birds moist by acting as automatic basters. If desired, remove the bacon for the last 15 minutes of roasting to allow the skin to become crisp.

Always warn your guests to bite gently into the meat and to be on the lookout for stray BBs. This especially applies to all imported Scottish game.

Scientifically, wild and farm-raised birds are the same, but when it comes to cooking them, they are as different as a flock of turkeys from a covey of quail. Farm-raised birds are less risky to cook because you know what you are getting. They are harvested at a young age, which ensures tenderness and takes the guesswork out of how long to cook them. This, plus their nonmigratory lifestyle and regular food supply, produces tender plump birds that taste more delicate than their wild counterparts. Some cooks miss the "wild" taste in these birds, others find it a blessing. I like both and find that farm-raised birds are a good way to introduce game to people who have never tried it before.

When buying game birds it is essential to purchase them from a reliable source. Buy birds that are plump and moist looking, without tears in the skin. If the birds are frozen, allow them approximately 2 days to thaw in the refrigerator. To defrost them quickly, submerge them in their wrappers in a large bowl of cold water. Change the water every 30 minutes. Never use warm water, which would encourage the growth of bacteria. Or, thaw the birds in the microwave according to the manufacturer's instructions, but cook the birds immediately. For safety, never store microwave-thawed birds for later use.

Many farm-raised birds, such as ducks, guinea hen, pheasant, squab, and quail can be roasted or braised just like chicken while others—like ostrich or emu—are best cooked for just a few minutes over searing hot heat. The best cooking method for each type of bird can be found in the following pages.

⚬ BLACK CHICKEN ⚬

Black chickens, marketed as "black silky chickens," are not named for their feathers, but instead for their black skin and bones. This unusual species of bantam chicken are sold almost exclusively to the Asian population who for centuries have cooked them for their curative powers. Traditionally, these farm-raised small chickens are used for making stock that is drunk as a cure for high blood pressure and, after childbirth, as an energy-inducing tonic. Barbara Tropp, noted authority on Chinese cooking, calls them "Chinese penicillin." Black chickens are steamed and stewed on their own but the rich meat is drier than the fattier chickens we are used to. While the birds are scrawny and unappealing to look at, they produce a rich, yellow stock that is so highly regarded, it is featured on the menu of the most famous dumpling house in Taipei.

AVAILABILITY: Frozen year-round.

HOW TO BUY: Black chickens are sold whole, 1 to 2 pounds in weight, with the head and feet on.

BEST COOKING METHOD: Black chickens have little meat and are best used to make stock or soups. One black chicken makes 3 cups of stock.

DOVE

Doves and pigeon are members of the same family, and their names are used interchangeably. In general terms, doves are smaller than pigeons with longer tails. The young of both are called squab.

For hunters the mourning dove is a favorite game bird in early fall. These small birds, named for their plaintive call, are widespread and the most common native dove on the continent.

Dove have succulent dark meat. Serve 1 to 2 per person. Substitute in any quail, or pigeon recipe.

BEST COOKING METHODS: Roast, braise, broil, or grill.

WILD DUCK

Of the 109 species of wild ducks worldwide, 44 live in North America. They are good swimmers and fliers, and always nest and breed near water.

American wild ducks are divided into three groups—dabbling or surface feeding, diving, and tree ducks. The most important group gastronomically are the dabbling ducks, named for their habit of tipping their bodies under the water with their tails sticking up to graze on vegetation in shallow waters. It includes some of America's most popular game birds—mallards, pintails, gadwalls, shovelers, black ducks, widgeon, and teal, to name a few.

Diving ducks are subdivided into two groups, bay ducks and sea ducks. Bay ducks, which prefer peaceful estuaries and lagoons, include the delicious canvasback duck, regarded as one of the finest wild ducks for eating because of its preferred diet of wild celery (commonly called eelgrass). Other bay ducks in this group, such as the scaup, are less discriminating, and their diet of marsh vegetation often can make their meat unappetizing. Sea ducks include the buffleheads, scoters, eiders (from which eider down comes), and mergansers, even though mergansers spend most of their time in freshwater, instead of saltwater, eating fish. Sea ducks eat a variety of food from mollusks to fish.

Bird Hunting on the Delaware

Tree ducks, such as wood ducks (also known as Carolina ducks) inhabit woodland areas and often nest in trees. They have long legs and necks and are better divers than swimmers. Their diet is varied and chiefly vegetarian. In fact, in areas where there are rice fields, they are known as pests. Cooks relish the fine taste of these colorful birds.

In early America, ducks were an important part of the lives of the Native Americans, providing meat, feathers for decoration, and down for domestic use. Typically the birds were roasted or stewed, but the Seminole Indians in Florida had their own unique method for cooking them. They individually wrapped the day's catch of ducks, feathers and all, in clay gathered from the riverbank, and put the clay-wrapped ducks in a smoldering fire to cook. When they returned, the fired clay was broken open. The feathers stuck to the clay and the birds were ready to eat.

Until the turn of the nineteenth century, wild ducks were commonly hunted for restaurant fare. Market prices varied from five to twenty-five cents a bird, with hundreds of thousands bagged every year. Fortunately, national and state laws enacted in the early 1900s prohibited the commercial hunting of wildfowl, saving many species from extinction.

Today, duck hunting is still popular in many regions of the United States but the number of birds shot, based on their sex and species, is strictly controlled by individual state departments of fish and wildlife.

BEST COOKING METHODS: My cousin in Nebraska calls duck "flying liver," because the deep reddish to brown color of uncooked duck does resemble liver. Ducks are constantly using their muscles flying and have large amounts of myoglobin, a red iron-containing protein of the muscles that stores oxygen. When ducks are properly cooked, the similarity to liver ends.

Allow one-half duck per person. Bring the ducks to room temperature. Remove any remaining pin feathers (a strawberry huller works well for this), and cut off the neck. Dry the ducks, including the cavities, with paper towels and season with salt and freshly ground pepper. Follow the recipe for Roast Wild Duck (page 42).

For boneless wild duck breasts, season the meat with salt and freshly ground pepper and sauté them over medium to high heat in a small amount of olive oil or butter until they are golden brown on the outside and the juices run a rosy color. Discard any accumulated fat and deglaze the pan with $1/4$ cup brandy, stirring constantly to release the caramelized cooking bits that stick to the bottom of the pan.

FARM-RAISED DUCK

The first domestic European ducks were introduced to North America by Spanish explorers, and by the Pilgrims, 150 years later. Ducks were highly prized, not only for their fine-tasting meat and useful fat but also for their down and feathers.

It was the offspring of those domesticated European ducks that provided the stock for the birth of the duck industry on Long Island, New York. The availability of good farmland, ready access to water, and a nearby market (the entire east coast) made the area attractive to duck farmers. By the beginning of the eighteenth century, Long Island ducks and geese had already developed a favorable reputation in New York City markets, but it wasn't until the mid-1800s that the industry began to flourish, due in part to the growing demand for ducks from Chinese immigrants. The birds were transported to New York City on the Long Island Railroad, packed twenty-five to thirty to a barrel with ice that was cut from ponds during the winter and stored in ice houses.

In 1873, M. J. E. Palmer of Stonington, Connecticut, in conjunction with a local trading company, brought a small flock of white Pekin ducks, also known as Peking ducks, to America on a clipper ship from China. These prized birds rapidly became the favorite of duck breeders for their fast growth rate, prolific egg production, and ability to live away from water.

By the 1970s three-quarters of all the white Pekin ducklings in the United States were being raised on Long Island by fifty duck farmers. But with sprawling urbanization, the industry began to shift to the Midwest. Sixty percent of the nation's duck farmers are now in Indiana and Wisconsin while the rest are divided among Long Island, California, and Pennsylvania.

The diet of farm-raised ducks has changed in the last sixty years from grass, seaweed, and corn to corn, soybean meal, and bran fortified with vitamins and minerals. Through genetics and better nutrition the birds are ready for harvest in 6 weeks, the equivalent age of a broiler chicken, instead of 14 weeks. The demand for duckling has been directly proportional to the increase in the Asian population in the United States. More than 17 million white Pekin ducklings are harvested each year. (A duckling is a young duck, 8 weeks or less. Since all ducks are marketed at a young age, duck and duckling are used interchangeably.)

Although white Pekin ducklings have a large amount of fat directly under their skin, there is no intramuscular marbling. Without the skin, the lean flesh has only 2 percent fat. The meat is delicately flavored with a lighter-colored flesh than either the moulard or muscovy duck.

Until recently, white Pekin duckling was the only duck served in American restaurants, but muscovy duck is gaining in popularity because American chefs like them for their plump breasts and distinctive flavor.

While all other domesticated ducks originated from the wild mallard, muscovy ducks are a distinct species of tree duck that came from the jungles of South America. They are named after the birds' musk gland that gives their meat a musky flavor when they are eaten during mating season. These birds are the largest of all domestic ducks with a plump turkey-like breast. They hiss like geese and have claws that allow them to roost like chickens.

These unusual birds were domesticated by South American Indians more than two thousand years ago. Early Spanish explorers liked them so much they took some home on their return voyage to Europe. Today muscovies are one of the most popular ducks in Europe. More than 70 percent of the ducks consumed in France are descendants of the *canard de Barbarie,* or the muscovy duck.

One American producer of muscovy ducks, Grimaud Farms of California, imports three thousand fertilized muscovy duck eggs every eighteen months from France. The ducks are naturally raised on a diet of wheat, corn, and soy and without hormones and antibiotics. The males are harvested at 12 weeks, or 8 pounds dressed, while the females are harvested at 10 weeks or 4 pounds dressed.

Both the muscovy duck and moulard, a cross between the Pekin and muscovy ducks, are used for making foie gras in the United States where it is illegal to use geese, the common foie gras–producing bird in France.

A magret is the succulent breast meat from any duck used to produce foie gras.

Although there is a thick layer of fat over the meat, there is little intramuscular fat, which makes this intensely tasty meat prized by cooks.

A few producers are raising mallard ducks that are marketed as Col-Vert, their French name.

AVAILABILITY: Muscovy, fresh and frozen year-round; moulard, fresh and frozen year-round; white Pekin, fresh and frozen year-round.

HOW TO BUY: One 4-pound muscovy duck hen serves four people; other cuts sold are whole drakes (7 pounds), boneless drake breasts (1³/₄ pounds a pair), boneless hen breasts (1 pound a pair), smoked breast, duck legs, boneless duck legs, duck liver, duck bones, duck fat, prosciutto, confit of duck drumette.

One 5-pound white Pekin duckling for two to three people; other cuts are sold as whole breasts.

One 8-pound moulard duck for seven to eight people; other cuts are sold boneless duck breast (magret: 2¹/₂ pounds), duck legs, and rendered fat.

The shelf life for a fresh domestic duck is 3 days in the refrigerator or 48 hours once it is opened, or up to 6 months if frozen. Duck prosciutto or smoked magret will keep for 3 weeks unopened, 9 or 10 days once it is opened and stored in the refrigerator.

BEST COOKING METHODS: Like chickens, ducks lend themselves to a variety of cooking methods, such as sautéing, grilling, broiling, or barbecuing. The exception is the white Pekin duck (the duck sold frozen at grocery stores), which has a thick layer of fat just under the skin; this is best when slow roasted (page 45).

Grill duck halves over hot coals until the skin is golden brown and the meat is still pink inside, about 20 minutes. Keep water in a spray bottle nearby in case dripping fat causes a flareup.

Score the skin of duck breasts and sauté skin side down, then brown the other side. Finish cooking in a 425°F oven or under the broiler.

For magret (breast from ducks used to make foie gras), score the skin and sauté the duck breast slowly, skin side down, for 20 minutes. Turn the breast over and lightly brown the other side for 5 more minutes.

Roast whole ducks approximately 15 minutes per pound unstuffed.

WILD GOOSE

The United States is the winter home to ten of the world's twenty species of wild geese. These migratory birds are excellent fliers and watching their undulating "V" pattern silhouetted against the autumn sky is always a thrill.

The most common geese in America are the Canadian geese, or honkers. There are seven subspecies in this family, with the birds ranging in size from 3 to 13 pounds. They have different geographic distributions and habitats as varied as their size, such as prairie sloughs, marshes, lakesides, tundra, farmland, and golf courses, to name a few. These geese often winter together in various regions of the United States, but when spring comes they head north to Canada and Alaska to their ancestral breeding grounds, often flying for thousands of miles.

Geese nest near water, but unlike ducks, they forage for food along the water's edge or on the ground instead of diving in the water. Their diet is mostly vegetarian and, depending on the subspecies, they eat stubble, grains and grasses that grow near water.

BEST COOKING METHODS: Braise, roast, or sauté. A 5-pound dressed wild goose will serve four.

FARM-RAISED GOOSE

Geese have been prized farm birds since colonial days for their meat, feathers and down, and fat. They have flavorful dark meat that should not be overcooked.

AVAILABILITY: Fresh around the holidays, frozen year-round.

HOW TO BUY: One 12-pound goose will serve six people; other cuts sold are boneless breast (24 to 28 ounces).

BEST COOKING METHODS: Roast whole, braise, or sauté.

WILD GROUSE

Grouse are members of the family Tetraonidae, which includes eighteen species world-wide with ten indigenous to North America: the ruffed, sharp-tailed, blue, spruce, and Franklin grouse of the upland woods; the sage grouse and two species of prairie chickens of the open terrain; and the ptarmigans, the subarctic cousins in the far north. All birds in this family prefer a cool northern climate.

These chicken-like birds are heavy-bodied and vary in size from the smallest—the white-tailed ptarmigan, about the same size as a quail—to the largest—the sage grouse weighing up to 7^1/$_2$ pounds. All the birds have slightly curved bills and large feet, both necessary for their terrestrial lifestyle and chiefly vegetarian diet of seeds, leaves, berries, and other wild fruits.

A ruffed grouse

Before the arrival of the white man, millions of grouse and prairie chickens inhabited the prairies and upland woods throughout North America, from the Gulf Coast to the Subarctic. These plentiful birds were highly valued for food by the Native Americans, who spoke of them in their myths and commonly used their feathers for decoration. The ceremonial dancing of some tribes even resembles the drumming and spectacular courtship dancing of the sharp-tailed grouse.

The most common grouse today are the ruffed grouse, the principal woodland game bird in the United States. (In New England these birds are called partridges, although they are not true partridges.) Their distinctive territorial drumming is a familiar sound to woodland hunters, but spotting the birds is a different story. Their russet-colored feathers blend almost completely into their woodsy surroundings. Ruffed grouse eat a diet of seeds, berries, and wild fruits, making them one of the best-tasting of all the grouse. In contrast, the spruce grouse and its western counterpart, the Franklin grouse, whose diet consists mainly of conifers, are the least desirable grouse to eat because their flesh can have a resinous flavor.

A pinnated grouse

The sage grouse, also known as the sage hen, is the largest member of the grouse family and the largest upland game bird, weighing almost 8 pounds each. They are indigenous to the Northwest, and the majority of their diet consists of different species of sagebrush.

The much smaller sharp-tailed grouse—known locally as prairie chicken—includes three species that inhabit prairies, open woodland, and brush lands. Their mostly vegetarian diet includes seeds, wild fruits, buds, and other foliage, making them highly esteemed by cooks who enjoy their dark meat.

Prairie chickens, or pinnated grouse, are North American game birds in the grouse family. There are two living subspecies: the greater prairie chicken (*Tympanuchus cupido*), inhabiting the shrinking prairies from southern Canada to Oklahoma, and the lesser prairie chicken (*T. pallidicinctus*), inhabiting the southern prairie states of Texas, Oklahoma, and New Mexico. Both of these chicken-like birds have a diet of insects and grains.

A blue grouse

The ptarmigans (*tar*-mi-gens) are the smallest grouse, ranging in size from 12 to 17 inches tall. Of the three—willow, white-tailed, and rock—the willow ptarmigan (the same bird as the highly regarded red grouse of Europe) is the most widespread. In North America, willow ptarmigans live in the tundra and alpine meadows in Alaska and Canada and subsist on leaves, wild fruits, and insects. Rock ptarmigans prefer rocky land near permanent snows, while the white-tailed ptarmigan is found from Alaska to New Mexico in the Rocky Mountain Range and in the coastal range to Washington.

All three are covered with snowy white feathers in the winter (with the exception of the willow ptarmigan, which has a black neck and red head) and sport autumn-colored feathers in the fall, summer, and spring.

BEST COOKING METHODS: Braise or roast whole; serve 1 bird per person.

⋅ FARM-RAISED GROUSE ⋅

Grouse are exported to the United States from shooting estates in the Scottish Highlands. The main diet of these highly regarded birds principally consists of the young shoots, seeds, and flowers of the lovely deep pink ling heather, which carpets the moors and gives the birds their distinct flavor.

The red grouse became a favorite hunting bird of the royals and nobility in 1892 when Queen Victoria determined August twelfth to be the start of the hunting season by moving her royal court to the Scottish Highlands from London. Since then, the shooting of the first grouse on August twelfth, better known as "the glorious twelfth," has signaled the start of hunting season.

Although exporters of red grouse scan the birds, always look for shot when eating them and warn your guests to be on the lookout for an errant BB.

AVAILABILITY: Fresh from September to early December.

HOW TO BUY: One bird per person; the birds are sold both young (10 to 12 ounces) and old (12 to 14 ounces).

BEST COOKING METHODS: Roast or grill young birds, braise older birds.

⋅ FARM-RAISED GUINEA HEN ⋅

Guinea fowl, guinea hen, pearl chicken, pintade, pintelle, faraona, and African pheasant are all names for the same bird. Its most common name in America is guinea hen, which refers to either the male or female bird.

These scrumptious chicken-like birds are native to the southern two-thirds of Africa and are named after Guinea in West Africa, where they are thought to have originated. One of the seven species in this family, the helmeted guinea fowl, has been domesticated for food since the fourth century B.C. It was eaten by the early Greeks and Egyptians, and subsequently in Italy it is known as *gallina faraona,* or "Pharaoh's hen," from its historic past.

By the sixteenth century, Portuguese traders had brought the birds to France where they were given several names. One was incorrectly *poules de Turquie,* which again was used incorrectly to name the American turkey later in the century. Guinea hens have remained popular in France—more than 50 million are consumed each year—where they are now called *pintade,* from the Portuguese *pintada,* or painted, referring to the birds' unique feathers. These colorful birds with their bold black and white polka dot feathers are often seen at zoos.

While guinea hens are slowly gaining in popularity as food, they are also used like peacocks as "watch birds" in the barnyard, essentially old-fashioned burglar alarms. Award-winning food journalist Waverly Root described their protective warning calls, which can be heard up to a mile away, as sounding like a rusty windmill.

Today a growing number of guinea hens are farm-raised in the United States. The most common are the pearl variety, one of the many variations of the domesticated helmeted guinea fowl. Pearls are large and fast growing, making them ideal market birds. They are raised without hormones on a diet of corn, soy, and wheat and are harvested at 10 to 12 weeks.

Of all the different meats that are said to taste like chicken, guinea hens really do, but I like them better than chicken. Their succulent light-colored breast meat is more flavorful and has more character with a much lower fat content, plus they have a higher meat to bone ratio. And, unlike some game birds, guinea hens do not develop an abundance of tendons in their legs. Even though the leg meat is dark, it is tender and exceptionally rich and flavorsome.

AVAILABILITY: Fresh year-round.

HOW TO BUY: Whole (2 to 4 pounds), buy ½ pound per person; boneless breast, bone-in legs. The legs and thighs will have a slightly bluish look to them.

BEST COOKING METHODS: Use any favorite chicken recipe. A 3-pound bird, for instance, will be cooked in 50 to 60 minutes when roasted at 375°F. The internal temperature should read 185° in the thickest part of the thigh.

❦ WILD PARTRIDGE ❦

The family Phasianidae includes partridge, quail, and pheasants—all chicken-like birds with long legs and strong bills, characteristics necessary for their terrestrial life. Partridges, larger than quail but smaller than pheasants, are native to the Old World and were first imported into the United States in the eighteenth century as game birds.

Of the three species of partridge found in America, the most common is the gray partridge *(Perdix perdix)*, also called English partridge as it is native to England, and known more commonly in America as the Hungarian partridge, Hun, or Hunkie, because it was brought from the wheat fields of the Hungarian plains to the United States. These ground-loving birds inhabit wheat fields, prairies, and open farmlands in the northern United States, from eastern Oregon and Washington to western New York. They feed primarily on seeds and stubble, supplemented by insects. The meat of the Hungarian partridge is darker and has a more delicate flavor than its cousins, the red-legged and chukar partridges.

The red-legged partridge *(Alectoris rufa)*, sometimes called the French partridge as it is indigenous to southern France and Spain (and named, as you might guess, after its red legs), prefers the woodlands and roosts in trees.

Chukar partridges *(Alectoris chukar)*, known as rock partridges, are named for their distinctive call—"chuk-karr, chuk-karr"—a familiar sound near dry river canyons. These birds were introduced to the United States from the Mediterranean and have readily adapted to the warm summer climate of the eastern Pacific Northwest and West. Chukars are fast runners and typically run uphill and then fly down, giving hunters a formidable challenge.

BEST COOKING METHOD: Braise, serve 1 bird per person.

❦ FARM-RAISED CHUKAR PARTRIDGE ❦

Chukar partridges are farm-raised naturally without antibiotics or growth stimulants. They are fed a high-protein diet and are harvested at 22 to 24 weeks. They have lean, light-colored meat.

AVAILABILITY: Fall.

HOW TO BUY: One bird per person (8 to 10 ounces); sold whole or semiboneless.

BEST COOKING METHODS: Braise or sauté.

⚘ WILD PHEASANT ⚘

Pheasant are not indigenous to the United States but were successfully introduced from their native Asia in the late nineteenth century. In 1831, an American diplomat posted in Shanghai, Judge Owen Denny, sent a flock of ring-necked pheasants on a ship from China to his brother's farm in Oregon's Willamette Valley. The birds did not survive and a second flock was sent in 1882. The latter group thrived and similar releases quickly took place throughout the country. The English pheasant, also a native of China, was introduced to England by the Romans, and brought to the United States shortly after the ring-neckeds arrived. The common pheasant found in the United States today is a hybrid of the two.

Today the ring-necked pheasant can be found throughout the United States, excluding the South where the blazing summer heat is unsuitable for the birds.

Pheasant are upland game birds, that is, they do not need to breed near water. They live in farmlands and open fields with brushy cover nearby. Their medium-sized bodies, with long legs and large feet, are well suited to a terrestrial life of scratching for grains, seeds and berries, and insects.

Until the 1980s pheasant were plentiful in the United States, but loss of habitat to development and harsh winters have taken a toll on these popular game birds. A recent boon to the declining pheasant population has come from the Conservation Reserve Program, a federal government program which started paying farmers in 1995 to not grow crops for ten years on highly erodible land to preserve the topsoil. It has left millions of acres undisturbed, providing the birds much needed wintering and nesting grounds. Pheasants Forever (page 292), which began as a regional conservation group in Minnesota, raises money for the protection and enhancement of pheasant and other upland wildlife.

Over the years, many people have unsuccessfully tried to introduce some of Asia's fifty different species of pheasant to America, but there is a recent newcomer that appears to be thriving. The Sichuan pheasant, which looks like a ring-necked without the ring, has adapted to the brushy habitat in the Michigan countryside.

BEST COOKING METHODS: Young pheasant can be cooked as you would chicken, but older birds, because they are less tender, require moist heat, such as braising. Pheasant are fast runners and the many tendons in their legs make them especially tough. If you are not sure of the age of the bird, try this method: Remove the breast meat and partially freeze. Slice the meat against the grain in 1/4-inch slices. Dredge in seasoned flour and fry over medium-high heat in a mixture of half butter and half olive oil. Use the carcass for stock, page 65. Serve 1 bird for two to three people.

FARM-RAISED PHEASANT

Farm-raised pheasant are consistently tender and have a more delicate flavor than wild pheasant. Young pheasant, sold as baby pheasant, are harvested at 6 to 8 weeks, while adult pheasant are harvested at 18 to 24 weeks. The majority are raised outside in flying pens and fed a high-protein diet.

Scottish pheasant are raised on barley (same as grain-fed Japanese Kobe beef), which gives the birds a rich, unique flavor.

AVAILABILITY: Baby pheasant, available midspring to summer fresh, frozen year-round; adult pheasant (2 to 4 pounds), whole and breasts, fresh and frozen year-round; smoked whole pheasant, frozen year-round.

HOW TO BUY: One pheasant (2 to 3½ pounds) for two to three people; other cuts available are boneless breast (8 to 10 ounces), airline breast (wing attached), and boneless thighs. Allow 1 baby pheasant (1 pound) per person.

BEST COOKING METHODS: Sauté or roast young birds; braise older birds.

WILD PIGEON

Pigeons are members of the large family Columbidae of which there are 290 species worldwide. Only eight are native to North America and three more have been successfully introduced. Typically the New World species are shades of gray or brown, while pigeons in other parts of the world are brightly colored.

When the colonists first came to America they found the sky was often black with flocks of passenger pigeons that consisted of more than a billion birds. There were more passenger pigeons in America than any other bird species on earth, but the decimation of forests and overhunting caused the birds to become extinct by the early 1900s.

BEST COOKING METHODS: Roast, sauté, grill, or braise; serve 1 to 2 birds per person.

FARM-RAISED PIGEON

The first domestic pigeons were most likely brought to the United States by the colonists. Today, the most popular farm-raised pigeons are a crossbreeding of the White King and Hubble varieties, which produce squab that are broad-breasted, the most desirable trait in market birds. Adult birds are fed a diet of soy- and alfalfa-based high-protein pellets, whole grain corn, and supplements, while the young birds are fed pigeon milk regurgitated from both parents. Squab or baby pigeons are harvested at 4 weeks just before they begin to fly. Once they have flown, they are called pigeons.

Squab are tender and intensely flavorful with finely textured dark meat. Most squab produced in the United States are sold to Asian markets and Chinese restaurants where they are considered a delicacy.

AVAILABILITY: Fresh and frozen year-round.

HOW TO BUY: One bird (12 to 16 ounces) per person; they are sold whole and semiboneless.

BEST COOKING METHODS: Roast, grill, or sauté.

WILD WOOD PIGEON

Wood pigeons are imported into the United States from Scotland. They are native to the Old World and are commonly seen flying among the trees that line Great Britain's country roads. They are a little larger than a quail with dark, intensely flavorful meat. Wood pigeons are not raised commercially.

AVAILABILITY: Frozen year-round.

HOW TO BUY: One bird (8 to 10 ounces) per person; the boneless breast (5 to 6 ounces)
   is marketed as a "wood pigeon crown."

BEST COOKING METHODS: Sauté young birds; braise older ones.

FARM-RAISED POUSSIN

Poussin is French for a very young chicken harvested at approximately 3$^1/_2$ weeks. Their white meat is fork-tender and delicately flavored.

AVAILABILITY: Fresh or frozen year-round.

HOW TO BUY: One bird (14 to 18 ounces) per person; sold whole and semiboneless
   (8 to 12 ounces).

BEST COOKING METHODS: Roast or grill.

· WILD QUAIL ·

Partridges, quail, and pheasant are all members of the family Phasianidae. Of the three, only the quail subfamily includes natives to both America and the Old World. Quail are migratory birds found in Eurasia, Australia, and Africa, while in the United States, the birds are slightly larger and they are nonmigratory.

Of the six species of quail native to North America—mountain, scaled, Gambel's, California, Montezuma, and bobwhite—only the bobwhite, named for its bobwhite call, is indigenous to the eastern half of the United States where it lives in forest edges, fields, and brushy areas. The bobwhite is the most populous American quail, but in the last thirty years its numbers have dropped by 30 percent due to loss of their habitat and vegetation. The bobwhite is the most popular game bird in the south, where it is called a partridge.

The California quail, while indigenous to California and Baja, have been successfully introduced into some regions of British Columbia, Oregon, and Nevada. They prefer brushy areas, coastal valleys, and oak canyons. Gambel's quail, which look like California quail, prefer the hot desert country of the southwestern United States. They live in desert brush near water sources which they visit mornings and evenings.

Mountain quail, the largest American quail, are similar in appearance to California and Gambel's quail but they inhabit the dense mountainous country of the Pacific Northwest. They breed high in the mountains in summer but walk up to 40 miles to winter in the milder valleys.

Montezuma quail (harlequin quail, Mearns' quail) are the smallest North American quail and have one of the smallest ranges, from southern Arizona and western Texas to Mexico. They inhabit grassy and brush woodland areas in semiarid land up to 9,000 feet.

Scaled quail (blue quail), named after their black and brown feathers which resemble scales, also prefer the arid regions of the Southwest, including parts of Texas, New Mexico, Arizona, and Colorado.

Quail are diminutive birds, each weighing just 5 to 10 ounces, and live in groups called coveys. They eat a diet of seeds, insects, and grain and, like other upland game birds, seldom fly except to escape danger.

These tasty little birds have succulent dark meat. Serve 2 birds (4 to 6 ounces) per person.

BEST COOKING METHODS: Roast, grill, or sauté.

Farm-Raised Quail

The most common farm-raised quail in the United States is the Coturnix quail (Japanese quail), native to Eurasia. They are the only farm-raised bird characterized by hens that are bigger than the males. These fast-growing birds are raised naturally without hormones, on a diet of grain—corn, wheat, and barley—and soybean meal. They are harvested at 6 to 7 weeks. Farm-raised quail are tender, succulent little birds with light-colored meat.

AVAILABILITY: Fresh or frozen year-round.

HOW TO BUY: Quail are often sold four to a package. Buy 2 birds per person; either whole (6 to 8 ounces), semiboneless (4 to 6 ounces), or whole smoked.

BEST COOKING METHOD: Quail can be roasted, grilled, or sautéed but be careful not to overcook these delicate birds.

Ratites (Ostrich, Emu, Rhea)

Ratites (*rat*-tights) are flightless birds that lack a keel bone to which flight muscles can attach. Instead they have a flat, raftlike breastbone (*ratis* is Latin for raft) which supports their long necks. Included in this group are ostriches, emus, and rheas, all relative newcomers to the American table.

The largest ratite is the ostrich—weighing on the average 300 pounds and reaching up to 8 feet tall, making it the largest bird in the world. It is indigenous to Africa where there is a single species, *Struthio camelus,* and four existing subspecies. The East African or Masai ostrich, heavily imported to the United States during the last twenty years and called rednecks here, and the South African ostrich, or bluenecks, are the two subspecies raised for their meat.

The commercial ostrich industry began in Cape Colony, South Africa, in the mid-nineteenth century where the birds were raised for their decorative feathers, which were the fashion rage at the time. Today, the birds are raised for their meat and leather, as well as their feathers. The majority of the world's total ostrich harvest still comes from South Africa, but production in other countries is increasing dramatically. In the United States, the industry started in the early 1980s and has rapidly matured from the breeding stage to a thriving livestock business. Currently there are between 350,000 and 500,000 ostriches in the United States. Texas is the largest producer, followed by California, Arizona, and Oklahoma. Although an ostrich lays thirty to fifty eggs annually until the age of fifty, the demand for American ostrich meat is greater in America than the current supply of a million pounds annually.

Ostriches are adaptable to a variety of climates and are almost always raised outdoors. They are fed a natural diet of pellets made from alfalfa, oats, barley, wheat, and corn. The birds are harvested at 10 to 14 months.

Although ostriches have huge rib cages, they do not have any breast meat. All 75 pounds of meat comes from the tenderloin and ten major muscles in the thighs and legs, which range in size from 2 to 20 pounds. But be aware that the primary muscles in the thigh are convoluted, which causes the grain to change within the muscle 90 degrees. If the meat is improperly butchered, it will be tough, like flank steak that is not cut against the grain, making it essential to buy from a knowledgeable source.

Ostrich is marketed as "the red meat from an egg." The deep cherry red color of uncooked ostrich muscle is due to its high myoglobin content (the protein in blood that carries oxygen to the muscle), making it slightly darker than beef, but with a similar texture and milder flavor. Because there is no intramuscular fat in ostrich meat, its fat content is almost negligible, just 1.2 percent, making it a healthy alternative to other meat.

The emu is the second largest ratite, weighing 130 pounds and standing more than 5 feet tall. It is native to Australia and Tasmania, where there exists the common emu and three subspecies. Like ostriches, they were first imported into the United States in the early 1800s. The meat has a slightly oilier bite than ostrich, but with a finer grain.

The smaller rheas are native to South America and are sometimes incorrectly called South American ostrich. Two species of rheas exist, the common rhea and Darwin's rhea. Both weigh about 50 pounds with a height of 4 feet. Both emus and rheas have delicately flavored, low-fat red meat—1.8 grams fat per 3-ounce portion for emus, 1.2 grams fat per 3-ounce portion for rheas.

The difference between the three ratites is most noticeable in the texture of the meat. The smaller the bird, the finer the texture. All three birds have red meat with a beeflike texture and flavor. The meat should be cooked quickly to rare to medium-rare doneness. Overcooking will make it tough and livery tasting.

Ostrich meat is sometimes sold as medallions or Perfect Portion medallions. These are made from the three most tender muscles rolled together and sold as 7-ounce steaks ($1/2$ to 1 inch thick and 4 inches in diameter) or 5-ounce steaks ($3/4$ to 1 inch thick and 4 inches in diameter).

AVAILABILITY: Fresh or frozen year-round.

HOW TO BUY: 3 to 4 ounces per person. The most tender cuts are the tenderloin (1-pound package), top loin, and fan fillet (4 pounds). Other cuts available are 5- to 7-ounce portioned steaks (two per package), thigh strip steak (good for fajitas, stir-fries, and satays), and ground.

BEST COOKING METHODS: Sauté or grill over hot and fast heat. Warm the meat to room temperature first, otherwise it will take too long to cook. Season with a dry rub or marinade. Serve rare or medium-rare.

COMMON SNIPE

Snipe are known by hunters as jack snipe or formerly as Wilson's snipe. These small shore birds, barely 9 to 11 inches tall, are widespread in most of the northern hemisphere where they inhabit coastal areas and freshwater marshes and bogs.

Their long skinny beaks allow them to probe along the shoreline for crustaceans, freshwater snails, and various types of marsh grasses.

These tiny birds have flavorful, dark meat. Serve one to two birds per person. Snipe are not available commercially.

BEST COOKING METHODS: Braise, broil, roast, or grill.

WILD TURKEY

Wild turkeys are the largest game birds in North America, the males reaching a height of 4 feet. There are only two species of wild turkey in the world: the North American wild turkey, with four subspecies, and the ocellated or Mexican turkey, with three subspecies.

When Cortez reached Mexico in the early 1500s, these huge birds were kept as pets by the Aztecs. He shipped wild turkeys back to Spain several years later. The English were unable to pronounce their Indian name, *uexolotl* (I can't imagine why not), and called them "turkie-birds" after the "Turkey merchants," another name for the Spanish and Portuguese explorers who traded in the eastern Mediterranean.

Before the arrival of the colonists, wild turkeys were abundant in the eastern and southeastern United States, but overhunting and loss of their native habitats markedly decreased their numbers. During the last decade wild turkeys have been reintroduced throughout America by the state departments of fish and game, and today these birds exist in every state but Alaska.

Wild turkeys inhabit a variety of woodlands throughout the United States including pine, oak, mesquite, Douglas fir, and cottonwood forests. While they roost in trees, noticeable by the characteristic hump on their chest, they feed on the ground, eating a diet of insects, seeds, grasses, leaves, and nuts. They spend most of their lives on foot since they are unable to fly long distances.

A wild turkey

BEST COOKING METHOD: Wild turkeys are extraordinarily lean with just 1 percent fat, making them a challenge for cooks. The best cooking method is to put the turkey in a roasting bag and cook in a preheated 325°F oven until a meat thermometer reaches 165°F (approximately 10 to 12 minutes per pound for unstuffed, 12 to 14 minutes per pound for stuffed). Remove the bird from the oven and let it sit at room temperature until the thermometer reads 170°F. Carve the bird as you would domestic turkey. It will have both light and dark meat. One pound of turkey on the bone will serve one person.

FARM-RAISED WILD TURKEY

Farm-raised "wild" turkey sounds like an oxymoron but it's not. Genetically similar to wild turkeys, these birds have a much more pronounced turkey flavor than domesticated turkey. These lean birds have the best features of both the wild and domesticated

An American
woodcock

turkey—intense flavor with substantially less fat than the domestic birds, making them a joy to eat. Wild turkeys are raised outdoors in large pens and eat a natural diet, including weeds. They are harvested at 12 months when the hens weigh 6 to 9 pounds and the gobblers 9 to 13 pounds.

AVAILABILITY: Fresh in November through advance orders; frozen year-round.

HOW TO BUY: 1 pound will serve one person; sold whole (7 to 16 pounds).

BEST COOKING METHOD: Roast as you would a wild turkey (see page 36) or a domestic turkey, basting often.

WOODCOCK

Woodcocks, slightly smaller than robins, are one of our smallest wild game birds. They are members of the same family as snipes and sandpipers. All three are wading birds with long legs and bills and plump bodies. Woodcocks are not available commercially.

There are five species of American woodcock—all of them inhabit the woodland areas of the eastern United States and eat a diet almost entirely of worms.

Woodcocks have intensely flavorful dark meat. Serve one bird per person.

BEST COOKING METHODS: Roast, broil, or grill.

TURKEY SHOOTS

Shooting competitions, known as "turkey shoots," have been an American tradition since colonial days. Competitive shooting as a sport, however, originated centuries ago with archery and crossbows. In the fourteenth century, after the invention of firearms, target shooting became a favorite sport of the European aristocracy. By the sixteenth century, guns, which had become ornate and outrageously expensive, were illegal for commoners, to protect the hunting privileges and lives of the nobility.

In colonial America, guns were required by all men for hunting and protection, an absolute necessity for survival. Every small village, as soon as weather conditions permitted, held shooting matches on weekends and holidays. These competitions drew locals into towns, creating commerce and a welcome social gathering after a week's hard work. Shooting contests quickly became the nation's number one sport, with participants paying a small fee to enter. Since money was scarce, turkeys, pigs, geese, and chickens were given as prizes. For big shoots the prize was beef, a rare commodity in those days. First-place winner got the hind quarters, second place the front, and so on.

As America's wilderness shrank with the swelling of its cities and the settlement of the West, hunting became a sport rather than a necessity. Shooting clubs were established for hunting and target competitions. Although the clubs decreased with the advent of World War I—a majority of the men were off fighting the war—they still exist today all across the country for America's fourteen million hunters. Turkey shoots are still popular but the rewards are simpler now, with a prepackaged turkey being the number one prize.

BRAISED GAME BIRDS: MASTER RECIPE

SERVES 4

Use this recipe for wild or farm-raised partridge, pheasant, grouse, and guinea hen, as well as rabbit and hare. All of these birds and animals have low-fat meat that is enhanced by braising. For an alternative method, in which the meat is taken off the bones and the bones are sautéed for the sauce, see Breast of Wood Pigeon with Mushrooms (page 75).

2 tablespoons olive oil

1 large onion, cut into eighths

5 tablespoons all-purpose flour

1 teaspoon coarse salt, plus more to taste

2 to 3 pounds game birds, chicken, rabbit, or hare, cut into 6 to 8 pieces

2 tablespoons unsalted butter

1 cup homemade chicken stock or reduced-sodium chicken broth

1/4 cup dry white wine

1 teaspoon chopped fresh thyme or rosemary, or 1/2 teaspoon dried

1/2 pound mushrooms, such as chanterelles, sliced

Chopped fresh parsley

Heat the olive oil in a large skillet over medium-high heat. Add the onions and sauté until golden brown, about 8 minutes. Transfer the onions to a bowl and set aside.

Stir the flour and salt together in a shallow bowl and dredge the bird pieces in the mixture.

Melt 1 tablespoon of the butter in the same pan. Add the meat and sauté the pieces until they are lightly browned. Layer the onion over the top and pour in the chicken stock, white wine, and thyme. Cover and simmer until the pieces are tender, 30 to 40 minutes.

Meanwhile, melt the remaining 1 tablespoon of butter in a small skillet and add the mushrooms. Sauté until they begin to soften. Season with a pinch of salt. Add the mushrooms and their cooking juices to the large pan 10 minutes before the game pieces are done. Serve garnished with chopped parsley.

DOVES BAKED IN A
HORSERADISH CRUST

SERVES 4

Paula Lambert is renowned for the fine cheeses she makes at her factory, the Mozzarella Company in Dallas, Texas. But she is also a terrific cook and when her husband brings home doves from west Texas this is one of the ways she likes to cook them.

12 doves, about 3 ounces each
Coarse salt
²/₃ cup prepared horseradish, drained
1 tablespoon brown sugar
2 tablespoons olive oil
2 bunches spinach, stemmed
Freshly ground black pepper
Polenta (page 281)
¹/₂ pound mascarpone

Preheat the oven to 400°F and heat a large platter.

Dry the birds, inside and out, with paper towels and rub the cavities with salt. Place in a large baking dish.

Combine the horseradish and brown sugar, and coat each bird with the mixture. Bake for 10 to 12 minutes, then turn the oven to broil and cook an additional 5 minutes, or until the mask is golden brown.

Heat the olive oil and sauté the spinach over high heat until it is wilted, which will take 1 to 2 minutes. Season with a pinch of salt and freshly ground pepper.

Pour the polenta onto a large platter and flatten with the back of a spoon. Spread the mascarpone over the polenta. Drain the spinach if necessary but leave the juices in the pan. Lay the spinach on top of the mascarpone. Arrange the doves on top of the spinach. Put the pan you cooked the birds in on top of the stove and add any spinach cooking juices. Reduce over high heat for 1 minute and drizzle over the birds. Serve immediately.

ROAST DOVES WRAPPED IN PEPPERED BACON

SERVES 4

Doves have dense, flavorful dark meat that goes particularly well with bacon. Serve these birds on toast that has been cut diagonally in half.

8 doves, about 3 ounces each or quail, about 6 ounces each

1 teaspoon coarse salt

1 teaspoon chopped fresh thyme or $^1/_2$ teaspoon dried, crushed

$^1/_2$ teaspoon freshly ground black pepper

2 tablespoons unsalted butter

8 slices meaty peppered bacon

4 slices of toast

Preheat the oven to 400°F.

Wipe each bird dry with paper towels. In a small bowl, mix the salt and thyme together. Rub the birds inside and out with the salt and thyme seasoning. Melt the butter with the pepper and brush 1 tablespoon of it on the birds. Wrap a piece of bacon around each bird and secure with a toothpick. Pour the remaining butter into a baking dish and place the birds in the dish so that none of them are touching.

Bake for 12 to 15 minutes, or until they are deep brown and the juices run a rosy color when the meat is poked with a fork.

Serve immediately on crisp pieces of toast.

MARKET HUNTERS

Market hunters played a prominent role in feeding America during the 1800s. The wild game they bagged was sold directly to wholesalers, who in turn supplied local markets and restaurants. But their role came to an end during the Theodore Roosevelt administration, when Congress enacted legislation establishing protection for the nation's wildlife. Since then it has been illegal to sell any wild game meat commercially in the United States.

ROAST WILD DUCK

SERVES 4

Serve wild ducks on toast to catch every drop of their succulent juices. Buy a round loaf of coarse-grained French bread and cut pieces approximately the same size as the birds. If the crust is overly tough, remove it before toasting the slices. Serve the birds with the thyme and lemon quarters inside their cavities. The tart, herb-flavored juices cut the richness of the ducks. For smaller birds decrease the cooking time.

4 mallard or other wild ducks, about 2½ pounds each
Coarse salt and freshly ground black pepper
8 sprigs fresh thyme
1 lemon, quartered
Four ½-inch-thick slices coarse-grained country-style French bread, lightly toasted

Preheat the oven to 475°F. Line a roasting pan with foil (this makes cleanup easy).

Pat the birds dry with paper towels. Season them inside and out with the salt and pepper, generously rubbing it into the skin. Divide the lemon quarters and thyme among the birds' cavities.

Roast the birds for 25 to 27 minutes, or until the juices run a rosy color for a medium-rare bird, clear yellow for a well-done bird. Broil for 3 to 5 minutes more to crisp the skin, if necessary.

Serve the birds whole on the toast.

Three canvasback ducks

DUCKY'S GRILLED WILD DUCK

SERVES 6

Dan Duckhorn, owner of Duckhorn Vineyards in St. Helena, California, gave me this great recipe. "One of our favorite meals consists of grilled wild or domestic duck, served with Port sauce," he said. "Allow one-half wild duck per person and accompany it with wild rice and sautéed greens."

3 wild ducks, about 2¹/₂ pounds each
Coarse salt and freshly ground black pepper
Ground cumin
3 tablespoons fresh orange or lemon juice
Ducky's Port Sauce (page 261)

Heat the grill or broiler.

Cut the ducks in half lengthwise and pat dry with paper towels. Season with the salt and pepper and rub with the cumin. Sprinkle the orange or lemon juice over both sides of the ducks.

Grill over very hot coals for 8 to 10 minutes, cut side down. Turn the birds over and grill for another 6 to 8 minutes, or until the juices run a rosy color when the bird is stuck with a fork. Keep a baster with a jar of water handy to keep the flames under control. The breasts should be firm to the touch but cooked until rare to medium-rare for best eating.

Place on a warmed platter, cut side down, and spoon some of the hot sauce over the grilled birds. Put the extra sauce in a gravy boat and serve with the birds.

HISTORIC HARVESTS

According to the Game Transfer Company, records for the San Francisco Bay Area show that 300,000 wild ducks were sold in 1900 for 50 to 80 cents each. Five years earlier in 1895, 47,565 mallards alone were sold at the amazing price of 25 cents per duck!

Fish and Wildlife Resources of the San Francisco Bay Area

Roast Mallard Ducks with Brandied Apples

SERVES 4

Of all the different recipes for wild duck I've cooked, this one is the simplest and the best. The apple and onion slices can be marinated in brandy the night before, leaving little preparation when you are ready to cook. One caveat, though: If the ducks are fatty, they will produce a lot of smoke, so don't try this recipe unless your oven has a good fan.

2 tart green apples, unpeeled, but cored and quartered
2 onions, quartered
$^1/_2$ cup apple brandy
4 mallard ducks, about 2$^1/_2$ pounds each, at room temperature
$^1/_2$ teaspoon coarse salt
1 teaspoon chopped fresh thyme, plus 4 sprigs for garnish
4 teaspoons unsalted butter, softened
2 cups homemade chicken stock or reduced-sodium chicken broth
Freshly ground black pepper

Soak the apples and onions in the brandy for at least 1 hour, or overnight.

Preheat the oven to 475°F. Line a roasting pan with foil (this makes cleanup easy).

Dry the mallards inside and out with paper towels. In a small dish, mix the salt and 1 teaspoon thyme. Rub the cavities of the birds with the salt and thyme seasoning and stuff with the apples and onion quarters, reserving the brandy. Rub the skin of the ducks with the butter.

Place the birds breast side up, not touching each other, in the pan. Roast for 25 minutes, or until the juices run a rosy color for a medium-rare bird, clear yellow for a well-done bird. Broil for 3 to 5 minutes more to crisp the skin, if needed. Transfer the ducks to a platter and place in a warm oven.

Mr. and Mrs. Mallard

Discard the fat from the cooking juices. Put the cooking juices back in the pan with the chicken stock and reduce by half, stirring constantly to release the caramelized bits stuck on the bottom of the pan. Add the reserved brandy and season with salt and pepper. Strain, if necessary. Put the sauce in a gravy boat and serve with the birds, which have been garnished with the thyme sprigs.

SLOW-ROASTED DUCKLING WITH RED CURRANT SAUCE

SERVES 4

I have adapted for homecooks the method that Tom Douglas, chef-owner of The Palace Restaurant, Ettas, and Dahlia Lounge in Seattle, uses for roasting ducklings. What makes the recipe unusual is the long roasting time at 500°F, then an even longer roasting time at 350°F. The former crisps the skin and renders much of the fat from the birds while the latter slowly cooks the meat to perfection. You will need a roasting rack to keep the ducks above the fat that accumulates in the bottom of the pan. Serve with Butternut Squash Risotto.

2 farm-raised ducklings, about 4 pounds each
Szechuan and Green Peppercorn Rub (page 248)
8 garlic cloves, peeled
Butternut Squash Risotto (page 277)
Red Currant Sauce (page 254)

Preheat the oven to 500°F.

Trim the wing tips and neck fat from the ducks and remove the giblets. Pat the birds dry with paper towels, then rub inside and out with the peppercorn rub. Place 4 garlic cloves in each neck cavity. Put the ducks on a rack in a roasting pan and roast for 25 minutes. Reduce the heat to 350°F and roast for an additional 40 minutes, or until the skin is golden brown and the juices are a rosy color. A meat thermometer should read 160°F to 165°F. Remove the birds from the oven and let them rest at room temperature for 15 to 30 minutes before carving.

Carve each duck into 2 boneless breasts and leg/thigh portions. Serve each person 1 breast and 1 leg/thigh. Arrange the duck over the risotto and ladle the hot currant sauce over the duck.

THE CANVASBACK FROM EAST TO WEST

"The canvas-back duck [*Aristonetta vallisneria*] is a most beautiful fowl, most delicious to the palate; it is found in considerable numbers in this neighborhood. It is of the same species with those of the Delaware, Susquehannah, and Potomack, where it is called the canvas-back duck, and in James' River [Virginia] it is known by the name of the shelled drake [sheldrake]. From this last mentioned river, it is said, however, that they have almost totally disappeared. To the epicure of those parts of the United States, where this game is in plenty, nothing need be said in praise of its exquisite flavor, and those on the banks of the Columbia are equally delicious. We saw nothing of them until after we reached the marshy islands [at the mouth of the Columbia.]"

The History of the Lewis and Clark Expedition by Meriwether Lewis and William Clark, 1804

Duck hunting on the Calumet River in Illinois, 1868

DUCK SHOOTING ON THE CALUMET RIVER. SKETCHED BY CHARLES KUNE. [SEE PAGE

ROAST PEKIN DUCKLING WITH DUCKY'S PORT SAUCE

SERVES 6

Although Pekin ducklings look large, they do not have a lot of meat for their size. You will need one bird for every two guests.

3 Pekin ducklings, about 5 pounds each
Coarse salt and freshly ground black pepper
Ground cumin
¹/₄ cup fresh orange or lemon juice
Ducky's Port Sauce (page 261)

Preheat the oven to 500°F.

Trim the wing tips and neck fat from the ducks and remove the giblets. Pat the birds dry with paper towels, then rub inside and out with the salt, pepper, and cumin. Sprinkle with the orange or lemon juice. Put the ducks on a rack in a roasting pan and roast for 25 minutes. Reduce the heat to 350°F and roast for an additional 40 minutes, or until the skin is golden brown and the juices are rosy-colored to yellow. A meat thermometer should read 160°F to 165°F. Remove the birds from the oven and let rest at room temperature for 15 to 30 minutes before carving.

Discard the fat from the drippings. Pour the drippings into the Port sauce and heat. When it is hot, pour the sauce in a sauce boat and serve with the roast duck.

Carve each duck into 2 boneless breasts and leg/thigh portions. Serve each person 1 breast and 1 leg/thigh.

Chippewa duck hunters in a birchbark canoe

ROAST MUSCOVY DUCK WITH
PERSIMMONS AND FIGS

SERVES 4

Roast duck has an affinity for fresh fruits that can be varied depending on the season. In the fall, I pair the brilliant flame-colored Fuyu persimmons with sweet nuggets of Black Mission figs; in summer I use fresh local tree fruits—peaches, apricots, cherries, plums—or cane berries, such as raspberries or blackberries, or a mixture of both. To bring out the best of the fruit, add fruit *eau de vie,* such as framboise with fresh raspberries and kirschwasser with fresh cherries.

1 muscovy duck hen, about 4 pounds
Coarse salt and freshly ground black pepper
²/₃ cup dry white wine
1 tablespoon brandy
1 teaspoon sugar
1¹/₂ cups chopped Fuyu persimmon (1 large persimmon), pitted and peeled, or other fresh
fruit, thinly sliced
¹/₂ cup fresh figs, chopped

Preheat the oven to 450°F.

Trim the wing tips and neck fat from the duck and remove the giblets. Pat the bird dry with a paper towel, then rub inside and out with the salt and pepper. Put the duck on a rack in a roasting pan. Roast for 15 minutes, then reduce the heat to 375°F and roast for 50 minutes more, or until the juices are a rosy color. A meat thermometer should read 160°F to 165°F. Transfer the duck to a platter and let it rest 15 to 30 minutes before carving.

To make the sauce, discard the fat from the drippings. Set the roasting pan over a burner and add the wine, brandy, and sugar. Bring to a boil. Reduce the liquid by half, stirring constantly to release the caramelized bits stuck on the bottom of the pan. Remove the pan from the heat and add the fruit. Season with salt and pepper.

Carve each duck into 2 boneless breasts and leg/thigh portions. Serve each person 1 breast and 1 leg/thigh with a spoonful of the persimmon and fig sauce over each serving.

A THANKSGIVING LETTER

During the Civil War, a Union soldier camping on Hilton Head Island with his regiment wrote to his sister on Thanksgiving Day:

Hilton Head, S.C.
(Thanksgiving) Nov. 26, 1863

Dear Sister,

With a light heart and a full stomach I take my pen to write an answer to your letter which arrived here yesterday together with one from Gal, both of which were very acceptable and shall try to answer both tonight. Well I suppose you would like to know [how] I spent Thanksgiving. So will tell you I had a big time and feel pretty well used up, having come off of picket this morning and dinner consisted of Turkey, ducks, Roast Pig, plum pudding and all the chicken fixings that is required to make up a thanksgiving dinner. We had one turkey that weighted 14 lbs. the other was small. The ducks I helped to shoot, three in number. The puddings were made of soaked bread with fixings, licking good sall, the pig was bought with the Co. fund, each man had a piece, all this for a mess of twelve men, we tried to put it all away but it was to much for us, consequently we had to go back on it, and we calculated the fragments which were gathered up after the feast will stand us for four meals more, so you can judge about what my feelings are at the present time, by the bye, I forgot to say that we had both Irish and sweet potatoes, squash and turnips. . . . I have thought of home a great many times today and have wondered if you were enjoying yourselves as well as I was, if you did then you had a good time. . . .

Your affectionate Brother, Eben

MUSCOVY DUCK WITH SWEET AND SOUR SAUCE

SERVES 4

Claude Bigo is a charming Frenchman from the Loire Valley who moved his family to Stockton, California, ten years ago to establish Grimaud Farms of California, a sister company to Groupe Grimaud—a world leader in the duck and rabbit industry. Every eighteen months Claude imports three thousand fertilized muscovy duck eggs—the duck known in France as *canard de Barbarie*—from Grimaud Ferme of France to ensure superior genetic breeding stock. This recipe for preparing the richly flavorful and low-fat muscovy duck is Claude's favorite.

1 muscovy duck, about 4 pounds
Savory Herb and Peppercorn Rub (page 249)
4 shallots, cut in half if large
¹/₄ cup balsamic vinegar
¹/₄ cup red wine vinegar
6 tablespoons heavy whipping cream
4 tablespoons honey
Coarse salt and freshly ground black pepper

Preheat the oven to 450°F.

Trim the wing tips and neck fat from the duck and remove the giblets. Pat the bird dry with a paper towel, then season inside and out with the rub. Put the bird on a rack in a roasting pan, breast side up.

Roast for 15 minutes, then reduce the heat to 375°F and roast for 50 minutes more, or until the juices run a rosy color when the duck is poked with a fork, or a meat thermometer reads 160°F to 165°F. Transfer the duck to a platter and let rest at room temperature for 15 to 30 minutes before carving.

Separate the fat from the cooking juices and discard the fat.

Put the roasting pan with the cooking juices on the stove. Sauté the shallots in the drippings for 2 to 3 minutes over medium heat. Turn the heat to high and deglaze the pan with the vinegars, scraping the bottom of the pan to release the caramelized cooking pieces. Reduce the juices by one-half. Lower the heat to medium and add the whipping cream. Cook for another 3 to 4 minutes until the sauce is slightly thickened. Stir in the honey and season with salt and pepper.

Carve each duck into 2 boneless breasts and leg/thigh portions. Serve each person 1 breast and 1 leg/thigh. Ladle a spoonful of the sweet and sour sauce over each serving.

A FAMILY DUCK POND

Almost fifty years ago, R. T. Morris of New Bern, North Carolina, and his good friend, Joe Blow (no kidding), bought twelve thousand acres of marshland for a duck camp on the Pamlico Sound. They built a rustic camp lodge and for forty-five years held "duck camp" for friends and relatives throughout hunting season. Several years ago they worked together with the state of North Carolina to control the mosquito population by putting up a dike in the marsh. They built a spillway with a pump, then sprigged the ponds with eelgrass, a favorite of the ducks. When water was pumped back in, the mosquito population decreased significantly and the duck population increased, just what they had hoped for. "Last year we saw twenty-five thousand ducks in these marshes, way up from previous years."

Here is one of the methods R. T. uses for preparing duck:

"Remove the breasts from the birds and pound them with a mallet. Roll them in flour, dust heavily with pepper, and quickly sauté in a hot pan with just a little oil. Put the duck meat on a platter and keep warm. Add a little flour to the pan. Scrape up the drippings as you brown the flour, then stir in a little water for the gravy. Ladle the gravy over the ducks and serve with hot biscuits. If you have guests who don't like the flavor of wild duck, sauté onions in the oil before cooking the breast meat."

MAGRET WITH ASPARAGUS AND SHIITAKE MUSHROOMS

SERVES 4

The magret is the breast from a duck commonly raised for foie gras. It is rich and flavorful, but the thick layer of fat under the skin makes it necessary to cook it fat side down for 20 minutes to slowly render the fat, which is then discarded. To substitute other domestic or wild duck breasts, simply season the meat with the rub, then sauté on both sides over medium heat until the juices run a rosy color. Discard any accumulated grease and, without wiping out the pan, follow the instructions below for cooking the vegetables.

1/2 magret breast, about 1 to 1 1/4 pounds
1 teaspoon Ground Porcini Rub (page 246) or coarse salt and
  freshly ground black pepper
1/2 pound asparagus, trimmed and broken into 2-inch pieces
3 ounces shiitake mushrooms, stemmed and sliced
Coarse salt
4 cups hot cooked rice, preferably half wild and half brown

Season the flesh of the magret with the rub. Place fat side down in a large ungreased skillet and turn the heat to medium to medium-low. Slowly cook the breast for approximately 18 to 20 minutes without turning. The bottom side will become dark brown and fat will accumulate in the pan as it cooks.

Remove the magret from the pan and carefully discard the rendered fat. Return the pan to the burner and cook the other side until the juices run a rosy color, 5 to 8 more minutes. Transfer the meat to a plate and keep warm.

Cut into thin slices against the grain.

Turn the heat to medium-high and, in the same pan, sauté the asparagus and mushrooms with a pinch of salt until the vegetables are barely cooked. The asparagus will still be crisp but slightly browned. Put the vegetables over the duck and serve with the rice.

ROAST WILD GOOSE

SERVES 8

In this unusual recipe for wild goose, the bird is placed in a hot oven which is immediately turned off. The result is a perfectly cooked goose that is moist— no small achievement for a bird that has very little, if any, fat in its flesh. If you have any goose left over, try making the Potted Game in a Bread Bowl (page 209). This method of roasting is only for unstuffed birds.

2 wild geese (see Note), about 5 to 6 pounds each
Coarse salt and freshly ground black pepper
1 tablespoon unsalted butter, softened

Preheat the oven to 500°F and adjust the rack to the lower one-third of the oven.

Pat the birds dry inside and out with paper towels and sprinkle the cavities with the salt and pepper. Put the birds breast side up in a large roasting pan and rub the skin with the butter. Place the birds in the preheated oven and turn the oven off. *Do not open the door for 1 hour*. Remove the geese from the oven and carve, as you would a turkey, immediately.

NOTE: Cook birds that weigh 10 to 12 pounds as you would domestic geese (page 23).

A group of
Nebraskan goose
hunters

A CHRISTMAS BARBECUE

"Deciding to winter in Clayoquot (Vancouver Island, 1791) Gray located a land-locked cove, had his men chop out a clearing on its shores, and there build a two-story log fort eighteen feet wide by thirty-six feet long. . . . The Indians seemed amiable enough. Dusky maidens supplied berries, salmon, and other comforts; Gray cured a sick chief. On Christmas the whites amazed the Indians by bedecking the fort, shops, and ship with evergreen boughs. Twenty geese were roasted on spits before a huge fire, and the local dignitaries and their ladies were invited to a feast on the ship. (Rather than board the Columbia, the women sat outside in their canoes, waiting for whatever their lords tossed down.) Chief Wicananish repaid the compliment by inviting some of the whites to a name-giving dance, during which he handed on his name to his son and assumed a new one. . . ."

Land of Giants by David Lavender

Snow geese
heading south
for winter

BAKED WILD GOOSE
WITH GINGERED BEANS

SERVES 5

This combination of goose baked with beans is a variation on a cassoulet, a specialty from the Languedoc region of France. Traditionally, a cassoulet is a slow-baked dish of beans and various meats including preserved goose, pork, lamb, duck, and sausage. I use duck confit legs that are now available commercially because they add a rich flavor to this dish. If you are unable to find them, use ¼ pound diced meaty bacon.

Wild goose has a savory, intense flavor which is enhanced when cooked with moist heat. Wild duck or upland game birds, such as grouse and pheasant, can also be prepared in this manner.

Like any bean dish, this recipe tastes best if it is made a day in advance. Reheat the covered Dutch oven at 350°F for 45 minutes, or until the mixture is piping hot. If it is a little dry, moisten with chicken stock before reheating.

1 pound Great Northern beans, cooked and drained (page 9)

⅓ cup tomato paste

1 teaspoon dry mustard

1 teaspoon ground ginger

2 garlic cloves, finely chopped

Coarse salt to taste

½ teaspoon freshly ground black pepper

1 onion, sliced

1 wild goose, about 3 pounds, quartered

3 duck confit legs or ¼ pound meaty bacon, cut into 1-inch pieces

1 cup homemade chicken stock or reduced-sodium chicken broth

½ cup dried bread crumbs

2 tablespoons melted unsalted butter

Preheat the oven to 300°F.

Place the beans in a large Dutch oven.

Combine the tomato paste, mustard, ginger, garlic, salt, and pepper and add to the beans. Stir gently to mix. Evenly layer the onion slices over the beans. Put the goose pieces on top of the onions, flesh side up. Put the 3 duck legs on top and pour the chicken stock over the mixture. Cover with a tight-fitting lid and bake in the preheated oven for 3 hours.

Mix together the bread crumbs and the melted butter. Spread the bread crumbs evenly over the top of the goose and bake at 300°F uncovered, until the surface is well browned, about 10 minutes.

Serve hot from the oven.

WILDFOWL BALL

The Wildfowl Ball is—no, not a dance where wild ducks and geese boogie the night away—one of the hottest conservation benefits in the nation. It is the brainchild of the Hilton Head chapter of the South Carolina Waterfowl Association. Attendees, encouraged to wear either black tie or camouflage, enjoy a spectacular game dinner prepared by their hosts, who are all hunters and cooks. Last year the culinary highlight was a 200-pound wild pig, spit-roasted for more than 10 hours, until tender chunks of meat fell off the bone when it was carved. After dinner, a raffle and an auction of art, hunting trips, and merchandise provide additional proceeds for South Carolina conservation programs.

HUNTING-CAMP
WILD GOOSE BREAST

SERVES 4

The best meals are often created out of necessity. Good friend Gerry Drummond shared this wild goose recipe that he and a friend devised one night while at a hunting camp.

1/2 cup orange juice

1/4 cup bourbon

1 whole wild Canadian goose breast (both sides), skinned and boned, about 1 pound

Coarse salt and freshly ground black pepper

1 tablespoon olive oil or unsalted butter

1 shallot, chopped

1 cup homemade chicken stock or reduced-sodium chicken broth

1 tablespoon marmalade or apricot jam

Pour the orange juice and bourbon in a bowl or sturdy self-sealing plastic bag large enough to hold the goose breast. Season the goose meat with salt and pepper, and marinate in the orange juice–bourbon mixture for 2 hours or overnight in the refrigerator (or in an ice chest if you are in hunting camp).

In a large skillet, heat the olive oil over medium-high heat. Sauté the goose breasts, turning once or twice as they cook, until the juices run a rosy color when the breasts are poked with a fork. Remove the goose meat and cover with foil while you make the sauce.

Return the skillet to the burner and add a little more oil if necessary. Sauté the shallot until it starts to brown, then pour in the chicken stock and marinade and reduce to 1 cup, scraping the bottom of the pan as it cooks to release the caramelized bits stuck to the bottom of the pan. To be safe, the marinade must be boiled for at least 10 minutes. Stir in the marmalade.

Slice the goose breast against the grain into thin slices and serve with the bourbon-orange sauce.

ROAST FARM-RAISED GOOSE

SERVES 6

One bite of sliced goose meat, with its rich, toothsome flavor, makes it easy to understand why this bird has been prized by cooks for centuries. While it is not as tender as domestic duck, roast goose is a gustatory delight. In this unusual recipe, the bird is placed in a hot oven and roasted for 45 minutes. The oven is turned off and, without opening the door, the bird is left to cook for another 35 minutes. The result is a perfectly cooked goose that is crisp and golden brown on the outside and perfectly moist within. This method can be used only with unstuffed birds. Make the dressing and cook it separately (see Sides and Salads). If you have any goose left over, try making the Potted Game in a Bread Bowl (page 209).

1 farm-raised goose, about 12 pounds
Coarse salt and freshly ground black pepper
1 bunch fresh thyme
1 lemon, quartered
3 cups homemade chicken stock or reduced-sodium chicken broth
1/2 cup Madeira

Preheat the oven to 500°F. Adjust the rack as low as necessary for the goose to fit in the oven.

Remove the neck and giblets, saving the liver for pâté (page 208). Remove the wing tips and cut off any visible fat. Pat the bird dry inside and out with paper towels and sprinkle the cavity with salt and pepper. Put the thyme and lemon wedges in the cavity. Arrange the bird in a large roasting pan, breast side up. Prick the breast of the bird to release any fat as it cooks. Stick a meat thermometer in the thickest part of the thigh. Put the bird in the oven and adjust the meat thermometer so that it is facing toward you. (This way you can read it through the oven glass even when the door is closed. This is not a necessity but it helps to determine when the bird is done without opening the door.)

Roast the goose for 45 minutes, then turn the oven off. *Do not open the door.* Leave the bird in the oven for 35 to 45 more minutes, until the meat thermometer reads 165°F. (It will rise to 170°F as the bird rests out of the oven.)

Remove the goose from the oven and transfer to a platter. Cover with foil and let rest for 15 to 20 minutes.

Separate the fat from the cooking juices and discard the fat. Put the roasting pan with the cooking juices on the stove over medium-high heat. Add the stock and Madeira, scraping the bottom of the pan to release any caramelized bits that stick to the bottom of the pan. Reduce to 2 cups.

Carve the goose as you would a turkey, and serve the sauce in a gravy boat.

GOOSE FEATHERS AND DOWN

Geese were prized by American pioneers for more than just their meat. Their down and feathers were used to stuff mattresses and pillows, and the feathers from the wings were greatly sought after for writing instruments. These prized feathers have a hard quill and a natural bend to them that gently arches over the back of the hand, making them ideal for writing.

THE GOOSE SOCIETY

The Hidatsa and Mandan Indians believed that during the fall migration, flocks of water birds flying south for the winter took the spirits of the corn and other crops with them. To ensure a bountiful season, it was the job of the Goose Society—women thirty to forty years old—to offer prayers and hold ceremonial feasts throughout the year. Their most important meeting was held in the springtime with the arrival of the water birds, which signaled both the end of winter and the return of the corn spirits.

SOUSED GROUSE

SERVES 4

Sharp-tailed grouse are distinctly flavorful with moist, dark-colored meat that has an affinity for blackberry brandy. I learned how to cook them from my friend Lynn Loacker, who is an avid hunter and the past-president of the Oregon chapter of the Ruffed Grouse Society, as well as a good cook. She roasts the birds and bastes them with blackberry brandy. The birds are served whole and each guest is instructed to make a 2-inch slit in the breast meat on both sides next to the breastbone. She passes the sauce boat and everyone ladles some of the savory blackberry sauce over their birds.

The cooking of the birds is done in two steps. First, they are browned on top of the stove, then they are transferred to a baking dish and put into the oven. While the birds are roasting, the blackberry sauce is prepared.

> *5 tablespoons unsalted butter or half olive oil and half butter*
> *2 cups blackberry brandy, plus more for pouring over the birds*
> *1/4 cup all-purpose flour*
> *1/4 teaspoon poultry seasoning*
> *1/4 teaspoon celery salt*
> *1/4 teaspoon garlic powder*
> *1/2 teaspoon salt, plus more to taste*
> *1/2 teaspoon freshly ground black pepper, plus more to taste*
> *4 sharp-tailed grouse or chukar partridges, about 8 to 10 ounces each*
> *3 shallots, chopped*
> *1 cup fresh or frozen blackberries, thawed on a paper towel for 20 minutes (optional)*

Preheat the broiler with the rack in the lowest position.

Melt 3 tablespoons of the butter in a 9 × 13-inch baking dish, add the shallots, and pour in 1/2 cup of the blackberry brandy; set aside.

Combine the flour, poultry seasoning, celery salt, garlic powder, salt, and pepper in a shallow dish. Dredge the birds in the seasoned flour.

Melt 2 tablespoons of butter in a large sauté pan over medium-high heat and brown the birds on all sides. Transfer the birds to the prepared baking dish, arranging them breast side up. Pour a little brandy over each bird. Bake for 20 minutes, basting every so often, until their juices run a rosy color when the meat is poked with a fork. If the legs start to get too brown, wrap in foil.

While the birds are broiling, make the sauce. Pour the remaining 1½ cups brandy into the sauté pan and reduce by half. When the birds are done, pour all the cooking juices into the sauté pan and continue reducing until the sauce is thick. Add the blackberries and gently heat for 1 to 2 minutes. Season the sauce with salt and pepper.

Serve 1 bird per person. Instruct each guest to make a 2-inch slit in the breast meat on both sides next to the breastbone. Pass the sauce boat and ladle a spoonful of sauce into the slits.

A sharp-tailed grouse

GUINEA HEN WITH
HAZELNUTS AND MUSTARD

SERVES 3

While guinea hen are not as common on the American table as they are on European tables, these juicy birds are slowly gaining in popularity, and with good reason. They are full-flavored with a high meat-to-bone ratio. Substitute guinea hens in any chicken recipe and the dish will taste even better.

2 whole boneless guinea hen breasts with or without drumette, about 1 pound

Coarse salt and freshly ground black pepper

¹/₄ cup grainy mustard

¹/₂ cup coarsely chopped hazelnuts, roasted (see page 11)

2 tablespoons unsalted butter

1 tablespoon extra virgin olive oil

2 tablespoons fresh lemon juice

Chopped fresh flat-leaf parsley, for garnish

Cut each whole breast in half and trim off any excess fat. Pat the meat dry with a paper towel and sprinkle with salt and pepper. Generously rub the mustard over the flesh. Put the chopped hazelnuts in a shallow dish and press onto the breast pieces, coating both sides.

Melt 1 tablespoon of the butter and the oil over medium to medium-low heat and sauté the meat for 10 to 15 minutes a side—carefully turning the breasts only once—until the juices run clear yellow and the nut coating is nicely browned. The nuts burn easily so watch to be sure the heat is not too high.

Transfer the meat to a warm platter. Scrape any of the coating that may have fallen off in the pan back on top of the guinea hen pieces.

Return the pan to the burner and turn the heat to medium-high. Melt the remaining tablespoon of butter and pour in the lemon juice. Stir it into the butter while scraping the bottom of the pan to release the caramelized bits stuck to the bottom of the pan. Immediately pour the sauce over the meat, sprinkle with chopped parsley, and serve.

CHUKAR PARTRIDGE WITH ARTICHOKE HEARTS AND MUSHROOMS

SERVES 4

Chukars have light-colored meat with a delicate flavor. In this recipe I cook them simply, braising them with fresh mushrooms and artichoke hearts.

3 tablespoons all-purpose flour

1 tablespoon chopped fresh rosemary or 1 teaspoon dried, crushed

1 teaspoon paprika

$^1/_2$ teaspoon coarse salt

$^1/_4$ teaspoon freshly ground black pepper

4 chukar partridges, about 8 ounces each, or grouse or Cornish hens, cut in half length-
*   wise, or 1 chicken, quartered*

1 tablespoon unsalted butter

$^1/_2$ pound fresh mushrooms, sliced

2 to 3 teaspoons olive oil

2 garlic cloves, coarsely chopped

1 cup homemade chicken stock or reduced-sodium chicken broth

1 (9-ounce) package frozen artichoke hearts, thawed, or 1 (14-ounce) can artichoke
*   hearts, drained and cut in half*

Hot cooked noodles

Combine the flour, rosemary, paprika, salt, and pepper in a shallow dish or bag. Dredge the birds in the seasoned flour and set aside.

Melt the butter in a large skillet over medium heat. Add the mushrooms and sauté until they just start to soften, about 5 minutes. Transfer the mushrooms and their cooking juices to a plate and set aside.

Return the pan to the burner and pour in the olive oil. Add the garlic and sauté for 2 to 3 minutes. Add the birds and sauté until golden brown on both sides. Pour in the broth. Add the mushrooms and artichoke hearts and cook for 5 to 10 more minutes, until the birds are just cooked and the vegetables are hot.

Put the noodles in a warm, large shallow bowl. Transfer the birds and vegetables to the bowl using a slotted spoon. Turn the heat to high and reduce the sauce by half. Pour the sauce over the birds, vegetables, and noodles and serve at once.

NOTE: Hunters often take only the breast meat and legs from chukars. For this recipe use 8 boneless, skinless chukar breasts and 8 chukar legs, skinned.

A TRAMP ABROAD

Mark Twain toured Europe in 1878 and subsequently wrote *A Tramp Abroad*. In his work, he reviewed the sorts of European cuisine which did not appeal to his American taste. "There is here and there an American who will say he can remember rising from a European table d'hôte perfectly satisfied," he wrote, "but we must not overlook the fact that there is also here and there an American who will lie." In *A Tramp Abroad* he listed more than sixty American dishes that he was looking forward to having when he returned home. Among them were roast wild turkey, canvasback duck, prairie hens, Missouri partridges, opossum, and raccoon.

A ptarmigan

POACHED PHEASANT

MAKES 3 CUPS BONELESS PHEASANT MEAT AND 3 CUPS PHEASANT STOCK

Wild pheasants are often dry because they have so little fat, but when they are cooked in chicken stock, the meat becomes pleasantly infused with moisture. Farm-raised pheasants can be cooked using the same method, as well as other game birds.

After the meat is pulled off the bones, it can be used in any recipe for cooked chicken. Try the Pheasant with Chanterelles and Herb Dumplings (page 68).

1 whole pheasant, about 3 pounds
1 onion, quartered
3^{1}/$_{2}$ cups homemade chicken stock or reduced-sodium chicken broth

Combine the pheasant, onion, and chicken stock in a large pot. Cover and bring to a boil. Boil for 2 minutes, then turn the heat off but do not take off the lid or remove the pot from the burner. Let sit at room temperature until the pan is cool.

Remove the bird from the stock and pull off the skin. Pull the meat from the bones and discard both skin and bones. Go through the meat a second time to check for any remaining small bones that might have been missed.

Strain the stock and use as you would chicken stock. It will keep for 3 to 5 days in the refrigerator or it can be frozen and stored for up to 3 months. I prefer to use the meat fresh, but if it is double-wrapped in plastic wrap and sealed in a plastic freezer bag, it will keep in the freezer for up to a month.

GAME BIRD EGGS—A DELICACY

Native Americans not only ate the flesh of pit-roasted game birds but they collected their eggs as well. The eggs were boiled in baskets or preserved in wet sand.

Upland game hunters enjoying their day

SAUTÉED PHEASANT WITH MUSHROOMS AND LENTILS

SERVES 4

 Once the lentils are cooked, assembling the rest of the ingredients is easy, making this dish especially good for entertaining.

2 tablespoons all-purpose flour

¹/₂ teaspoon coarse salt

Freshly ground black pepper

1 teaspoon chopped fresh rosemary or ¹/₂ teaspoon dried, crushed

1 wild or farm-raised pheasant or chicken, about 3 pounds, cut into 8 pieces

2 teaspoons unsalted butter

¹/₂ pound fresh crimini mushrooms, cleaned, trimmed, and sliced

2 teaspoons olive oil

1 garlic clove, chopped

Lentils (recipe follows), about 1 cup

³/₄ cup homemade chicken stock or reduced-sodium chicken broth

Combine the flour, salt, pepper, and rosemary in a small bag or shallow dish. Pat the pheasant pieces dry and dredge in the seasoned flour. Set aside.

Melt the butter in a large skillet over medium heat. Add the mushrooms and sauté until they become tender, about 8 minutes. Transfer to a plate and set aside.

Return the skillet to the heat and pour in the olive oil. Add the garlic and sauté for a minute, then add the pheasant and sauté on each side for 3 to 4 minutes.

Add the mushrooms, lentils, and chicken stock. Cover and continue to cook until the meat is cooked throughout and the mixture slightly thickened, about 45 minutes. The pheasant or chicken will be opaque and clear yellow juices will run if the meat is poked with a fork. Serve at once.

LENTILS

MAKES ABOUT 1 CUP

I prefer the texture of the tiny green lentil above all others. In this recipe I cook them in chicken stock with bacon to give them additional flavor. If you have the time, cook them a day or two in advance and they will taste even better.

¹/₃ cup French green lentils

2 teaspoons olive oil

1 meaty piece of smoked bacon, trimmed of excess fat and coarsely chopped

¹/₂ cup chopped leek

1¹/₂ cups homemade chicken stock or reduced-sodium chicken broth

¹/₄ teaspoon coarse salt (omit if you are using commercial chicken broth)

Rinse and pick over the lentils.

In a small saucepan, heat the olive oil over medium heat and sauté the bacon pieces and leeks until they start to soften and turn brown, about 8 minutes. Add the lentils and chicken stock and simmer, covered, until the lentils are tender, about 40 minutes. Season with salt and toss.

Set aside to cool, then store covered in the refrigerator.

Pheasant with Chanterelles and Herb Dumplings

SERVES 4

Old-fashioned dumplings are good on any stewed or braised game dish because they are cooked floating in all those savory cooking juices.

4 tablespoons unsalted butter

3 tablespoons all-purpose flour

2 cups homemade chicken stock, reduced-sodium chicken broth, or pheasant broth
   (page 65)

1 cup cream or half-and-half

1/2 teaspoon coarse salt

1 cooked wild or farm-raised pheasant (see page 65), skinned, boned, and cut into bite-
   size pieces

1/4 pound fresh chanterelles, sliced vertically

HERB DUMPLINGS

2 cups all-purpose flour

2 teaspoons baking soda

1 teaspoon salt

1/4 teaspoon freshly ground black pepper

1/2 cup shortening

1 cup milk

2 teaspoons finely minced fresh rosemary or 1 teaspoon dried

2 teaspoons finely minced fresh thyme or 1 teaspoon dried

Heat 3 tablespoons of the butter in a sauté pan over medium heat and stir in the flour. Cook for 3 minutes, then stir in the chicken stock, cream or half-and-half, and salt. Continue stirring until the mixture thickens. Add the pheasant.

In a small skillet, melt the remaining 1 tablespoon butter and sauté the chanterelles over medium heat until they begin to soften, about 8 minutes. Add the chanterelles and their juices to the pheasant. Keep simmering while you prepare the dumplings.

To make the dumplings, combine the flour, baking soda, salt, and pepper in a bowl. Cut in the shortening with a pastry blender or two knives. Stir in the milk and fresh herbs. Alternatively, combine the flour, baking soda, salt, and pepper in a food processor. Pulse 4 to 5 times to blend. Add the shortening and pulse 8 to 10 times until the mixture resembles cornmeal. Turn the machine on and slowly pour in the milk and herbs.

Make 8 small mounds with the dumpling batter on top of the pheasant-mushroom mixture. Cover with a lid and simmer for 20 minutes, or until the dumplings are thoroughly cooked.

Serve hot in warm, shallow soup bowls.

BEAUTIFUL FEATHER QUILTS

Peter Lindstrom, a European geographer, talks about the beautiful feather quilts of painted bird feathers. They were made by old people because they required patience and dexterity: "In the first place they tie them with mesh-like nets, yet very fine; then they fasten the feathers in the meshes so neat and strong that not one feather came loose from it."

From *Peter Lindstrom: A Geographer who came to America 1654–1655*

A ring-neck pheasant

ROAST SQUAB WITH ARTICHOKES AND OLIVES

SERVES 4

In this recipe, the birds' cavities are filled with fresh lemon wedges, sprigs of rosemary, and garlic cloves and then roasted. The stuffing is not eaten, but left inside the cavity when the birds are served. The lemony juices add a tangy bite to the thick slabs of toasted French bread tucked beneath each bird.

4 squab, approximately 12 ounces each, necks and wing tips removed
Paprika
Coarse salt and freshly ground black pepper
2 lemons, quartered
10 sprigs fresh rosemary
4 garlic cloves
1 tablespoon olive oil
1 pound baby artichokes, tips removed
4 ounces pitted kalamata olives
Four 1/2-inch-thick slices coarse-grained country-style French bread, lightly toasted

Preheat the oven to 425°F and put the rack in the center of the oven

Remove the giblets and pat the birds dry inside and out with paper towels. Sprinkle the cavities with paprika, salt, and pepper. Put 1 lemon wedge, 1 sprig of rosemary, and 1 garlic clove in each. Tie the legs together, and sprinkle the birds with paprika, salt, and pepper.

Heat the olive oil in an ovenproof skillet over medium-high heat and brown the birds on all sides. Arrange the birds breast side up and put the artichokes and remaining lemon wedges around them. Remove the leaves from 2 sprigs of rosemary and coarsely chop. Sprinkle the rosemary over the birds.

Roast the birds for 15 minutes. Sprinkle the olives over all and bake for another 10 minutes. Remove from the oven and discard the strings on the birds and the lemon quarters in the pan. Leave the stuffing inside the birds.

Serve each bird on a piece of toast accompanied by artichokes and kalamata olives. Garnish with sprigs of fresh rosemary.

NOTE: Baby, or cocktail, artichokes are completely edible. If they are any larger, steam them first until they are almost tender, remove their chokes, and cut them into quarters.

STOOL PIGEON

The term "stool pigeon" comes from the early American practice of attaching a live pigeon to a stool, strategically placed under a net, in order to attract large flocks of pigeons flying by.

Two chukar partridges slip by a hunter in the rolling hills of eastern Washington

ROAST SQUAB IN BHUTANESE RED RICE

SERVES 4

ike all game birds, roast squab have succulent juices that should not go to waste. In this recipe, every drop is captured in "mounds" made from Bhutanese red rice enhanced with fresh mango and chopped cilantro. If you like, substitute basmati rice or half wild and half brown rice.

4 whole squab, about 1 pound each, necks and wing tips removed
Coarse salt and freshly ground black pepper
1/4 cup red pepper jelly
1/2 teaspoon ground ginger
1 teaspoon fresh lime juice
Bhutanese Red Rice (page 279)

Preheat the oven to 450°F. Adjust the rack to the middle of the oven.

Remove the necks and pat the birds dry inside and out with paper towels. Discard any excess fat. Rub the flesh and cavities with salt and pepper. Put the birds in a roasting pan breast side up.

Roast for 15 minutes. Reduce the heat to 350°F and continue roasting for another 22 minutes, or until the juices run a rosy color when the meat is poked with a fork.

While the birds are roasting, soften the red pepper jelly in a small pan over medium heat. Stir in the ginger and lime juice. Generously brush the glaze on the birds during the last 2 to 3 minutes of roasting time.

Serve the birds in a mound of Bhutanese red rice.

GRILLED SQUAB CHINESE-STYLE

SERVES 4

 Serve these birds right off the grill or at room temperature—they are equally good either way. I serve them on a bed of fresh cilantro leaves.

4 squab, about 12 ounces each, or 4 Cornish hens, about 1¹/₂ pounds each

2 teaspoons coarse salt

2 teaspoons ground five-spice powder

3 tablespoons hoisin sauce

3 tablespoons plum sauce

1 garlic clove, minced

2 bunches fresh cilantro

Heat the grill or broiler.

Pat the birds dry inside and out with paper towels. Blend together the salt and five-spice powder. Sprinkle a pinch into each cavity and rub the remainder over the birds. The birds can be grilled immediately or covered and refrigerated overnight.

Stir together the hoisin sauce, plum sauce, and minced garlic. Set aside.

Grill the birds over a medium-hot fire for 20 minutes, turning every 5 minutes, or until the birds are almost done—the juices will be a dark rosy color when the breasts are poked with a fork.

Turn the birds breast side up and brush with the sauce. Continue grilling for 5 minutes, or until the juices run a rosy color.

Trim the long stems off the cilantro and spread the leaves on a large platter. Arrange the birds on top of the cilantro and serve immediately.

GRILLED SQUAB WITH GORGONZOLA AND ORECCHIETTE

SERVES 4

I serve these succulent birds in shallow bowls on a bed of pasta so that none of the flavorful juices are wasted. Orecchiette, meaning "little ears," after its disklike shape, is a type of pasta from southern Italy that has a firm texture with a slight indentation for holding tiny nuggets of sauce and cheese.

4 whole squab, 12 to 16 ounces each
Coarse salt and freshly ground black pepper
2 tablespoons extra virgin olive oil
2 garlic cloves, coarsely chopped
8 ounces uncooked orecchiette
1/2 cup chopped fresh basil leaves, plus 8 fresh whole leaves for garnish
3 ounces crumbled Gorgonzola cheese
12 cherry tomatoes, cut in half vertically

Pat the birds dry inside and out with paper towels and put them in a shallow bowl. Rub with salt and pepper and pour the olive oil and chopped garlic over the birds. Marinate in the refrigerator for 1 hour.

Heat the grill or broiler.

Grill the birds over a medium-hot fire, turning every 5 to 7 minutes, until they are brown on the outside and the juices run a rosy color when a bird is poked with a fork, about 25 minutes.

Cook the pasta in boiling water. Drain well. Toss the pasta with the chopped basil leaves, Gorgonzola cheese, and tomato halves. Adjust the seasoning with salt and pepper. Divide the pasta among 4 shallow bowls and put 1 squab in the center of each. Garnish each bowl with 2 basil leaves, or chop the remaining 8 leaves and sprinkle over the top of the birds. Serve at once.

Breast of Wood Pigeon with Mushrooms

SERVES 4

Here is a basic recipe that every good game cook should make. It comes from Bain of Tarves, a game export company in Aberdeenshire, Scotland, which specializes in prime Scottish wild game. Instead of cooking only the breasts of the birds, which is a common practice for many hunters, the flavorful bones are used, too. After the breasts are removed, I cut the remaining carcasses into quarters and sauté them with vegetables. The mixture is enhanced with a dash of brandy, then simmered in stock. The resulting sauce is rich and full-bodied, a consequence of extracting every bit of flavor from the bones that usually go to waste. Although the company suggests wood pigeons, any medium-size or small game bird can be used, such as quail, squab, partridge, grouse, or wild ducks.

4 wood pigeons, 8 to 10 ounces each
Coarse salt and freshly ground black pepper
2 tablespoons olive oil
1 small onion, chopped
1 small carrot, chopped
3 tablespoons brandy
2 cups homemade chicken stock or reduced-sodium chicken broth
1 tablespoon tomato puree
1 bay leaf
1 teaspoon chopped fresh thyme or 1/2 teaspoon dried, crushed
1 tablespoon unsalted butter
8 ounces mushrooms, such as chanterelles
Chopped fresh flat-leaf parsley

Remove the breast meat from the birds by running a sharp knife along the breastbone on both sides. Discard the skin and run your fingers over the meat and pull or cut away any small bones. Sprinkle the meat with salt and pepper and set aside. Cut the carcasses into quarters with a kitchen scissors or sharp knife.

In a medium saucepan, heat 1 tablespoon oil over medium heat. Add the carcasses, onion, and carrot and sauté for 8 minutes, until the vegetables start to brown. Carefully pour in the brandy and flame with a long fireplace match, holding the pan away from you. Add the chicken stock, tomato puree, bay leaf, and thyme. Turn the heat to high and reduce by half. Strain and adjust the seasoning with salt and pepper. Keep warm.

In a large skillet, heat the remaining 1 tablespoon of oil over medium-high heat and add the breasts. Sauté for 1 minute on each side. Season with salt and pepper. Remove from the pan and keep warm. Add the butter or a little more oil and the mushrooms to the pan. Sauté until they are soft and lightly browned.

Divide the breasts among 4 dinner plates. Pour any juices that may have accumulated from the cooked birds into the sauce. Cover the pigeon breasts with a mound of sautéed mushrooms, a spoonful of sauce, and a pinch of parsley. Serve immediately.

PASSENGER PIGEONS IN MASSACHUSETTS, 1634

"These birds come into the country to go to the north parts in the beginning of our spring, at which time (if I may be counted worthy to be believed in a thing that is not so strange as true) I have seen them fly as if the airy regiment had been pigeons, seeing neither beginning nor ending, length or breadth of these millions of millions. The shouting of people, the rattling of guns, and pelting of small shot could not drive them out of their course, but so they continued for four or five hours together. Yet it must not be concluded that it is thus often, for it is but at the beginning of the spring, and at Michaelmas when they return back to the southward; yet are there some all the year long, which are easily attained by such as look after them. Many of them build amongst the pine trees, thirty miles to the northeast of our plantations, joining nest to nest and tree to tree by their nests, so that the sun never sees the ground in that place, from whence the Indians fetch whole loads of them."

New England's Prospect by William Wood

GRILLED POUSSIN WITH PEACH CHUTNEY GLAZE

SERVES 4

The combination of the spicy rub with the sweet-and-sour jolt from the chutney glaze makes these mild-tasting birds a meal worth remembering. The rub is spread over each bird, even between the skin and flesh. This not only flavors the meat, but the circulating air makes the skin exceptionally crisp and irresistible.

4 poussin, each weighing 14 to 16 ounces
4¹/₂ teaspoons curry powder
2 teaspoons coarse salt
1 cup peach chutney
2 tablespoons mild olive oil
1 tablespoon unsalted butter, melted
2 tablespoons champagne vinegar
1 teaspoon ground ginger
1 garlic clove, crushed

Remove the necks and the livers. Pat the birds dry with paper towels and trim off any large pieces of fat. In a small dish, blend the curry powder and 1¹/₂ teaspoons salt. Rub the mixture over the birds and inside the cavities. With a small knife or with your fingers, carefully lift the skin up and season the flesh under the skin. Let the birds sit for 30 minutes.

Heat the grill or broiler.

Grill the birds slowly, turning every 10 minutes, over a medium fire until they are golden brown on the outside, and the juices run a clear yellow when a bird is poked with a fork, about 45 minutes.

Meanwhile, stir together the peach chutney, olive oil, melted butter, vinegar, ginger, garlic, and ¹/₂ teaspoon salt. Brush with half of the glaze during the last 5 minutes of cooking. Transfer the birds to a platter and brush with the remaining glaze.

Serve hot or at room temperature.

NOTE: Store the necks in a plastic bag in the freezer for stock at a later date. Just before serving, sauté the livers in a small amount of butter and serve them spread on a piece of toast as an appetizer.

POUSSIN WITH SPINACH

SERVES 4

W hat I like most about this recipe is eating the pungent mustard-coated spinach leaves that become warm from the roasted poussin resting on them.

4 poussin, 14 to 16 ounces each
2 tablespoons grainy mustard
2 garlic cloves, chopped
1 tablespoon chopped fresh thyme or 1 teaspoon dried, crushed
$^1/_2$ teaspoon paprika
1 teaspoon olive oil
1 teaspoon pink peppercorns, crushed
5 ounces baby spinach leaves
1 tablespoon extra virgin olive oil
1 teaspoon sherry vinegar
Pinch of coarse salt and freshly ground black pepper

Preheat the oven to 350°F and lightly grease a large baking dish—the birds need to be baked in a single layer.

Pat the birds dry with paper towels and cut each in half vertically. Combine the mustard, garlic, thyme, paprika, olive oil, and crushed peppercorns in a small bowl. Rub the mustard coating over both sides of the birds and place them cut side down in the baking dish.

Bake for 30 minutes, or until the juices run clear yellow when a bird is poked with a fork.

Five minutes before the birds are done, combine the extra virgin olive oil, vinegar, salt, and pepper. Toss the spinach with the vinaigrette. Equally divide the spinach among 4 dinner plates or large salad plates. Arrange 2 poussin halves on each plate and sprinkle with pepper. Scrape any of the cooked mustard coating left in the baking dish over the birds and serve.

GRILLED QUAIL SALAD WITH NECTARINES AND PLUMS

SERVES 4

The rich yet delicate flavor of grilled quail has an affinity for fruit. In this recipe, I pair the birds with fresh plums and nectarines cooked in their skins, which gives the fruit a slightly sweet-and-sour flavor, and serve them on a bed of spinach and radicchio.

2 teaspoons fresh lime juice

4 teaspoons extra virgin olive oil

1/2 teaspoon coarse salt

1/4 teaspoon freshly ground black pepper

2 tablespoons nonfat plain yogurt

1/2 cup fresh cilantro leaves, coarsely chopped

8 quail, 4 to 6 ounces each (preferably semiboneless)

Grilled Fruit (page 283)

SPINACH SALAD

6 ounces baby spinach

1 head radicchio, torn into bite-size pieces

1 tablespoon extra virgin olive oil

1 teaspoon fresh lime juice

Coarse salt and freshly ground black pepper

1 avocado, peeled and sliced lengthwise into thin slices

In a small bowl, stir together the lime juice, olive oil, salt, pepper, yogurt, and cilantro. Pat the birds dry with paper towels and put them in a shallow dish. Thoroughly brush or rub the quail with the marinade. Marinate for at least 30 minutes or up to 24 hours in the refrigerator.

Heat the grill or broiler. Grill the birds for approximately 7 minutes a side over medium heat until lightly brown on the outside and the juices run a rosy color when a bird is poked with a fork.

Combine the spinach and radicchio in a salad bowl. Mix together the olive oil, lime juice, salt, and pepper and toss with the salad.

To serve, equally divide the salad among 4 dinner plates, placing it in a mound in the center of each plate. Put 4 slices of avocado on each mound radiating out from the center of the salad like spokes in a wheel. Sprinkle the avocado with a pinch of salt. Lay 2 quail opposite each other on top of the greens and in between the avocado slices. Arrange 2 grilled plum halves and 1 piece of grilled nectarine, cut side up, around the rim of each plate, alternating the pieces. Serve at once.

A brace of quail

QUAIL WITH WHITE AND GREEN BEANS

SERVES 4

In this unusual recipe, I combine three of my favorite foods: sautéed quail, marinated white beans, and green beans with crispy bits of bacon. When I have time, I prepare the beans a day or two in advance to allow their flavor to develop; then I sauté the quail in olive oil instead of bacon fat.

> 6 ounces haricots verts or fresh green beans, trimmed and cut in half
> 1 cup Great Northern beans, cooked and drained (see page 9), or 1 (15-ounce) can, drained
> 2 tablespoons extra virgin olive oil
> 2 teaspoons fresh lemon juice
> 1 garlic clove, finely chopped
> 1 teaspoon chopped fresh thyme or $^{1}/_{2}$ teaspoon dried, crushed
> $^{1}/_{2}$ teaspoon coarse salt
> 3 pieces meaty bacon
> 8 semiboneless quail, 4 to 6 ounces each, or 4 semiboneless poussin, cut in half lengthwise
> Freshly ground black pepper

Steam or boil the haricots verts in a small amount of salted water until tender, 6 to 8 minutes. Drain and transfer to a bowl with the Great Northern beans. Whisk together the olive oil, lemon juice, garlic, thyme, and salt and toss with the bean mixture.

Cook the bacon in a large sauté pan until crisp. Transfer to a paper towel to drain. When cool enough to handle, crumble the bacon and toss with the beans. (The beans can be prepared up to this point 2 days in advance—just toss them again before serving. Add a few more drops of olive oil and a squeeze of lemon juice if they look a little dry. Always serve them at room temperature or warmer.) Transfer the beans to a large platter and set aside.

Discard the bacon fat but do not wipe out the pan. Rub the birds with salt and pepper and sauté over medium heat until their juices run a rosy color, about 4 minutes a side. (For poussin, the juices will run clear yellow when done.)

Arrange the birds over the beans and serve.

QUAIL IN POTATO NESTS WITH TOMATO-SAFFRON SAUCE

SERVES 4 AS A FIRST COURSE

You will need a good nonstick skillet, at least 6½ inches wide, to make the potato "nests" for this recipe. The potatoes are first sautéed on one side, then baked on a cookie sheet with a quail in the middle of each nest. As the birds cook, two things happen. Their savory juices run down into the potato nests while the potatoes brown on the bottom. When the birds are done, I transfer them to large shallow bowls and ladle the tomato-saffron sauce over the top of each. One caveat: Don't use prepackaged grated potatoes, fresh or frozen, for this recipe. They don't hold together as well as freshly grated potatoes. To serve this dish as a main course, roast 2 whole quail in each nest per person.

4 semiboneless quail, 4 to 6 ounces each
Coarse salt and freshly ground black pepper
1 teaspoon fresh thyme, stemmed and chopped
4 tablespoons olive oil plus 1 teaspoon
4 cups peeled and shredded Yukon Gold potatoes
2 shallots, chopped
½ onion, diced
4 tomatoes, skinned, seeded, and chopped (see Note)
½ to ¾ cup homemade chicken stock or reduced-sodium chicken broth
Hefty pinch of saffron
4 sprigs fresh thyme

Preheat the oven to 450°F. Spray a cookie sheet with nonstick cooking spray.

Pat the quail dry with paper towels. Season the inside cavities with a pinch of salt, pepper, and fresh thyme.

Heat 1 tablespoon of the olive oil over medium-high heat and sauté the quail until they are lightly brown on all sides, about 5 minutes. Set aside.

Heat 2 teaspoons of oil in a 6½-inch nonstick skillet (or spray with nonstick cooking spray). When the oil is hot, add 1 cup of shredded potatoes to the skillet. Push the potatoes down so that they lie flat in the pan and season with a pinch of salt and pepper. Cook the bottom side of the potatoes until golden brown, 5 to 8 minutes, then invert the pan onto the cookie sheet so that the uncooked side of the potatoes are down. If the nest does not completely hold its shape, push it back together with your fingers. Repeat with the other 3 cups of potatoes, adding more oil to start. Arrange 1 quail, breast side up, on top of each potato nest, leaving space around each. Put the birds in the oven.

While the birds are roasting, make the sauce by heating the remaining 2 teaspoons olive oil in a sauté pan. Add the shallots and onion and sauté until they start to brown, about 8 minutes, then add the tomatoes, chicken stock, and saffron. Season with salt and pepper. Cook the sauce over medium heat until it is slightly reduced, about 15 minutes.

When the birds are golden brown and their juices run a rosy color when the birds are poked with a fork, remove them from the oven. Put the quail and their potato nests in shallow bowls or on dinner plates and ladle a spoonful of sauce over each. Garnish each plate with a sprig of fresh thyme.

NOTE: To remove the skins from the tomatoes, drop them in boiling water for 25 seconds to loosen their skins. Peel the skins away from the flesh with a paring knife. Cut the tomatoes in half horizontally and squeeze to remove the seeds.

EARLY SPRING DOVES

"Where I grew up near Fresno, California, we hunted *muchaloni*, the Italian word for all small wild game birds, like dove, quail, and snipe. Our favorite were the doves who began arriving in the early spring on their return flight from wintering in Mexico. The wild fennel was just coming up then, and we would pick some seeds to season the birds with. My mother would make a polenta cake and we'd roast the birds standing upright so all their savory juices would drip down into the polenta."

Michael Chiarello, chef/owner, Tra Vigne,
St. Helena, California

QUAIL ROASTED IN POLENTA

SERVES 6

This remarkable game dish comes from Michael Chiarello, executive chef of Tra Vigne in St. Helena, California. The birds are browned in olive oil, then cooked standing upright in polenta. They make a stunning presentation at a casual dinner party with guests who don't mind eating the tiny birds with their fingers.

The secret is to bake the polenta in a small enough dish—for instance, a 9-inch baking dish—so that it is at least $1^1/_2$ inches thick to support the birds. Be careful not to crowd the birds—they can be slightly touching on the sides, but if they are too close, they won't cook evenly.

If you wish, add some roasted but slightly undercooked spring vegetables to the polenta, such as small onions, baby carrots, or raw peas, and the dish will be an entire meal. Or, serve it with a tomato-based vegetable dish, such as ratatouille.

12 wild or farm-raised quail or other small game birds, necks removed, 6 to 8 ounces each

2 to 3 tablespoons Coriander-Fennel Rub (page 247) or seasoning of choice

2 tablespoons olive oil

1 large garlic clove, chopped

Polenta (page 281)

Fresh rosemary or parsley sprigs for garnish

Preheat the oven to 425°F and grease a 9 × 9-inch baking dish.

Season the birds with the rub of your choice. Set aside while you prepare the polenta. Pour the polenta into the baking dish.

In a large skillet, heat the oil and garlic over medium-high heat. Add the birds and thoroughly brown them on all sides. Remove the pan from the heat and let the birds cool until they can be handled without burning your fingers. This step can be done several hours in advance.

Arrange the quail in a circle by taking each bird and standing it upright in the polenta, breast meat facing out. Gently push the bird down into the polenta until it can stand by itself. Put the next bird alongside the first and repeat for the remaining quail.

Bake for 12 to 15 minutes, or until the juices run a rosy color when a bird is poked with a fork. Garnish with sprigs of fresh rosemary or parsley.

OSTRICH SATAY

SERVES 4 AS AN APPETIZER, 2 AS A MAIN COURSE

I love to make this appetizer for unsuspecting guests who haven't eaten ostrich before. They are always amazed at how tasty it is.

PEANUT DIPPING SAUCE

1/4 cup bean sauce or hoisin sauce

1/4 teaspoon crushed garlic

2 tablespoons sugar

1/4 teaspoon salt

1/2 teaspoon corn oil

2 tablespoons creamy peanut butter

2 tablespoons crushed, roasted peanuts (optional)

6 ounces ostrich thigh, inside round, or emu, or lean beef, such as flank or round steak, sliced against the grain, 4 1/2 inches by 1/2 inches by 1/4 inches

3 tablespoons low-sodium soy sauce

1/4 teaspoon ground ginger

1/2 teaspoon brown sugar

Pinch of coarse salt and freshly ground black pepper

3 sprigs fresh cilantro

First, make the sauce. In a small saucepan, stir together the bean or hoisin sauce, garlic, sugar, salt, oil, and peanut butter. Stir in 1/2 cup water. Cook over medium heat for 3 minutes. Let cool.

Pat the meat dry with paper towels. In a small bowl, combine the soy sauce, ginger, brown sugar, salt, and pepper to make a marinade. Put the meat in the marinade, turning once to coat both sides, and marinate in the refrigerator for 30 to 60 minutes.

Heat the grill or broiler.

Thread each piece of meat onto individual bamboo or metal skewers, as if you were basting a hem, and grill over hot coals until the meat is medium-rare, about 1 1/2 minutes a side.

Serve on a plate garnished with the cilantro sprigs, accompanied by a small bowl of the dipping sauce, garnished with the chopped peanuts.

GRILLED OSTRICH MEDALLIONS

SERVES 4

Even though the ostrich is a bird, its red meat tastes more like beef than chicken. Be careful not to overcook it.

1¼ pounds ostrich or emu medallions or Perfect Portion fillet (page 34), partially frozen (so it slices more easily)
¼ cup extra virgin olive oil
1 tablespoon fresh lemon juice
1 teaspoon chopped fresh rosemary or ½ teaspoon dried
3 garlic cloves
½ teaspoon coarse salt
¼ teaspoon freshly ground black pepper

Cut the medallions in ³⁄₈-inch horizontal slices and pat dry with paper towels. In a shallow dish, whisk together the olive oil, lemon juice, rosemary, garlic, salt, and pepper. Put the ostrich slices in the marinade, turning them once to coat both sides. Cover the dish with plastic wrap and marinate in the refrigerator for 30 to 60 minutes.

Heat the grill or broiler. Lightly grease the grill.

Grill the meat for 1 minute a side over medium-hot coals or until the inside is still slightly pink. Serve hot.

NOTE: Perfect Portion fillets are precut into 1-inch-thick, 3-ounce or 5-ounce medallions.

CIDER-BASTED WILD TURKEY

SERVES 6 TO 8

Good friend Dottie Trivison is the food editor of Hilton Head's local newspaper, *The Island Packet*. Several years ago she developed this stellar wild turkey recipe for her Thanksgiving column. The bird is roasted surrounded with apple halves that are basted with cider and Calvados, and served with a wild rice, pecan, and cranberry dressing. After she cooks the cranberries for the dressing she makes Kir Royales by stirring 1 to 2 tablespoons of the cranberry syrup into a glass of champagne.

1 wild turkey, farm-raised wild turkey, or domestic turkey, about 8 pounds, neck, giblets, and wing tips removed

1 teaspoon coarse salt

1/2 teaspoon freshly ground black pepper

1 medium onion, sliced

1 medium green apple, such as Granny Smith, cored and sliced

1 teaspoon dried sage or 1 tablespoon chopped fresh

9 tablespoons unsalted butter, softened

2 cups hard cider, or 1 cup dry white wine and 1 cup sweet cider

1/2 cup plus 2 tablespoons Calvados or applejack

6 large baking apples, such as Rome or Golden Delicious, peeled, cored, and halved lengthwise

1 cup homemade chicken stock or reduced-sodium chicken broth

3 tablespoons all-purpose flour

Preheat the oven to 325°F.

Pat the bird dry with paper towels and pull off any remaining pin feathers and excess fat. Season the cavity with 1/2 teaspoon salt and 1/4 teaspoon pepper. Place the onion, sliced green apple, and sage in the body cavity. Cover the large cavity opening with a small piece of aluminum foil. Using a thin metal skewer, pin the turkey's neck skin to its back. Fold the turkey's wings akimbo behind the back. Tie the drumsticks together with kitchen string. Rub the turkey all over with 6 tablespoons of the softened butter. Season with the remaining 1/2 teaspoon salt and 1/4 teaspoon pepper. Put the turkey on a rack in a large, shallow roasting pan. Combine the hard cider with 1/2 cup of the Calvados; pour

1 cup of this mixture into the bottom of the pan. Loosely cover the turkey breast with aluminum foil.

Roast the turkey, basting often, first with the remaining cider mixture, then with the pan drippings, for 2 hours. Remove the aluminum foil and surround the turkey with the apple halves; baste the apples well with the pan drippings. Continue roasting, basting often, until the turkey tests done and the thigh meat registers 170°F, approximately another 40 minutes. The juices will run clear yellow. Remove the turkey to a carving board, loosely cover with foil, and let stand for 20 minutes before carving.

Meanwhile, pour the pan drippings into a large measuring cup and skim off the clear fat that rises to the surface or use a fat separator. Add enough of the stock to total 3½ cups liquid. Set aside.

Heat the remaining 3 tablespoons butter in the roasting pan over medium-high heat. Whisk in the flour and cook for 3 minutes. Slowly whisk in the pan drippings and stock and simmer to a gravy-like consistency. Add salt and pepper to taste. Pour in a gravy boat and pass with the turkey. Carve the turkey and arrange on a platter surrounded by the roasted apples.

TURKEY GIRL

There is a mountain near Santa Fe, New Mexico, called Turkey Track Mountain by the Pueblo Indians who live nearby. Pablita Velarde, in her book *Old Father Story Teller*—a collection of Indian legends she remembers hearing from her grandfather and great-grandfather—explains that the tracks are from the escape of Turkey Girl from her evil foster mother. The flock of turkeys she took out every day to forage for food helped their beloved Turkey Girl escape to a better land. Even today hunters can still hear gobbling in the canyons and see turkey tracks, but they always return empty-handed.

Woodcock with Lingonberry Stuffing

SERVES 4

We do not have woodcocks on the West Coast so I have never cooked one. When I do, I plan to use this recipe, which was given to me by John Poister, author of *The Pyromaniac's Cookbook*.

9 tablespoons butter

1 cup dried bread crumbs

Coarse salt and freshly ground black pepper

Pinch of fresh thyme or rosemary

²/₃ cup lingonberries, drained

1 tablespoon heavy cream

6 woodcocks, 8 to 10 ounces each

¹/₄ cup all-purpose flour

1 onion, finely chopped

2 garlic clove, minced

2 cups Game Stock (page 263) or beef or chicken stock

1 cup dry red wine

¹/₃ cup Cognac

Preheat the oven to 300°F.

Melt 2 tablespoons butter in a large skillet and brown the bread crumbs. Transfer to a mixing bowl, season to taste with salt, pepper, and a pinch of thyme or rosemary. Mix well. Add the lingonberries and the cream to help bind the mixture. Spoon the stuffing into the cavities of the woodcock. Truss the birds so that the legs and wings are held close against the bodies.

Melt 4 tablespoons butter in the skillet used to brown the bread crumbs. Dredge the birds in 2 tablespoons of the flour and sprinkle with salt and pepper. Brown them in the skillet over high heat.

Place the chopped onion, garlic, stock, and wine in a roasting pan. Arrange the woodcock in the pan and roast until the birds are tender when the breasts are pierced with a fork, about 30 minutes. Baste the birds frequently with the pan juices. When the woodcock are done—the juices will run a rosy color—remove the twine and place them on a heated platter. Keep hot.

Put the roasting pan on top of the stove and boil the juices to reduce slightly.

Blend 3 tablespoons butter with the remaining 2 tablespoons flour in a heavy-bottomed saucepan and cook over moderate heat until the flour is slightly browned. Remove the saucepan from the heat and cool slightly. Strain the juices from the roasting pan and very gradually add to the saucepan, stirring constantly, until the sauce is thick, creamy, and smooth.

Arrange the woodcock on a heated flameproof platter. Warm the Cognac in a small saucepan, ignite with a long fireplace match, holding the pan away from you, and pour the flames, very slowly, over the birds. Pour the hot sauce over the birds and serve immediately.

A strutting tom turkey

LARGE GAME

❦ ❦ ❦

Bear · Farm-Raised Beefalo · Bison (American Buffalo) · Farm-Raised Bison

Wild Boar and Other Pigs · Farm-Raised Wild Boar · Caribou

Wild Deer (Venison) · Farm-Raised Deer · Wild Elk · Farm-Raised Elk

Wild Moose · Wild Mountain Goat · Farm-Raised Goat · Wild Musk-ox

Peccary (Javelina) · Wild Pronghorn · Farm-Raised Antelope · Wild Sheep

Snow falling on bull moose

ARGE GAME USED to refer to commonly hunted wild animals that weighed over 40 pounds, but today it includes farm-raised large game as well.

The quality of all game is affected by everything that happens from the second the finger pulls the trigger. The animal, whether it be a 40-pound peccary or an 1,800-pound moose, needs to be field-dressed immediately to allow the inside to cool, decreasing the chance of spoilage. Once the animal is eviscerated, it is hung at 40°F or lower for about 5 days to age. Hanging game diminishes the chance of spoilage by allowing it to cool quickly. During that time, the tissue begins to break down, releasing enzymes that enhance the flavor and tenderize the meat. The meat will continue to slowly age in the freezer.

Because there is so little fat in large game, it can be stored at 15°F or lower for up to 2 years. Sausage and hamburger, however, should be eaten within 3 to 4 months, or the fat will deteriorate. Always defrost the meat slowly in the refrigerator.

For detailed information on cutting up your animal, contact your state department of fish and game or local extension service. Both are listed in the telephone directory.

Cooking large game, either wild or farmed, is easy because there are only two basic rules to follow. The tender cuts—that is, the meat farthest away from the head and feet: the loin, tenderloin, steaks, and chops—are cooked hot and fast. Large game is exceptionally lean, without intramuscular fat or marbling, as it is known in domestic animals. Without the fat layers to cook through, the heat rapidly penetrates through the muscle, cooking the meat to rare or medium-rare in just minutes and minimizing the loss of cooking juices. When game meat is overcooked, the connective tissue in the muscle contracts, squeezing out all the juices, making the meat dry and tough with a livery taste and texture. And even if you like liver, you won't enjoy overcooked game meat.

The best hot-and-fast cooking methods are sautéing, grilling, and broiling. Preparations for the three are the same: Bring the meat to room temperature and pat dry with paper towels. Season with coarse salt and freshly ground black pepper, or with a spicy rub or marinade (see Marinades and Rubs). Marination is not necessary, but it will slightly tenderize and flavor the meat.

To sauté steaks, heat 1 to 2 tablespoons of olive oil in a skillet over medium-high heat. Cook on one side and do not turn over until cooking juices start to collect on the top side of the meat. Turn over and cook the other side. The entire process should not take more than 3 or 4 minutes, depending on the thickness of the meat. The meat is done when it is browned on the outside and medium-rare within. Deglaze the pan with stock or brandy to make a sauce (see Sauces).

For grilling and broiling, first brush the meat with a thin layer of olive oil. Cook about 4 inches from the heat source turning it only once, when the juices start to collect on the top side of the meat.

An easy way to determine if meat is done is to press down in the center of the cut. If it pushes back with some resistance, the meat is done. It takes some practice to get the feel for this, but the best place to start is with a raw piece of meat. When you press down with your fingertip, there is no resistance—your finger sinks into the muscle tissue. Next, try it with cooked meat.

The tougher cuts—or those closest to the head and feet: the neck, shoulder, chuck, and shank—are cooked slow and low. These are the muscles the animals use the most, making them well developed and loaded with connective tissue, the part of the muscle that makes meat tough. When these cuts are cooked for a long time at a low temperature, the connective tissue is broken down into gelatin.

The two most important slow-and-low cooking methods are braising and stewing, both with moist heat. The difference between the two is that stews are made from small cuts of meat cooked in a covered pot in a large amount of liquid, while braises, such as the classic pot roast, are larger cuts cooked the same way but with less liquid. For both braising and stewing, brown the meat first in hot oil before adding the liquids to give it additional flavor.

There are two secrets to successful game cookery: First, do not overcook the meat; and second, let the meat rest for at least 10 to 15 minutes before carving it. In New Zealand, I was advised to let venison rest for the same amount of time it cooks.

Although farmed and wild large game are generally cooked by the same methods, there are some differences that affect tenderness and flavor. Farmed large game are harvested at approximately 2 years of age, before their muscles have time to completely develop. This young age, plus their less active lifestyle and ready food source, contributes to the tenderness of these animals. And, like beef, farmed game carcasses are tenderized with electrical stimulation, making the meat twice as tender as wild game of the same species.

The flavor of wild and farmed large game is surprisingly similar, but wild game is more intense because of its diverse diet in the wild. Large game animals, raised free-range on ranches where they lead a wild life, fall into this same category. These animals have the best qualities of both wild and farmed game—complex flavor from foraging but tenderness since they are tenderized through electrical stimulation.

Many of the most popular large game animals—deer, elk, moose, caribou, and pronghorns (American antelope)—belong to the family Cervidae, and their recipes are interchangeable. They are classified by their even-toed cloven hooves and branched antlers that are grown annually and shed after the mating season. The flesh of these mammals is referred to as venison, a meat that is highly prized by cooks worldwide for its delicious flavor. The venison recipes in this chapter are for wild, ranched, or farm-raised large game.

Note: Trichinosis is a parasitic disease caused by the larva of the trichina worm encysted in infected meat. Some game animals can carry the risk of trichinosis, most notably black bear, caribou, boar, and wild pigs. To be safe, always cook at-risk game to 170°F. Freezing the meat is not adequate because the trichinae larvae found in wild game are often resistant to cold temperatures.

A bear overlooking his territory

• BEAR •

Black bears are the most common bears in the continental United States. They are secretive creatures that live in the mountainous and forested areas in the West, where they can also be cinnamon colored, and in forested and swampy areas in the East. These nocturnal animals weigh 200 to 500 pounds (but only 10 ounces at birth) and subsist largely on vegetarian fare, including berries, fleshy fruits, nuts, acorns, and their favorite snack, honey. Meat and fish are only a small part of their diet.

Hunters should avoid bears that have been feeding on large quantities of fish as their meat will taste fishy. Bear meat is at its prime in the late fall when they have stored up large quantities of fat just before hibernating. Both the pioneers and the Indians prized bear fat for cooking. Bear meat is dark like venison, but has its own unique taste.

AVAILABILITY: Bear meat, culled from game reserves for population control, is available frozen year-round. A limited number of bear are raised commercially for meat which is available frozen year-round.

BEST COOKING METHODS: Allow 3 to 6 ounces per person. Substitute bear meat in any pork recipe, but trim off excess fat before cooking. Preferred cuts are roasts and loins. Bear meat can carry trichinae and must always be cooked to 170°F. Never serve it rare or medium-rare. And, unlike the strains of trichinae found in pork, the *T. spiralis* that infects Alaskan bears is not destroyed by freezing because it has become cold resistant.

· FARM-RAISED BEEFALO ·

Beefalo are a breed of cattle developed in the 1960s by crossing American buffalo with domestic cattle. In 1985, the USDA approved labeling for beefalo as "Beefalo Beef" or "Beef from Beefalo," if the animal is at least 17 percent to 35 percent buffalo. The basis for the industry is the full-blood beefalo, defined as $3/8$ American buffalo and $5/8$ bovine of any breed.

These hybrids have the best qualities of both cattle and buffalo—hardiness, fertility, no intramuscular fat, and they are fast-growing. Beefalo, raised naturally without steroids or hormones, are pastured during grazing season but are fed supplemental hay in the winter. At 13 to 15 months, when they weigh approximately 650 pounds, they are ready for the market, at a much younger age than for either buffalo or cattle.

Beefalo have red meat that tastes like beef but with just 4 percent fat compared to 15 percent fat for beef.

AVAILABILITY: Frozen year-round. Fresh beefalo is available only in some regions of the country because of limited beefalo breeding stock.

HOW TO BUY: 3 to 6 ounces per person. Cuts available are the same as for beef.

BEST COOKING METHODS: Beefalo can be cooked using any recipe for beef, but reduce the temperature to 325°F for roasts.

· BISON (AMERICAN BUFFALO) ·

Buffalo are the largest terrestrial animals in North America, weighing close to 2,000 pounds and standing $6^{1}/_{2}$ feet tall at the shoulder. Although they are commonly called American buffalo, they are not related to either the Asian water buffalo *(Bubalus bubalis)* or the African Cape buffalo *(Syncerus caffer)*. Their closest relative is the European bison *(Bison bonasus)*, or wisent. All members of the buffalo family—the American bison, the wood bison, and the European wisent—belong to the family Bovidae, which is composed of large-hoofed animals, including domestic cattle, sheep, and goats.

Before the arrival of the settlers, more than 60 million buffalo roamed throughout North America's prairies and valleys from northern Mexico to Canada's Northwest Territories. On the Great Plains, the migratory herds carpeted the rolling hills as far as the eye could see, like an enormous brown rug. These majestic animals were the staff of life for the Plains Indians, providing food, shelter, clothing, tools, fuel, and a basis for their spiritual life. In return, the Indians were strong and healthy from their readily available high-protein diet.

In Santa Fe, as early as the middle 1600s, the Indians were driving wagons loaded with buffalo hides, dried meat, and salted buffalo tongues south on the Camino Real to barter for goods in the cities of Old Mexico.

But by the turn of this century, the buffalo population had plummeted to fewer than five hundred from overhunting (for both meat and robes) and the government's policy of eliminating the main food supply of the Plains Indians to allow for expansion in the West.

Through private and governmental conservation, buffalo herds have rebounded from near extinction to more than 200,000 today. Recent research has shown that while other species have suffered from severe genetic problems when their numbers were close to extinction, modern buffalo are genetically strong and even have a unique gene that makes them resistant to most cattle diseases.

Only limited hunts are allowed for culling the herds on game reserves, as in Yellowstone National Park and the Nation Bison Reserve.

BEST COOKING METHODS: Cook as you would farm-raised bison or beef (see below).

✦ FARM-RAISED BISON ✦

Even though buffalo are being raised in every state in the union, the herds are not yet big enough to meet the growing demand for buffalo meat. In a welcome twist to some of America's most unpleasant history—the lifestyle of the Plains Indians was destroyed in the late 1800s when the buffalo were decimated to near extinction—forty-two Native American tribes are currently raising buffalo commercially. The largest herd belongs to the Crow Indians in the Big Horn country of Wyoming.

Unlike cattle, buffalo are efficient grazers, eating only the top grass, making them the ideal environmentally correct animal for the twenty-first century. They consume about 30 pounds of grass a day, supplemented by browsing on twigs, leaves, berries, and lichens. In the winter their diet is supplemented with grain pellets.

After vaccination against brucellosis and a worming shot, buffalo are handled as little as possible. They are raised hormone free—the National Bison Association recently passed a resolution against using chemicals and hormones.

Male calves are harvested between 18 and 24 months. The meat, which is state and USDA inspected the same as beef, is aged for a week before it is butchered. Young cows are saved for breeding stock.

Although the average market weight is 1,200 pounds, a good portion of it comes from the animals' large bones and heavy skin. Surprisingly, an average buffalo will yield only 545 pounds of boneless meat. They carry most of their weight in the front half of their bodies, with their huge heads and shoulders, while their back halves are comparatively small. Because the prime cuts come from the back of the animal, the limited premium meat is extremely expensive.

The hump is composed of five different muscle groups: two in the front that hold up the head, which are tough; two rear muscles that are comparable to prime rib; and one muscle group in the middle back that is like a tenderloin.

Uncooked buffalo meat has a high iron content, making it darker than raw beef. Once it is cooked, the two look almost identical, but buffalo tastes slightly sweeter.

Bison have an extremely low fat content of less than 2 percent. Unlike beef, they have no intramuscular fat, so the meat cooks quicker because the heat does not have to penetrate through fat layers.

AVAILABILITY: Fresh and frozen year-round.

HOW TO BUY: 3 to 6 ounces of meat per person. Cuts available are the same as for beef.

BEST COOKING METHODS: Substitute buffalo in any beef recipe but cook it at slightly lower temperatures. Steaks and roasts should always be served rare or medium-rare. Cook roasts at 325°F until a meat thermometer reads 135°F, approximately 12 to 15 minutes a pound. When you are testing for doneness, don't let the dark red cooking juices deceive you. It will look rarer than it is because of the high iron and myoglobin levels.

Bison burger contains 8 to 12 percent fat, about the same as lean ground round. Make the patties a little thicker than normal and don't overcook them.

⋅ WILD BOAR AND OTHER PIGS ⋅

All pigs (boars are male pigs), domestic and wild, are descendants from eight species of Old World swine that are native to Eurasia and Africa. Pigs, as well as cattle and horses, were introduced to the New World by the early Spanish explorers and friars in the fifteenth and sixteenth centuries. The razorback hogs of the southeastern United States are thought to be the descendants of the herd of pigs Spanish explorer Hernando de Soto drove from Florida to Arkansas in 1539.

Swine readily adapted to the Americas, thriving on the abundant variety of indigenous food. As their numbers rapidly increased—pigs reproduce two to three times a year with an average of eight to ten piglets—the colonists had a welcome source of nourishing meat to supplement their diet of wild game.

Throughout the settlement of America, small pockets of feral pig populations formed whenever the pigs escaped captivity. In less than a year on the lam, domestic pigs revert back to their wild state: Their tails straighten out, they grow body hair, and the males develop fierce-looking tusks, which they use as weapons and to dig for food.

To add to the mix, European boars, imported into the United States over the years to stock game preserves, also escaped into the wild. They subsequently interbred with neighboring wild pigs and created a wild hybrid pig population. As one member of the Texas Department of Fish and Wildlife said: "There are a lot of mongrel feral pigs out there."

Today, wild pigs, often reaching weights of up to 300 pounds, live in a wide range of locations in North America from wooded wilderness areas, to dry brush lands, to steamy swamps. Their eclectic diet includes wild nuts, fruits, crayfish, ground-nesting birds, roots, and tubers.

Male wild pigs, commonly called boars, have a strong disagreeable-tasting meat during the mating season due to large amounts of testosterone in their system. The best-flavored wild pigs are sows and piglets, which taste like domestic pork.

BEST COOKING METHODS: Serve 3 to 6 ounces per person. Cook as you would domestic pork but always until the internal temperature reaches 170°F. If the pig has been skinned, marinate and wrap in foil before cooking. Wild pigs can carry trichinae so always cook the meat to 170°F. Never serve the meat rare or medium-rare.

FARM-RAISED WILD BOAR

Since the 1800s, wild Russian boars, a subspecies of the European boar, have been imported into the United States for game preserves. Today these animals are being raised on ranches where they live in the wild under free-range conditions, without steroids, hormones, or antibiotics. The succulent meat of wild boar is lean and exceptionally flavorful. Both the wild Russian boar and feral wild pigs, also sold as boar, are available.

AVAILABILITY: Fresh and frozen year-round.

HOW TO BUY: 3 to 6 ounces per person. Cuts available are leg, bone-in, shoulder, tenderloin, striploin strip, rack, saddle, bacon, chops, spareribs, back ribs, and stew meat; whole, head on (30 to 50 pounds).

BEST COOKING METHODS: Cook as you would domestic pork. Farm-raised wild boar can carry trichinae so it must always be cooked to 170°F. Never serve it rare or medium-rare. Always let roasts rest for 10 to 15 minutes before carving.

CARIBOU

Caribou are native to both Eurasia and North America and have recently been reclassified as the same species as the domesticated reindeer of Siberia. They are members of the deer family that were named by the Micmac Indians of Canada: *caribou* is their word for shoveler. These animals, which are famous for their seasonal migrations, use their hooves as shovels to paw through deep snow to find lichen, their main source of food in the winter.

There are four subspecies of caribou additionally named after the habitat they prefer. The woodland caribou reside in coniferous forests in northeastern Washington, northern Idaho, Alaska, and throughout most of Canada and migrate short distances up and down mountain slopes depending on the seasons. At one time they inhabited the forests of every Canadian border state, but logging, hunting, fires, and disease have taken their toll on the population.

The barren ground caribou winter with the woodland herds but make their famous migration in the summer to the tundra in the upper far North American continent. The Greenland caribou are restricted by the terrain to Greenland, while the Peary caribou, named after American explorer Robert Peary, inhabit several islands in the northern Arctic.

For centuries, the caribou of North America have played the same vital role for the Eskimos, Indians, and Aleuts of the far north as the bison did for the Plains Indians. Their survival has depended upon the caribou for their meat, clothing, and tools and as a basis for their cultural life. Today, every family in Alaska is allowed five caribou per year.

The majority of the caribou sold commercially comes from the Canadian wilderness. Young bulls are culled from the herd during controlled hunts orchestrated by the Department of Fish and Wildlife.

North American caribou are larger than deer but smaller than elk, weighing up to 240 pounds. Their meat has a superb flavor and should be cooked like deer. Caribou are not raised commercially but their meat becomes available when herds are culled to control the population.

AVAILABILITY: Dependent upon when the controlled hunts are held.

HOW TO BUY: 3 to 6 ounces per person. Cuts available are shoulder roast, saddle, striploin, tenderloin, stew meat, ground chuck, roast, French rack, and trim.

BEST COOKING METHODS: Use in any venison recipe. Caribou can carry trichinae and must always be cooked to 170°F to destroy this parasite. Never serve caribou rare or medium-rare.

⸱ WILD DEER (VENISON) ⸱

Deer, elk, pronghorns, moose, and caribou all belong to the family Cervidae—ruminant, even-toed hoofed animals that have antlers which are shed each year. The flesh of these animals is commonly called "venison." (For more information on elk, pronghorns, moose, and caribou look under their individual listings.)

Of the two species of deer native to North America—the mule deer and the white-tailed deer—the latter is the most widespread, inhabiting the entire United States with the exception of the Pacific coast. White-tailed deer played a critical role as a source of food and clothing for Native Americans and early settlers. These hardy animals with gourmet appetites have readily adapted to the encroachment of mankind as they supplement their diet by eating domestic crops and gardens, as well as by foraging on shrubs, grasses, and wild fruits. They weigh from 75 to 300 pounds and are distinguished by their tan triangular-shaped tails that raise as a warning flag, exposing their white underside when danger is imminent and by their unbranched main antler beam.

Their larger cousins, the stocky mule deer, weigh from 125 to 400 pounds and were named for their large mulelike ears. Other distinguishing characteristics are their ropelike tails with a black tip and equally branched antlers. They inhabit a large portion of the western half of North America and live in varied habitats, from the rugged mountains to the rolling foothills.

Black-tailed deer, a subspecies of the mule deer found only along the Pacific coast, look more like the white-tailed deer with the exception that their triangular-shaped tails are dark on the upper surfaces instead of light. Flavorwise the three deer—white-tailed, mule, and black-tailed—are almost indistinguishable.

A limited amount of wild Scottish red deer meat is imported into the United States. The deer, culled from herds on Scotland's six hundred game estates, is purchased by a game buyer, transported in a refrigerated truck to a plant where the meat is aged, inspected, and processed for export. Its distinct flavor comes from their diet of heather and bracken ferns that cover the windswept highland moors where they live.

BEST COOKING METHODS: The extremely low fat content of wild deer requires either a fast cooking time for tender cuts or a long, slow cooking time for the tougher cuts of meat (see page 94).

• FARM-RAISED DEER •

Of the five different species of deer being raised in America today—fallow, axis, sika, red, and white-tailed—fallow deer are the most common. The name "fallow" comes from the Anglo-Saxon word *fealo* referring to the dominant reddish-brown color of their coat. These diminutive but hardy animals are native to Europe and Asia, where for centuries royalty kept them on their estates for hunting and ready access for feasts. Their signature palmated antlers and permanent white spots on their back distinguish them from native North American species of deer. Fallow deer weigh from 60 to 200 pounds and subsist on a high-fiber diet of grains, brush, and pasture grasses. These deer are prized for their tender and mild-flavored meat.

Red deer, like fallow deer, consume large quantities of grass. They are native to Europe, Asia, and Africa and were introduced to New Zealand with the fallow deer by English immigrants in the latter 1800s. New Zealand exports large quantities of red deer, which they market, throughout the world, including to the United States, where red deer are also being farmed.

Axis deer are natives of the forests and grasslands of India and Sri Lanka. They are currently being raised in Texas and Hawaii, where they thrive in the warm weather that is similar to that of their homeland. These small deer (35 to 37 inches at the shoulder) have delicately flavored meat that is not readily available in most of the United States.

Smaller yet, only 31 to 34 inches tall at the shoulder, are the sika deer, native to forests of southeast Asia. These diminutive animals have been successfully introduced into several regions of the United States. Large herds exist in Texas, while smaller numbers inhabit regions of Kansas, Oklahoma, Wisconsin, Maryland, and Virginia. Sika deer have a fine flavor that is more pronounced than that of the meat from the axis deer.

In the last twenty years, the number of deer farms in America has been increasing at a rapid pace. Today, the North American Deer Farmers Association Inc.—founded by Jupp Kerckerinck-Borg in 1983—has more than five hundred members who maintain the high standards required for superior-quality venison. Deer are raised drug free (no steroids or hormones) on pastures or range land with a diet of alfalfa, clover, and grass mix. They are harvested at 22 to 24 months for bucks, and 26 to 28 months for does.

Because many deer farmers have small operations, they have formed cooperatives to market their venison. Brand names are often given to the meat, such as Northern Velvet, Fallow Venison from the Pacific Northwest, or New York Fallow Venison, to distinguish their meat from other producers'.

The majority of venison sold in the United States is Cervena venison, imported from New Zealand. The word "cervena" (sir–venn–ah) comes from the combination of Cervidae (the scientific family name for deer) and venison, from the Latin, *venari*, meaning to hunt. In 1983, the New Zealand Game Industry Board coined the term Cervena as an appellation to designate premium cuts of the saddle and leg from deer and elk raised and processed under strict guidelines, modeling the program after the French appellation system. The appellation in this case refers in general terms to New Zealand. Cervena venison is only sold in the United States, Australia, and New Zealand. Ninety-seven percent of New Zealand venison is exported.

More than half of New Zealand's 4,300 deer farms are located on the South Island in the Canterbury Plains and adjoining high country. The average herd of three hundred is made up of red deer—brought to New Zealand in the late 1870s from Angus, Scotland, for game hunting—North American elk (wapiti)—introduced to Fiordland by President Theodore Roosevelt in 1905—and hybrids of the two animals. Hybrids are produced by crossing a red hind (female red deer) with a wapiti (North American male elk) bull. They are marketed as elk or relk.

Deer and elk meat sold as Cervena are raised naturally without hormones or steroids, in free-range conditions where they are grass-fed. To insure optimum flavor and tenderness, the animals are harvested at 3 years of age or younger.

After processing, the meat is vacuum-packed in packaging with gold stripes if it is shipped fresh, or with silver stripes if it is shipped frozen.

Venison from New Zealand is exported to the U.S. in chilled sea containers at 0°C or 32°F. It takes about three weeks for the ships to get to the United States, during which time the meat continues to age.

AVAILABILITY: Fresh and frozen year-round.

HOW TO BUY: 3 to 6 ounces per person. Cuts available are steaks, rack, flank steak, medallions, shortloin, shanks, saddles, stew meat, shoulder roasts, tenderloin.

BEST COOKING METHODS: Sauté or grill steaks simply seasoned with salt and freshly ground black pepper or with a spicy rub over a hot fire, 1½ to 2 minutes a side. Marination is not necessary, but it will add extra flavor. For roasts, sear them first in hot oil, then finish cooking in a preheated 425°F oven, allowing 3½ minutes per half-inch of thickness. Roast until a meat thermometer reads 136°F. Remove the meat from the oven. Cover and let rest for approximately the same amount of time the meat has been cooked.

WILD ELK

Little did the English settlers know the confusion they would cause when they named the American elk *(Cervus canadensis)*, "elk." In Europe, moose are referred to as elk. The misnomer has stuck over the years despite the disparity. American elk are also called "wapiti," a Shawnee word meaning "white rump," which refers to the distinguishing white patch of hair on their behinds.

As the herds of North American elk headed west and south to avoid the freezing grip of the last ice age, they became isolated in four distinct regions: the northwestern coast, western and interior California, the southwestern U.S. and Mexico, and east of the Cascades and the Sierra Nevada. From these regions developed six subspecies of elk: Rocky Mountain, Roosevelt, Tule, Manitoban, eastern, and Merriam. The Merriam is extinct, the eastern is thought to be extinct (one source recorded that the last eastern elk died in Pennsylvania in 1867), and the Manitoban exists only in Canada. During colonial days, elk were the most populous members of the deer family in North America.

Of the remaining three subspecies—the Rocky Mountain, Tule, and the Roosevelt—the largest are the Roosevelt, with an average weight of 1,000 pounds. They live in the Pacific Northwest from Humboldt County in northern California to Alaska. Their range extended farther south to San Francisco before the arrival of the hungry '49ers during the gold rush days.

Although the Rocky Mountain elk is smaller, around 730 pounds, their antlers are larger, making them prized as a game animal. They are named after their primary habitat in and around the Rocky Mountains, specifically near Yellowstone National Park and Jackson Hole, Wyoming, where the rugged isolation of the region has kept the herds from being overharvested by early settlers. Today these animals inhabit a narrow strip of land from northern New Mexico and Arizona extending up into Canada and west to eastern Washington and Oregon.

Both the Rocky Mountain and Roosevelt elk spend the winters at lower elevations where food is more accessible and the summers high in the mountain meadows where they graze on grasses and forbs. From winter to summer they can cover a distance of up to 60 miles.

The smallest elk is the Tule elk, a former inhabitant of central California. Large herds used to roam from the San Joaquin and Sacramento valleys to the foothills of the

Sierra Nevada mountains, but a combination of overhunting, competition for the land with domestic livestock, and encroachment by mankind has driven the herds to near extinction. Today the Marin County Tule Elk Refuge in Inverness, California, has a large and healthy herd. Tule elk are not hunted except by special permit to cull the old and sick.

BEST COOKING METHODS: Use in any venison recipe.

₰ FARM-RAISED ELK ₰

While elk are not raised commercially in the United States, elk meat is imported into the United States from New Zealand, where they are raised naturally without hormones or steroids, in free-range conditions. North American elk (wapiti) were introduced to Fiordland on the South Island of New Zealand by President Theodore Roosevelt in 1905. Hybrids, produced by crossing a red hind (female red deer) with a wapiti (North American male elk) bull, are marketed as elk or relk.

Deer and elk meat are sold as Cervena. To insure the optimum flavor and tenderness, the animals are harvested at 3 years of age or younger.

AVAILABILITY: Fresh and frozen year-round.

HOW TO BUY: 3 to 6 ounces per peson. Cuts available are the same as for venison.

BEST COOKING METHOD: Use in any venison recipe.

₰ WILD MOOSE ₰

Bull moose, the largest game animals in North America, weighing up to 1,800 pounds, are members of the deer family. Their enormous palmated antlers spread out like a regal crown above their massive bodies.

Four separate subspecies inhabit North America—the Alaskan (Yukon), northwestern, eastern, and Wyoming (Shiras) moose. Before overhunting and loss of habitat displaced them, moose also populated the wooded areas of New York and Pennsylvania. Today these colossal animals inhabit the upper regions of North America with some found in the Rocky Mountains of northeast Utah and northwest Colorado.

Moose typically live in wooded areas with water—swamp, lakes, or streams—nearby. Their diet consists of twigs (some say the name moose comes from the Algonquin Indian word meaning twig eater or to strip away), bark, willows, and aquatic vegetation. Their meat tastes sweeter than deer.

In Europe these same animals are called elk.

BEST COOKING METHODS: Use in any venison recipe.

Cascade wild mountain goat

❦ WILD MOUNTAIN GOAT ❦

American mountain goats are not true goats, but are descendants of the Old World antelope, including the chamois of Europe and parts of Asia, that crossed the land bridge between Eurasia and North America thousands of years ago. They live at the highest elevation of any animal in North America on sheer rocky ledges above timberline in the Cascade and Rocky Mountains, and in several other regions of the United States where they have been successfully introduced. Mountain goats weigh between 120 and 160 pounds and eat a vegetarian diet of lush grasses in the summer and brush in the winter. Native Americans prized them for their beautiful white woolly hair and underfur which they used in making goat-hair blankets, a valuable trading item. It is currently illegal to hunt mountain goats for food. Their flesh is considered by some to be unpalatable. They are not raised commercially.

◦ FARM-RAISED GOAT ◦

Only a limited number of goats are sold commercially. The majority of goats are sold to markets for Hispanic and Greek communities which traditionally roast them whole on a spit. Boer goat and Chevon, a cross between a South African Boer goat and a Spanish goat, are both raised in small numbers in the United States today. Australian wild goat is imported into the United States in limited numbers It is only available frozen.

Young goats are kids up to the age of 6 months, when they are completely weaned. Yearlings and under have tender, dark meat that is mildly flavored with just 1 percent fat.

HOW TO BUY: Only sold whole, approximately 40 pounds.

BEST COOKING METHODS: Cook yearlings and under as you would lamb; braise the tough and strong-tasting older goats.

◦ WILD MUSK-OX ◦

Musk-oxen, named after the strong scent emitted by the males, belong to the same family as cattle, buffalo, sheep, and goats, although they are more like the mountain sheep, or takin, of Tibet. At one time, musk-oxen were circumpolar but today they are found only in northern Greenland, Canada, and northwest Alaska where they were reintroduced in 1929. These stocky animals, weighing 900 pounds, stand 5 feet tall at the shoulder and have long brown hair with a thick layer of wool underneath. They eat grasses, lichens, and willows and tend to stay in one place during the winter.

Overhunting has drastically reduced these herds, which were important economically to the Eskimos. Today musk-oxen are recovering under strict government protection. Thirty years ago, Banks Island in the Northwest Territories had only 100 head of musk-ox but the herd has increased to 95,000 today. Most of the animals sold commercially come from strictly controlled hunts culling the herds on the island or from similar hunts in Alaska. The hunts are managed by the Canadian or Alaskan departments of fish and wildlife.

The time of the hunt is dependent upon the weather. The Inuit Indians corral and harvest the animals, and process the meat in a tent. It is so cold the meat is completely frozen in less than 3 hours.

Musk-oxen have red meat with intramuscular marbling that tastes like beef.

AVAILABILITY: Dependent upon the weather and the time of the controlled hunts; frozen year-round.

BEST COOKING METHODS: Substitute in any venison recipe.

PECCARY (JAVELINA)

Javelina is the common name for peccary, North America's only native wild pig. They are not related to domesticated pigs and wild boars, but belong to an entirely separate family indigenous only to the New World. The Indians used to ambush them around oases, where these small wild pigs would come to drink water. Early Spanish explorers called them "musk hogs" after the smelly odor they produce to mark their territory and identify herd members.

There are three species of peccary, but the only one of significance for North American hunters is the smallest of the three, the collared peccary, named for its yellowish-white markings above its shoulders that resemble a collar. The adults are only 18 inches tall and weigh from 40 to 55 pounds.

Although collared peccaries are the most widespread of the three species, ranging from Argentina to the southwestern United States, they inhabit only three states: New Mexico, Arizona, and Texas. Extensive cattle grazing has destroyed native grasses, allowing desert scrub lands to spread, thus expanding peccary habitat northward.

Because peccaries inhabit areas that are usually warm most of the year, it is imperative for hunters to skin (which automatically removes the smelly musk gland on their rump that can taint the meat with musk oil), eviscerate, and put the animal on ice immediately to keep the meat from spoiling even during the winter.

Peccaries are mainly vegetarian, eating acorns, roots, grasses, and wild fruits, but they will also eat eggs, worms, insects, and toads. Their meat is dark like venison and the adults have a strong taste, making those under a year the most desirable for the table.

They are not raised commercially.

BEST COOKING METHODS: Many hunters like to use the meat for chili or slice it thinly and fry it like venison. Javelina can carry trichinae so always cook it to 170°F. Never serve it rare or medium-rare.

WILD PRONGHORN

Pronghorns (*Antilocapra americana*) are commonly called antelope. The genus name *Antilocapra* means antelope goat, but they are not related to either goats or antelopes or to any other living animal. Instead they are the surviving members of an ancient family that is native to North America and more than 20 million years old. They are named for the male's curvaceous black horns, which have pronglike protrusions halfway up their shaft. These slight animals weigh only 75 to 120 pounds, but they can run up to 70 miles per

Pronghorns on the prairie

hour, making them the fastest animal in the Western Hemisphere and second fastest in the world, after the cheetah.

In 1803, when Lewis and Clark made their historic journey across the United States in search of direct river access to the Pacific Ocean, they found vast herds of pronghorns, as well as buffalo, elk, and deer, grazing on the Great Plains. The Indians preferred buffalo meat and hunted pronghorns only occasionally for clothing, thus allowing the herds to remain large. But by the turn of the century, as the plains were settled and fences went up, the numbers of pronghorn rapidly declined.

During the past one hundred years, extensive game management has rescued the diminished herds. Over a half million now inhabit the plains and high desert areas, from Montana to west Texas and from eastern Oregon to western North Dakota. The pronghorn is once again hunted as a game animal but under strict regulations.

Pronghorns are browsers and prefer open terrain, such as grasslands and sagebrush areas. The majority of their diet is sagebrush, followed by foliage and twigs of woody plant species, grasses, weeds, and nonwoody plants. Pronghorn meat can have a strong flavor, and some hunters prefer to use it for sausage and jerky. These four-legged vegetarians have the lowest fat content of all game animals, a trifling 1 percent. They are not raised commercially.

BEST COOKING METHODS: Use in any venison recipe.

FARM-RAISED ANTELOPE

Two species of antelope, the black buck and nilgai—both native to India—are now being raised commercially on game ranches in the United States. Black bucks, named for the dark color males turn during the mating season, are one of the smallest members of the venison family, weighing only 55 to 100 pounds. They are thriving in their new Texas homeland, exceeding in numbers the small herds found in India, where they are endangered.

The nilgai, weighing 150 to 500 pounds, is the antelope most commonly sold commercially. Although both animals subsist on grasses in their free-range environment, the nilgai, which is sometimes marketed as the South Texas Antelope, has a slightly milder flavor with tender and savory light-colored meat that can almost pass for veal.

AVAILABILITY: Frozen year-round.

HOW TO BUY: 3 to 6 ounces per person. Cuts available are saddle, boneless shoulder roast, leg, and Denver leg.

BEST COOKING METHODS: This tender meat has a delicate flavor that should not be masked by overpowering seasonings and sauces. Substitute in any venison recipe.

WILD SHEEP

North America has two native wild sheep—the bighorn of the Rocky Mountains and the Sierra Nevadas and the larger Dall sheep of the Pacific Northwest. Both have hair like a deer instead of the typical wool of domestic sheep.

Before the arrival of the pioneers, large herds of bighorn lived in remote areas stretching all the way from northern Mexico to Canada. Today, there are six subspecies isolated into small herds with varied habitat from the desert floor to steep rocky slopes above timberline. They are named for the male's large curvaceous horns, with spirals over 3 feet long, which are used in battle to determine their rank in the herd. These stocky animals, weighing 250 pounds, are strictly vegetarian, eating a diet of grasses, shrubs, or cacti depending upon the animals' surroundings.

A wild ram

The smaller Dall sheep weigh 200 pounds and inhabit the mountainous regions from British Columbia to Alaska.

Overhunting and loss of habitat have drastically reduced populations of both these wild sheep. Through strict conservation efforts, the animals are on the rebound. In the United States, tags for hunting bighorn are drawn by lottery and only one per lifetime is issued.

Both bighorn and Dall sheep are prized by hunters for their succulent meat, which is dark like venison and tastes similar to elk.

BEST COOKING METHODS: Cook as you would venison.

Grilled Garlic-Herb Buffalo Ribs

SERVES 4

My godfather—Art Ford, who owns the Humboldt Hereford Ranch in northern California—introduced me to the secret of using pureed garlic on grilled meat. He has always been a good cook and this recipe proves it. The garlic not only adds a savory, complex flavor, but it doubles as a paste, keeping the herbs on the meat while the ribs are slowly roasted over the hot fire.

3 pounds buffalo, beefalo, or beef ribs
3 tablespoons pureed garlic
2 tablespoons chopped fresh rosemary or ³/₄ tablespoon dried, crushed
2 tablespoons chopped fresh thyme or ³/₄ tablespoon dried, crushed
1¹/₂ teaspoons coarse salt
1 tablespoon cracked black pepper

Pat the ribs dry with paper towels.

Mix the garlic, rosemary, thyme, and salt together and rub all over the ribs to coat. Sprinkle the cracked pepper over all. Cover and let the ribs sit in the refrigerator for 1 hour.

Heat the grill. Adjust the grill rack at least 6 inches above the coals and slowly grill the ribs over medium-low heat for approximately 45 minutes, turning frequently, until the juices run clear when the meat is poked with a fork, and the ribs are crusty and thoroughly brown on the outside. Serve hot.

Buffalo hunters under the White Wolf skin

GRILLED BUFFALO STEAKS

SERVES 4 TO 6

The spicy chile-flavored dry rub on these steaks is not for the timid palate. If you want an even bolder flavor, add a pinch of red pepper.

Four 8-ounce buffalo, beefalo, or beef ribeye steaks
1½ teaspoons ancho, California, or Chimayo chile powder
1½ teaspoons ground cumin
1 teaspoon cracked black pepper
1 teaspoon coarse salt

Pat the steaks dry with paper towels. Mix the chile powder, cumin, cracked pepper, and salt together in a pie pan. Press the mixture into each steak, coating both sides.

Heat the grill or broiler. Grill over a hot fire for 3 to 4 minutes on each side, or until the steak is cooked on the outside and rare or medium-rare within. Be careful not to overcook.

A COLD WINTER'S NIGHT

". . . having built a slight lean-to of brush, and dragged together dead timber to burn all night, we cut long alder twigs, sat down before some embers raked apart, and grilled and ate our buffalo meat with utmost relish. Night had fallen; a cold wind blew up the valley; the torrent roared as it leaped past us, and drowned our words as we strove to talk over adventures and success; while the flame of the fire flicked and danced, lighting up with continual vivid flashes the gloom of the forest about."

The Wilderness Hunter by Theodore Roosevelt

BUFFALO T-BONE STEAK SMOTHERED WITH MUSHROOMS AND ONIONS

SERVES 4 HUNGRY EATERS

I buy one steak per person and send my guests home with their leftovers wrapped in foil and instructions on how to fix it the next day in a sandwich. Remove the meat from the bone and coarsely chop it. Put the chopped steak in a bowl with a pinch of salt and pepper and bind together with a dollop of Chipotle Mayonnaise (page 260). Spread the mixture on a thick slice of sour dough bread and top with slices of red onion and avocado.

> 1 teaspoon unsalted butter
>
> 1 teaspoon olive oil, plus more for brushing on steaks
>
> 1 yellow onion, sliced
>
> 1/2 pound fresh shiitake mushrooms, stemmed and sliced
>
> 1/4 pound mushrooms, sliced
>
> 1 teaspoon chopped fresh rosemary
>
> Coarse salt and freshly ground black pepper
>
> Four 8-ounce buffalo, beefalo, or beef T-bone steaks

Preheat the grill or broiler.

Heat the butter and olive oil in a nonstick pan and sauté the onion and mushrooms for 3 to 4 minutes until the onion starts to turn translucent. Sprinkle with half the fresh rosemary and sauté for another 8 to 10 minutes, until the mushrooms are soft and lightly browned. Season with salt and pepper and toss in the remaining 1/2 teaspoon of rosemary. Set aside but keep warm.

Pat the meat dry with paper towels and rub a sprinkling of salt and pepper into the meat with your fingers. Lightly brush each side with a small amount of olive oil. Grill the steaks over a medium-hot fire for 3 to 4 minutes a side, or until the steaks are cooked on the outside and medium-rare within.

Put the steaks on the warm plates and equally divide the mushroom-onion mixture on each.

Native American hunting buffalo on horseback

A BUFFALO HUMP DINNER

"The buffalo was the quintessential animal of the North American continent, the symbol of the Great Plains, more than any other animal save the beaver the magnet that drew the men to the West. It was not new to science, but of the men of the expedition only the French voyagers had previously seen one. Lewis immediately detailed twelve men to accompany him to the site of the kill to bring the carcass back to the river. That night, for the first time, the party dined on buffalo hump, buffalo tongue, buffalo steaks. Next to the tail of the beaver, buffalo hump and tongue at once became the meat of choice."

Undaunted Courage: Meriwether Lewis, Thomas Jefferson, and the Opening of the American West by Stephen E. Ambrose, p 153.

GRILLED BUFFALO RIBEYE BURRITOS

SERVES 4

Two buffalo steaks can feed at least four people in this recipe from Border country.

2 buffalo, beefalo, or beef ribeye steaks, 8 ounces each
Coarse salt and cracked black pepper
Ground cumin
8 fresh flour tortillas
2 cups hot refried beans or 1 (16-ounce) can
2 large pasilla chiles, grilled and peeled (see Note)
2 medium tomatoes, stem-end removed and chopped
1 avocado, pit removed, peeled and sliced vertically
Tomatillo Salsa (page 117)
4 ounces fresh arugula leaves

Heat the grill or broiler.

Pat the meat dry with paper towels. Season with salt and a good dusting of cracked pepper and cumin.

Grill the meat over medium-high heat for 2 to 3 minutes a side, until the meat is brown on the outside and medium-rare inside. Let the meat rest for 10 minutes. Slice the meat against the grain in $1/4$-inch slices.

Put the tortillas between 2 paper towels and sprinkle the outsides of the towels lightly with water. Microwave on high for 30 seconds. To serve, put out all the fixings and let folks make their own. I like to spread a warm tortilla with refried beans, followed by a few strips of meat and chiles, chopped tomato and avocado, a spoonful of tomatillo salsa, a couple of arugula leaves, then roll the burrito up.

NOTE: Grill the pasilla chiles over high heat until they are completely charred on the outside. Put them into a plastic bag and wrap them up to steam for 15 minutes. Take them out of the bag and pull the charred skin off. Discard the seeds and stems. Cut into long strips.

The American Buffalo

TOMATILLO SALSA

MAKES ABOUT 1 CUP

Tomatillos are small, husk-covered green fruit related to the tomato and the cape gooseberry. They are used in Mexican cooking for their acidic bite, which makes for a tangy salsa and a good counterbalance to rich game meat.

¹/₄ pound fresh tomatillos, husks removed
1 garlic clove, skinned
1 jalapeño chile, stemmed and seeded
2 tablespoons chopped red onion
¹/₂ cup fresh cilantro leaves
2 tablespoons fresh lime juice

Put the tomatillos in a small dish with 2 tablespoons water. Microwave on high for 1 minute, just to heat through or blanch in boiling water for 15 seconds; drain and cool under cold water. Combine the garlic, chile, and red onion in the bowl of a food processor. Process to mince, 5 to 10 seconds. Add the cilantro and lime juice and pulse 8 to 10 times, until coarsely chopped. Let stand for at least 15 minutes at room temperature. If the mixture is too thick, add a few teaspoons of water.

DURHAM RANCH
BUFFALO TENDERLOIN

SERVES 6 TO 8

More than 3,800 buffalo graze on the sprawling 55,000-acre Durham Buffalo Ranch south of Gillette, Wyoming. The ranch belongs to the Flocchini family, who own and operate the Durham Meat Company in San Jose, California, the largest distributor of wild game meat in the United States. Rich Flocchini, son of the founder Armando Flocchini, manages the company with his brother Armando Junior. When Rich entertains, he enjoys cooking bison tenderloin for his guests. This is his prize recipe, "And whatever you do," he says, "don't overcook it."

4 pounds buffalo or beefalo tenderloin
Extra virgin olive oil
2 teaspoons coarse salt
1 teaspoon lemon pepper
2 tablespoons minced garlic
3/4 to 1 cup Madeira
1 cup beef stock

Preheat the oven to 325°F.

Trim off any silverskin, the silvery tissue covering the muscle, and pat the meat dry with a paper towel. Thoroughly brush the meat with olive oil. In a small bowl, mix together the salt, lemon pepper, and garlic. Coat the tenderloin with the mixture.

Put the meat in a roasting pan, fat side up, and roast for 50 to 60 minutes, or until a meat thermometer registers 135°F. Remove the roast to a platter and allow it to rest while you make the sauce.

Pour the Madeira into the roasting pan. Light a match and flame, holding the pan away from you. Add the beef stock and cook over high heat, scraping the bottom and sides of the pan to release the caramelized cooking bits stuck to the bottom, until the sauce is reduced by half.

Carve the roast by slicing against the grain and transfer the meat to a warmed platter. Ladle a few spoonfuls of the sauce over the meat and pass the remaining sauce in a gravy boat.

DISTANT THUNDER

"The almost countless herds of these animals that are sometimes met with on these prairies, have been often spoken of by other writers, and may yet be seen by any traveller who will take the pains to visit these regions. The 'running season,' which is in August and September, is the time when they congregrate [sic] into such masses in some places, as literally to blacken the prairies for miles together. It is no uncommon thing at this season, at these gatherings, to see several thousands in a mass eddying and wheeling about under a cloud of dust, which is raised by the bulls as they are pawing in the dirt, or engaged in desperate combats, as they constantly are, plunging and butting at each other in the most furious manner. In these scenes, the males are continually following the females, and the whole mass are in constant motion; and all bellowing (or 'roaring') in deep and hollow sounds; which, mingled altogether, appear, at the distance of a mile or two, like the sound of distant thunder."

North American Indians by George Catlin

A buffalo herd moving toward water, from *Harper's New Monthly* magazine, January 1869

BUFFALO AND BEER
POT ROAST

SERVES 4 TO 5

I'm not sure which is better—smelling the savory aroma of pot roast cooking or actually eating it. If there is any meat left over, it can be made into tasty sandwiches by spreading two pieces of sourdough bread with Chipotle Mayonnaise (page 260) and layering with pieces of cold pot roast. Sprinkle the meat with coarse salt and freshly ground black pepper and top with slices of red onion and avocado and a piece of crisp lettuce.

> *4½ pounds boneless chuck buffalo, beefalo, or beef pot roast*
>
> *3 tablespoons all-purpose flour*
>
> *1½ teaspoons coarse salt*
>
> *1 teaspoon cracked black pepper or ¾ teaspoon freshly ground black pepper*
>
> *1 tablespoon olive oil*
>
> *2 garlic cloves, smashed*
>
> *4 medium onions, quartered*
>
> *2 teaspoons chopped fresh thyme or ½ teaspoon dried thyme, crushed*
>
> *1 (12-ounce) can beer*
>
> *4 to 6 carrots, cut into 2-inch lengths*

Preheat the oven to 350°F and position the rack in the lower half.

Pat the meat dry with paper towels. Measure the flour, salt, and pepper into a plastic bag and mix. Put the meat in the bag and completely coat with the seasoned flour.

In a Dutch oven, heat the oil over medium heat and brown the roast on all sides. Arrange the garlic and onions around and on top of the meat, sprinkle with the thyme, and pour in the beer. Cover the pan and roast for 2½ hours. Put the carrots around the meat, pushing them down into the beer and cooking juices, and roast for 30 more minutes or until the meat and carrots are tender when pierced with a fork. If you prefer, simmer the roast on top of the stove following the same directions, but turn the meat after it has cooked for 1½ hours. When the meat is done, transfer the roast and vegetables to a warm platter and cover with foil.

Remove any grease that has accumulated in the cooking juices by tilting the pan and skimming it off with a spoon or use a fat separator. Heat the remaining cooking liquid over medium-high heat, scraping the bottom and sides of the pan to release the caramelized bits stuck to the bottom, and cook until the sauce is reduced by a third. Pour the sauce in a warm gravy boat to accompany the meat.

El Cibolero, a New Mexican buffalo hunter painted on a door in Santa Fe around 1835

BUFFALO BURGERS WITH SAUTÉED ONIONS AND CHIPOTLE MAYONNAISE

SERVES 4

Put extra napkins on the table for these juicy burgers. Chipotles are smoked jalapeño chiles and their robust flavor is a perfect counterbalance to the grilled sweet onions. If sweet onions are not available, use yellow onions, but sprinkle ½ teaspoon sugar over them while they are cooking to sweeten and help them caramelize as they cook, enhancing both their flavor and color.

1 tablespoon olive oil

1 pound Walla Walla Sweets or other sweet onions, sliced (about 4 cups)

1½ pounds extra-lean ground buffalo, beefalo, or beef

1 teaspoon ground cumin

½ teaspoon coarse salt

¼ teaspoon freshly ground black pepper

4 onion hamburger buns

Chipotle Mayonnaise (page 260)

Preheat the grill or broiler.

Heat the oil in a nonstick pan and slowly sauté the onions until they are soft and a deep golden brown color. This will take about 20 minutes.

While the onions are cooking, put the ground meat in a bowl and sprinkle with the cumin, salt, and pepper. Using your hands, thoroughly mix the seasonings into the ground meat and form 4 patties at least ½ inch thick. Wash your hands thoroughly.

Grill the burgers over a medium-hot fire for about 4 minutes a side, or until they are cooked on the outside and medium-rare within. Put the buns on the grill, cut side down, during the last minute or so to lightly toast them, or place under the broiler, cut side up.

Serve the burgers on buns with a generous amount of mayonnaise and smothered with the sautéed onions.

STAFF OF LIFE

"The buffalo meat, however, is the great staple and 'staff of life' in this country, and seldom (if ever) fails to afford them an abundant and wholesome means of subsistence. There are, from a fair computation, something like 250,000 Indians in these western regions, who live almost exclusively on the flesh of these animals, through every part of the year. During the summer and fall months they use the meat fresh, and cook it in a great variety of ways, by roasting, broiling, boiling, stewing, smoking, &c.; and by boiling the ribs and joints with the marrow in them, make a delicious soup, which is universally used, and in vast quantities."

North American Indians by George Catlin

Indian women stretching buffalo hides while the meat dries on racks in the heat of the sun

BUFFALO ROCKY MOUNTAIN OYSTERS WITH BOURBON SAUCE

SERVES 4

Rocky Mountain oysters, a regional name for bull testicles, are considered a delicacy by those who have tried them. In taste and texture they are similar to sweetbreads. Beverly Cox, author of the award-winning cookbook *Bounty of the West*, and her husband often go to brandings at neighboring ranches in northern Wyoming. "That's where Rocky Mountain oysters are traditionally served," she told me, "since the calves are castrated and branded at the same time."

Both buffalo and venison "bull fries" are available year-round, although in limited quantity (see Mail-Order Sources, page 294).

8 buffalo bull fries
¹/₄ cup all-purpose flour
¹/₂ teaspoon coarse salt
Freshly ground black pepper
1¹/₂ tablespoons salted or unsalted butter
¹/₄ cup bourbon

Preheat the oven to 350°F.

Soak the bull fries in salted water (1¹/₂ quarts water and 2 teaspoons coarse salt) in the refrigerator for 1 hour to remove any blood. Drain and rinse in cold running water. Remove the outer membrane of each bull fry with a paring knife. Cut the fries in half lengthwise. Peel away the outer coating on each half and discard it.

Stir together the flour, salt, and pepper. Roll the bull fries in the seasoned flour.

Melt ³/₄ tablespoon butter in an ovenproof pan over medium heat and sauté the bull fries for 2 minutes a side, until they are lightly browned. Put the pan in the oven and bake for 15 to 20 minutes, until they are golden brown and cooked throughout. Remove the pan from the oven and transfer the bull fries to a platter.

Return the pan to the stovetop over medium-high heat. Scrape the bottom of the pan to release the caramelized bits stuck to the bottom and pour in the bourbon. Cook for 1 to 2 more minutes, then stir in the remaining ³/₄ tablespoon butter and season with salt and more pepper, if necessary. Pour the bourbon sauce over the bull fries and serve immediately.

UNEXPECTED GUESTS

Bonnie Orem of Prineville, Oregon, had this to say about the package of Rocky Mountain oysters she had in her freezer from a neighboring ranch:

"Rocky Mountain oysters are to us country folks what caviar is to the wealthy. The last branding/castration we were at, I decided to freeze a bunch for my friends and relatives who don't believe you can actually eat these things. If you ever have unexpected company show up for dinner, do you have a surprise for them! Rocky Mountain oysters, fried potatoes, and corn-on-the-cob. They may take you out for pizza, even if the pizza parlor is 50 miles away."

The Oregonian, July 31, 1990, Barbara Durbin

An American buffalo drawn by a Spanish artist from the description given to him by returning explorers

GRILLED WILD BOAR CHOPS WITH JUNIPER-PEPPER RUB

SERVES 4

There is not much fat on wild boar chops, which makes them easy to grill. I generously brush each side after they cook to keep the sugar in the glaze from burning.

8 wild boar or pork chops, about 4¹/₂ ounces each
1 heaping tablespoon Juniper-Pepper Rub (page 248)
¹/₄ cup apricot jam
1 tablespoon balsamic vinegar
1 garlic clove, crushed

Heat the grill or broiler.

Dry the chops with a paper towel and coat with the rub. Tuck the narrow strip at the end of each chop up against the meat in the center and secure with a toothpick to keep it from overcooking.

To prepare the glaze, stir the jam, vinegar, and garlic together in a small microwave dish and cover with plastic wrap. Microwave on high for 30 seconds. Or, cook for 2 minutes over medium heat until hot.

Put the chops on the grill over a medium fire. Grill for 6 to 7 minutes. Turn them over and brush the cooked side with the apricot glaze. Grill for another 5 to 6 minutes. Remove the chops from the grill and thoroughly coat the second side with the glaze. Recoat the first side and serve immediately.

HOG WALLS

In the early 1800s, slaves from plantations in rural Virginia built stone "hog-walls" to control the feral hogs that foraged for wild nuts in nearby oak and chestnut groves. Remnants of these rambling stone fences still stand in the Virginia countryside.

ROAST LEG OF WILD BOAR

SERVES 8

ild boar meat is dark and intensely flavorful with practically no fat. The leg is spectacular to serve for a dinner party when it is cloaked with homemade cranberry sauce spiked with Grand Marnier.

MARINADE

1/2 cup dry red wine

1/2 cup extra virgin olive oil

2 teaspoons chopped fresh thyme or 1/2 teaspoon dried, crushed

2 teaspoons chopped fresh rosemary or 1/2 teaspoon dried, crushed

1 teaspoon coarse salt

1 teaspoon freshly ground black pepper

5-pound leg of wild boar or domestic pork

1 tablespoon Savory Herb and Peppercorn Rub (page 249) or a commercial seasoning mix

1 cup beef broth

Warm Cranberry-Orange Compote (page 262)

Combine all the ingredients for the marinade. Pour over the meat, turning to coat well. Marinate the meat in the refrigerator for 1 to 3 hours or overnight, turning the meat occasionally.

Preheat the oven to 325°F. Remove the meat from the marinade and pat dry with paper towels. Generously season with the rub. Put the meat in a roasting pan.

Roast the meat until a meat thermometer reads 155°F. Take the meat out of the oven and transfer to a platter. Cover with foil and let rest for 10 minutes.

Separate any accumulated fat from the cooking juices and discard the fat. Put the roasting pan on a burner and add the cooking juices and beef broth. Cook over high heat, scraping the bottom and sides of the pan to release the caramelized bits stuck to the bottom, until the sauce is reduced by half.

Remove the foil from the meat and pour enough of the compote over the top to make a thin layer. Carve and serve with the sauce in a gravy boat on the side.

WILD BOAR STEW

SERVES 6 TO 8

Chef Kaspar Donier, who owns one of Seattle's finest restaurants with his wife, Nancy, gave me this wonderful recipe for wild boar stew. Serve it in a soup bowl over a mound of polenta or garlic mashed potatoes, or simply accompanied by a wedge of homemade cornbread.

MARINADE

3 bay leaves

2 poblano chiles, finely diced

8 garlic cloves, peeled

2 1/2 cups V-8 juice

1/4 cup balsamic vinegar

1/4 cup Worcestershire sauce

3 tablespoons smoked or sun-dried tomatoes, chopped

4 to 6 chipotle chiles in adobo sauce (see Note on page 260) or dried, seeds removed

2 tablespoons chili powder

1 tablespoon ground cumin

1/4 cup brown sugar

8 fresh sage leaves or 1 tablespoon ground sage

3 tablespoons coarse salt

4 pounds wild boar stew meat or boneless shoulder meat, cut into 1 1/2-inch cubes

3 tablespoons canola oil

6 large onions, diced

Combine all the marinade ingredients in a large bowl and mix well. Add the meat, turning to coat well. Cover and marinate in the refrigerator for 24 hours.

Heat the oil in a large pot over medium heat. Add the onions and sauté for about 1 hour and 15 minutes, until the onions are lightly brown and caramelized. Add the marinated meat and liquid to the onions and stir to mix. Cover the pot and simmer over low heat for 2 hours or until the meat is tender, stirring occasionally. Serve hot.

HAWAIIAN PIGS

More than ten thousand wild pigs inhabit Hawaii's lush tropical rain forests and grasslands, where they are still hunted the ancient way with knives or spears and dogs. Pigs were introduced to Hawaii by the Polynesian settlers who brought small sacred pigs with them when they crossed the eastern Pacific Ocean more than a thousand years ago. Over time the pigs have interbred with larger feral European swine, creating a fierce wild pig population.

Pigs have always played an important cultural role in Hawaii, providing both substance and a strong spiritual source. Even today, at every event of importance, from baptisms to funerals, the traditional sacrificial pig roasted in the ground is still served.

A wild boar

Venison Osso Buco with Mushrooms and Rigatoni

SERVES 4 TO 6

Deep in the heart of the Texas hill country is Broken Arrow Ranch, the largest game ranch in the United States. The owner, Mike Hughes, makes the best osso buco—a savory Italian stew—using venison shanks instead of the traditional veal shanks. He cooks them with porcini and shiitake mushrooms, then adds Italian pasta and cannellini beans—white kidney beans—during the last half hour. The result is a thick and savory stew with meat so tender it just falls off the bone.

Commercial venison shanks are available in two sizes: the smaller fore shanks and the meatier hinds. I prefer the hinds because they have more meat on them, but either can be used.

Hunters who have their deer cut up for them should instruct the butcher to leave the shank meat on the bone for osso buco. The shanks can be left whole or cut across the bone into 1½-inch-thick pieces. For the larger elk, moose, or caribou, the bones would have to be cut into the smaller pieces.

1 cup dry white wine

1 ounce dried porcini mushrooms

3 ounces shiitake mushrooms, sliced

*5 pounds venison (wild or commercial) shanks, either whole or cut across the bone
    1½ inches thick, or veal, beef, or lamb shanks*

3 tablespoons all-purpose flour

1 teaspoon coarse salt

Freshly ground black pepper

4 tablespoons olive oil

1 large onion, coarsely chopped

1 tablespoon chopped fresh rosemary or 1 teaspoon dried, crushed

2 bay leaves

1 (28-ounce) can Italian plum tomatoes or peeled and diced tomatoes with juice

*1½ cups homemade Game Stock (page 263), homemade chicken stock, or reduced-
    sodium chicken broth*

¹/₃ cup chopped sun-dried tomatoes packed in oil, drained if necessary

2 (15-ounce) cans cannellini beans (white kidney beans), drained and rinsed

³/₄ pound rigatoni pasta, cooked

4 ounces freshly grated Parmigiano-Reggiano cheese (about 1 cup)

1 tablespoon chopped fresh rosemary, for garnish

Preheat the oven to 350°F.

Pour the wine in a bowl and heat in the microwave on high for 10 seconds. Add the dried mushrooms to rehydrate for 30 minutes. Drain and chop, reserving the wine, and combine with the shiitake mushrooms and coarsely chop. Set aside.

Pat the meat dry with paper towels. Combine the flour, salt, and pepper and coat each shank with the mixture.

Heat 2 tablespoons of the olive oil in a large ovenproof saucepan or Dutch oven over medium-high heat. Add the meat, brown well, and transfer to a plate.

Pour another tablespoon of oil into the saucepan and add the onion, rosemary, and bay leaves. Sauté until the onion starts to brown, about 8 minutes. Add the mushrooms with their soaking liquid, the canned tomatoes and their juice, the stock, and sun-dried tomatoes. Break up the canned tomatoes with a spoon. Return the shanks to the pan, spooning the tomatoes and liquid over the meat. Bring to a boil, cover, and put the pan in the oven.

Cook the meat for 1¹/₂ hours, until it is almost tender. Add the beans and push them down into the broth with a spoon. Uncover the pan and cook for another 30 minutes, until the meat easily pulls away from the bone and the sauce is slightly thickened. Discard the bay leaves.

Toss the pasta with the remaining tablespoon of oil and the cheese. Divide the pasta among 4 large plates or shallow soup bowls and top each with a venison shank, or several pieces if they have been cut up. Spoon the sauce over the top of the meat and pasta. Sprinkle each serving with the chopped rosemary.

NOTE: This dish can either be baked in the oven or simmered over medium-low heat on top of the stove. Both cooking methods will take approximately 2 hours.

Ancient petroglyph of deer being chased by dogs to a waiting hunter

LOIN OF VENISON WITH CRANBERRY-CHIPOTLE SAUCE

SERVES 8 TO 10

This recipe comes from Dallas chef Stephan Pyles, whose restaurant, Star Canyon, is known for its sensational game dishes. Stephan is a fifth-generation Texan who grew up hunting and eating game.

2 to 3 tablespoons clarified unsalted butter or vegetable oil

1 venison loin or beef tenderloin, 4 to 5 pounds

Coarse ground salt and freshly ground black pepper

2 tablespoons minced shallots

2 garlic chives, minced

2 cups fresh cranberries

3 tablespoons sugar

1 cup dry red wine

2¹/₂ cups reduced Game Stock (page 263)

1 teaspoon to a heaping tablespoon chipotle chile puree (page 260)

1 tablespoon chopped fresh sage or 1 teaspoon dried

3 tablespoons unsalted butter, at room temperature

Preheat the oven to 350°F.

Heat the clarified butter or oil in a large skillet over medium heat until lightly smoking. Season the venison loin with salt and pepper, and sear on all sides for 30 to 45 seconds each side. Remove from the skillet and place on a baking sheet. Place in the oven for about 15 minutes for medium-rare venison (136°F), or beef (145°F).

Pour out all but 1 tablespoon of the butter from the skillet. Add the shallots and garlic chives and cook for 20 seconds. Add the cranberries and sugar and cook for 30 seconds longer.

Deglaze with the wine and reduce by three-quarters over high heat (about 8 minutes). Add the stock, chipotle chile puree, and chopped sage. Reduce by one-third and strain through a fine sieve. Press the cranberry mixture with the back of a spoon to force as much of the sauce through the sieve as possible. Return the sauce to a clean saucepan and heat it to boiling. Whisk in the butter, remove from the heat, and season with more salt and pepper if necessary.

When the venison has been removed from the oven and has rested for 5 minutes, slice and serve with the sauce.

NOTE: A simple substitute for reduced venison or brown veal stock is to reduce two (14½-ounce) cans of Swanson's Beef Broth over high heat to 2½ cups. Or, use canned beef broth with commercial demiglaze (page 253).

PEMMICAN

Pemmican was an energy-packed pressed cake made by the North American Indians. They pounded strips of sun-dried buffalo or venison into a paste and mixed it with dried fruit and melted suet.

A gangly moose

LOIN OF VENISON WITH MUSTARD-PEPPER MARINADE

SERVES 4

When I visited New Zealand's South Island several years ago, I met a lovely couple, James and Anna Guild, who raise deer on their station—ranch—in the pristine high country at the base of Mount Cook. At lunchtime, James seared a venison loin on all sides in a huge cast-iron skillet. He wrapped the meat in foil and let it rest for as long as he cooked it, then sliced it into thick slabs, which Anna served with new potatoes sprinkled with chopped garlic and capers (page 276). It was a memorable meal and one that I've made many times since. I embellish the sauce with fresh huckleberries, but blueberries or high-quality dried cherries would be good, too.

A loin is sometimes called a backstrap in wild animals. This long slender muscle is tucked against the backbone where it gets little use, making it exceptionally tender and the prime piece of meat. Of course, they will range in weight depending on the size and species of the animal it comes from. You can use the whole piece or cut off the amount you need.

1/2 cup red wine
2 tablespoons grainy mustard
2 tablespoons cracked black pepper
1 1/4 pounds venison loin
2 teaspoons mild olive oil
1/2 cup Game Stock (page 263) or beef broth
2 tablespoons raspberry jam
1 cup fresh or frozen and thawed huckleberries or blueberries
Coarse salt

Pour the red wine into a large nonreactive dish and stir in the mustard. Pat the meat dry with paper towels and generously rub with the pepper. Add the meat to the marinade; turn to coat all sides. Let marinate for 1 to 3 hours in the refrigerator.

Remove the meat from the marinade and pat dry with paper towels. Heat the oil in a large sauté pan over medium-hot heat. Sear the meat on all sides. This should take about 4 minutes. The cooking time will vary with the thickness of the loin but the meat should be quite pink in the center. Remove the meat from the pan and wrap tightly in foil. Let sit for at least 10 minutes; it will continue to cook.

Return the pan to the stove with the stock. Turn the heat to high and reduce by half. Add the raspberry jam and huckleberries and season with salt, if necessary.

Slice the loin into 1/2-inch medallions and serve immediately.

A TRIP FROM NEW ZEALAND TO NEW YORK

In 1984 the first large shipment of New Zealand deer was shipped to New York. The order was for one thousand dressed-out deer, heads on. The carcasses, wrapped in white cotton stockinette and frozen, were stacked—floor to ceiling—in a refrigerated locker in the bowels of the ship. The ship sailed for New York and arrived on schedule. As soon as the ship docked, longshoremen came on board to unload the cargo. Immediately upon opening the door to the locker, all one thousand ghostly deer carcasses came crashing forward, causing the longshoremen to promptly flee. It took another three days before a second crew could be assembled to unload the cargo.

Rocky Mountain elk

LOIN OF VENISON DANISH-STYLE

SERVES 6

I met Esther Ferguson, known affectionately as the "Danish Cheese Lady" for the many years she spent teaching Americans about Danish cheeses, while staying at a friend's home in the Napa Valley. Esther fondly recalled how venison was prepared in her home when she was growing up in Denmark. This was her family's cook's favorite venison recipe. Canned chicken stock and some blue cheeses can be salty so do not add salt to this dish until the sauce is reduced and tasted.

2 pounds venison or pork tenderloin

4 slices meaty smoked bacon or pepper bacon

1 to 2 teaspoons unsalted butter

$^1/_2$ cup Game Stock (page 263), homemade chicken stock, or reduced-sodium chicken broth

$^1/_4$ cup heavy (whipping) cream

2 ounces Danish blue cheese

1 tablespoon ketchup (optional)

Coarse salt and freshly ground black pepper (optional)

Dry the meat with paper towels. Wrap the strips of bacon around the tenderloin and secure with toothpicks or wooden skewers. Melt the butter and brown the bacon-wrapped meat until the bacon is brown on all sides. Discard the fat. Pour in the stock and cover the pan. Simmer over low heat for 35 minutes, or until the tenderloin is medium-rare (136°F for venison, 148°F for pork). Transfer the meat to a warm plate and cover with foil to keep warm while you make the sauce.

Scrape the bottom of the roasting pan to release the caramelized bits stuck to the bottom. Pour in the cream and turn the heat to medium-high, watching to be sure the sauce does not boil over. Reduce the sauce by half, or until it will coat the back of a spoon. It will thicken slightly. Turn the heat down and stir in the cheese and ketchup, if using. Season with salt and pepper, if necessary. Pour into a warm gravy boat.

Slice and arrange the meat on a platter. Pour a small amount of the blue cheese sauce over the meat and serve the remainder from a sauce boat.

A COMMUNAL EFFORT

Although the Napa Valley of northern California is no longer thought of as a haven for hunters, game used to be abundant there. The indigenous Wappo Indians hunted deer in the Napa hills with bow and arrows from blinds built overlooking deer trails. Unlike fishing holes, which often belonged to only one family, hunting territory belonged to everyone and hunting was a communal effort.

GRILLED LOIN OF VENISON IN PANCETTA

SERVES 4

One of the most prized cuts of venison is the backstrap, or loin. The following method of preparing it, marinated in a Chinese-inspired sauce and then barbecued, is especially good. Serve it with a cold Chinese noodle salad and tender spears of fresh asparagus.

1 garlic clove, crushed
2 tablespoons soy sauce
3 tablespoons hoisin sauce
1 tablespoon honey
1¹/₂ pounds venison or pork loin
4 pieces pancetta, about 8 ounces

Combine the garlic, soy sauce, hoisin sauce, and honey. Rub the mixture generously into the meat and let it marinate in the refrigerator for 5 to 6 hours, turning the meat every hour or so.

Soak 6 to 8 toothpicks in water for 15 minutes. Wrap the pancetta strips around the middle and ends of the meat and secure with the soaked toothpicks.

Heat the grill or broiler. Grill over a very hot fire until the meat is crusty brown (136°F for venison, 148°F for pork), and the juices run a rosy color, 15 to 18 minutes for a 2¹/₂-inch-thick piece of meat.

Slice into medallions and serve.

LOIN OF VENISON WITH PUREED ROOT VEGETABLES

SERVES 4

In this recipe, adapted from one given to me by Chef Philippe Wagenfuhrer, the executive sous chef at the Sheraton Grand's Grill Room Restaurant in Edinburgh, Scotland, venison is roasted and served with a puree of root vegetables and fresh apples, plus a tangy, ruby-red sweet-and-sour onion jam. They are all bold, earthy flavors that are perfect paired with venison or other large game, such as wild boar.

> 1 pound venison, boar, or pork loin
> Coarse salt and freshly ground black pepper or 1 teaspoon Ground Porcini Rub
>   (page 246)
> 2 tablespoons olive oil
> Sweet Onion Jam, (page 269)
> Potato, Celeriac, and Apple Puree (page 273)

Preheat the oven to 350°F.

Pat the meat dry with paper towels and season with salt and pepper or the porcini rub.

Heat the olive oil in a large skillet over medium-high heat and brown the meat on all sides. Transfer to a roasting pan and put in the preheated oven. Roast until a meat thermometer reads 136°F for venison, 160°F for boar, or 148°F for pork. Remove the meat from the oven and let rest for 10 to 15 minutes before slicing.

To serve, put a mound of the onion jam and a mound of apple-vegetable puree on each plate with 2 to 3 slices of meat.

DEER DINNERS

"In addition to his fondness for mushrooms, the deer is also a great devourer of hazelnuts, chestnuts, acorns of many kinds,—especially those of the white oak and the live oak—beechnut pine mast, and the like. Occasionally he will eat apples; and I have known peach-trees to be wholly stripped of their half-ripe fruit by deer. Of domestic crops the deer will eat anything green and succulent; he delights in wheat, rye, buckwheat, oats, alfalfa, rice, sweet potato vines, young corn, timothy, turnips, beans, and peanut-vines. Deer have been known to pull up peanut-vines in order to get at the nuts, which they greedily relish."

Plantation Game Trails by Archibald Hamilton

Sacramento Valley Indian stalking an antelope

LOIN OF VENISON WITH HUCKLEBERRIES

SERVES 2

We always pick huckleberries in the Mount Adams wilderness area on Labor Day weekend. Other berries and fruits can be used, such as currants, raspberries, blackberries, blueberries, or halves of sweet cherries, if huckleberries are unavailable. Fresh berries are preferable but if you can't find them, substitute dried or frozen ones. Thaw the berries in a single layer on a paper towel for 20 minutes, or use dried sweet cherries.

4 ounces mesclun

8 ounces venison or pork loin

1 teaspoon coarse salt

Freshly ground black pepper

1 teaspoon dried thyme, crushed, or 3 teaspoons chopped fresh

2 tablespoons oil

2 tablespoons extra virgin olive oil

1 shallot, coarsely chopped

1 tablespoon balsamic vinegar

$^1/_2$ cup fresh or frozen huckleberries, blueberries, currants, raspberries, or blackberries

Preheat the oven to 350°F.

Divide the greens between 2 dinner plates and set aside.

Trim the meat of any silver skin and pat dry with paper towels. Mix together the salt, pepper, and thyme and rub it into the meat.

Heat the 2 tablespoons oil in a large skillet over medium-high heat. Add the meat and brown on all sides, then transfer to a baking dish. Roast for about 7 minutes, until a meat thermometer reads 136°F for venison or 148°F for pork. Remove the meat from the oven and let rest while you make the sauce.

Return the skillet to the stovetop and heat the olive oil over medium-high heat. Add the shallot and sauté until it starts to brown. Add the balsamic vinegar and huckleberries and gently stir. When the berries are warm, pour the dressing over the greens and toss.

Slice the meat into $^1/_2$-inch slices and arrange them over the greens. Serve immediately.

INDIANS, BEARS, AND STRAWBERRY SEASON, 1634

"For bears, they be common, being a great black kind of bear which be most fierce in strawberry time, at which time they have young ones. At this time likewise they will go upright like a man, and climb trees, and swim to the islands; which if the Indians see, there will be more sportful bear-baiting than Paris Garden can afford. For seeing the bears take water, an Indian will leap after him, where they go to water cuffs for bloody noses and scratched sides; in the end the man gets the victory, riding the bear over the watery plain till he can bear him no longer."

New England's Prospect by William Wood

Elk hunters in Jackson, Wyoming

VENISON STEAK WITH CRACKED PEPPER AND BRANDY

SERVES 3 TO 4

Venison steak simply seasoned with freshly cracked black pepper and a light brandy sauce proves that you don't need a fancy recipe for game to taste good. The secret of keeping the meat juicy is to sear it quickly to keep the juices in.

1 pound venison sirloin or round steak or beef flank steak

2 tablespoons unsalted butter or olive oil

Freshly cracked black pepper

2 teaspoons olive oil

$1/4$ teaspoon salt

$1/4$ cup brandy

Chopped fresh flat-leaf parsley, for garnish

Pat the meat dry, then rub it with the butter or oil and a light coating of pepper. Marinate for at least 1 hour in the refrigerator.

Heat the oil in a large skillet over moderately high heat. Add the meat to the pan, sprinkle with salt, and cook for 2 to 3 minutes, or until the juices begin accumulating on the top. Turn and cook for another 2 minutes. Do not turn again. Transfer the meat to a warm platter.

Scrape the bottom of the pan to release the caramelized bits stuck to the bottom and add the brandy. Cook over high heat for 1 to 2 minutes, then season with salt and more pepper, if necessary. Pour the sauce over the meat.

Garnish the steak with chopped parsley. Slice and serve immediately.

Two South Carolina hunters waiting in the winter sunshine.

PAN-FRIED VENISON STEAK WITH HORSERADISH-MUSTARD SAUCE

SERVES 3 TO 4

Venison's savory flavor is a perfect match with the robust but simple country-style horseradish sauce.

3 tablespoons all-purpose flour

½ teaspoon coarse salt

Freshly ground black pepper

1 pound venison sirloin steaks, or pounded venison round steaks, or beef flank steak, cut into ½-inch-thick slices

2 teaspoons olive oil

½ cup Game Stock (page 263), homemade chicken stock, or reduced-sodium chicken broth

1 teaspoon grainy mustard

½ teaspoon prepared horseradish

2 tablespoons sour cream (reduced-fat is acceptable)

Chopped fresh flat-leaf parsley

Combine the flour, salt, and pepper in a shallow dish. Dredge the meat in the seasoned flour.

Heat the oil in a large skillet over medium-high heat. Add the meat and quickly sauté until the meat is medium-rare, about 2 minutes a side. Remove the meat to a warm platter and set aside.

Successful pronghorn hunters

Add the stock to the skillet and stir with a fork to release the caramelized bits stuck to the bottom of the pan. Turn the heat to low and stir the mustard, horseradish, and sour cream into the stock. Continue cooking the sauce over low heat until it is hot but not boiling. Pour over the meat, sprinkle with chopped parsley, and serve.

STIR-FRIED VENISON WITH PENNE AND BEANS

SERVES 4

I love the combination of bright bold flavors in this dish—venison, arugula, and sun-dried tomatoes—with the contrasting mild and soft-textured Great Northern beans and penne pasta. Although there are several different steps involved in the preparation, it doesn't take long once you get organized. Serve it family-style in a shallow bowl that has been warmed in the oven.

1 1/2 tablespoons extra virgin olive oil

1 1/2 teaspoons red wine vinegar

1/4 to 1/2 teaspoon coarse salt

1 pound boneless venison or beef sirloin steaks, cut against the grain in 2 × 1/4-inch strips

1/2 cup penne pasta, cooked according to the manufacturer's instructions

1/4 cup sun-dried tomatoes packed in oil, chopped

8 ounces fresh arugula or baby spinach, chopped

1 cup cooked Great Northern beans (page 9), or canned, drained

1/2 cup Game Stock (page 263) or beef broth

Salt and freshly ground black pepper

Stir together the olive oil, vinegar, and salt in a shallow dish and add the meat. Toss to coat. Marinate the meat in the refrigerator while you prepare the remaining ingredients.

Drain the meat and sauté in a nonstick pan without adding any oil, until the strips are cooked on the outside and rare within, about 1 minute. Add the cooked pasta, tomatoes, arugula, beans, and broth. Cook over low heat for 2 to 3 minutes, tossing constantly, until all the ingredients are hot and the meat is cooked through. Season with salt and pepper and serve.

GRILLED VENISON CHOPS

SERVES 4

These very simple grilled venison chops go well with baked potatoes and green salad.

Two 8-ounce double venison chops
1 teaspoon Spicy Texas Rub (page 246)

Pat the meat dry with paper towels and season both sides with the rub. Let sit for 30 minutes.

Preheat the grill or broiler. Grill over medium-hot coals or until the meat is rare to medium-rare, about 10 minutes. Split the chops and serve immediately

CHRISTMAS PIE CENTERPIECE

By the late 1800s, Chicago's Prairie Avenue had become the home for some of Chicago's most prominent citizens, including John Glessner—partner in International Harvester—Marshal Field, George Pullman, Philip Armour, and Joseph Sears. Their elaborate mansions were staffed with servants who did the cooking and serving except on certain occasions.

"Christmas of 1888 was a festive time at Glessner House. Holly decorated all the doorways, and twenty-one stockings were hung for children and servants. Mrs. Glessner had concocted her usual Christmas pie centerpieces, a pie tin chock full of little presents all buried in sand, and trimmed with a bouquet of flowers. For Christmas dinner, she cooked venison in a chafing dish at the dinner table."

Prairie Avenue Cookbook by Carol Callahan

Mixed Game Grill with Double Venison Chop, Quail, and Rabbit Sausage

SERVES 4

I discovered the advantages of serving a mixed game dinner quite by accident. For months I had been raving about the superior flavor of buffalo to some close friends, but on the day they were to come to dinner, my buffalo supplier was out of it. Not wanting to disappoint them, I bought some fresh quail and a double venison chop and thawed a piece of rabbit sausage from my freezer. As it turned out, sampling the three types of game at one sitting was a gustatory delight. And it was easy too, because all three took approximately the same amount of time to cook on the grill.

> 4 semiboneless quail, 4 to 6 ounces each
> Coarse salt
> 4 sprigs fresh rosemary plus 1 heaping teaspoon chopped
> 1/4 cup extra virgin olive oil
> 2 garlic cloves, minced
> 8-ounce double venison loin chop (bone-in)
> 1 tablespoon dried green peppercorns
> 1 pound rabbit sausage or other type of game sausage

Remove the necks from the birds, if necessary and pat the birds dry with paper towels. Sprinkle each cavity with a pinch of salt and stuff with a sprig of fresh rosemary. Tuck the legs of the quail up next to the body with a toothpick or tie with string. Stir together the chopped rosemary, olive oil, and garlic in a shallow dish. Set aside 1 tablespoon of the oil mixture. Arrange the quail in the dish and thoroughly coat each bird with the seasoned oil. (A pastry brush works well for this.) Cover the dish with plastic wrap and set aside.

Pat the chop dry with paper towels. Blend 1/2 teaspoon salt and the dried green peppercorns together in a shallow dish. Coarsely crush the peppercorns with the back of a spoon or by gently pressing down on them with a mallet. Rub the chop in the salt-peppercorn mixture and set aside for 30 minutes.

Heat the grill or broiler. Brush each side of the venison chop and the quail with the reserved tablespoon of herbed olive oil. When the fire is hot, put the venison, quail, and sausage on the grill and grill for 8 to 10 minutes, or until the chop is browned on the outside and juicy pink on the inside. Turn all 3 after 4 minutes. Brush the quail with the oil while it cooks. It will be done when it is golden brown on the outside and the juices run a rosy color when a bird is poked with a fork. Cook the sausage until the outside is brown and the juices run a clear yellow.

Cut the game into 4 portions and serve.

THE REST IS HISTORY

One chilly wintry afternoon in 1981, Jupp Kerckerinck-Borg, owner of the Lucky Star Ranch in New York and founder of the American Deer Farmers Association, drove to Manhattan with a dressed fallow deer carcass in the trunk of his car. He ate dinner that night at La Côte Basque, and during the course of the evening he asked the chef if he would consider putting venison on his menu. The chef replied that he would like to, but fresh venison was not available. The following morning Jupp, dressed in a suit and tie, drove back to the restaurant. He threw the deer carcass over his shoulder and delivered it to the chef with the instructions that if he liked it, the restaurant could buy the next one. The rest, as they say, is history.

Venison Stew with Radiatore and Arugula

SERVES 4

Radiatore is a type of pasta named for its resemblance to a radiator. The wavy multiple crevices of each nugget are ideal pockets for holding the flavorful sauce of the stew. If you can't find it, substitute corkscrew pasta.

1 tablespoon all-purpose flour

1 tablespoon Hungarian paprika

$1/2$ teaspoon coarse salt, plus more to taste

$1/2$ teaspoon freshly ground black pepper, plus more to taste

1 pound venison or beef stew meat

1 tablespoon olive oil

$1/2$ teaspoon dried thyme, crushed, or 1 teaspoon fresh

1 large garlic clove, minced

1 onion, cut into eighths

3 cups Game Stock (page 263) or beef broth

1 tablespoon unsalted butter

12 ounces fresh mushrooms, cleaned and sliced

4 ounces arugula or fresh spinach, stemmed and coarsely chopped

4 ounces radiatore, cooked according to the manufacturer's instructions and drained

Preheat the oven to 350°F.

Combine the flour, paprika, $1/2$ teaspoon salt, and $1/2$ teaspoon pepper in a shallow bowl. Dredge the meat in the seasoned flour. Heat the oil in a large Dutch oven over medium heat. Add the meat and brown in the hot oil. Add the thyme, garlic, onion, and stock. Gently stir to blend the ingredients and release any pieces of meat that might be stuck to the bottom of the pan. Cover with a lid and bring to a boil. Put the stew in the oven and bake for 2 to $2^{1}/_{2}$ hours, or until the meat is tender.

Melt the butter in a large skillet. Add the mushrooms and sauté over medium heat until tender. Stir in the arugula and cook for another minute, until the arugula wilts. Add the mushrooms, arugula, and radiatore to the stew and stir to mix. Season with salt and pepper, if necessary, and serve immediately.

WHERE THE ANTELOPE PLAY

"The buffalo herds, which graze in almost countless numbers on these beautiful prairies, afford them an abundance of meat; and so much is it preferred to all other, that the deer, the elk, and the antelope sport upon the prairies in herds in the greatest security; as the Indians seldom kill them, unless they want their skins for a dress."

North American Indians, by George Catlin

Animals of the woods

GRILLED VENISON KEBABS

SERVES 4

My good friend Barbara Durbin, food writer for *The Oregonian*, makes these colorful kebabs with elk meat for summer barbecues, but any venison, beef, or buffalo can be used as well.

1/4 cup balsamic vinegar

1/4 cup red wine vinegar

2 cups red wine, such as Burgundy, merlot, or zinfandel

1 teaspoon sugar

1/2 cup olive oil

1 large onion, divided (chop smaller inner pieces of onion for marinade; save larger
outer pieces for skewering, 2 layers at a time)

2 garlic cloves, minced

3 tablespoons minced fresh herbs, such as rosemary, oregano, marjoram, or a mixture

1/2 cup minced fresh flat-leaf parsley

1 bay leaf

1 teaspoon coarse salt

1/2 teaspoon cracked black pepper

2 pounds venison loin or beef tenderloin, cut into 1-inch cubes

1 medium red bell pepper, seeded and cut into 1-inch pieces

1 medium yellow bell pepper, seeded and cut into 1-inch pieces

In a medium bowl, combine the balsamic vinegar, red wine vinegar, red wine, sugar, olive oil, about 1 to 1 1/2 cups chopped onion, garlic, herbs, parsley, bay leaf, salt, and pepper. Add the meat, cover, and refrigerate for at least 4 hours.

Soak bamboo skewers in water for at least 30 minutes so they won't burn.

Heat the grill or broiler. Thread the meat onto the skewers alternating with the pepper and onion pieces. Discard the marinade.

Grill the kebabs over medium-hot coals, turning once, until medium-rare, about 8 minutes.

Serve hot, over seasoned rice.

ESTOFADO

SERVES 4

The first Spanish families in California made hearty stews of rabbit, pheasant, and venison by using a master recipe like the one below. They just varied the main ingredient depending on what the hunters in the family brought home that day. This recipe comes from a cookbook written in 1938 by Ana Béqué Packman called *Early California Hospitality—The Cooking Customs of Spanish California with Authentic Recipes and Menus of the Period*. Other than dredging the cubes of meat in flour for browning, this wonderful recipe is exactly as she wrote it fifty years ago.

Serve estofado over a mound of warm polenta. If you push the top of the polenta in with the back of a large spoon the indentation will conveniently hold the meat and its robust rich brown sauce.

3 tablespoons all-purpose flour

1 teaspoon coarse salt

1/2 teaspoon freshly ground black pepper

1 1/2 pounds venison or beef stew meat, cut into 1-inch cubes

2 tablespoons olive oil

1 onion, cut into eighths

1 garlic clove, minced

1 small red or green jalapeño chile, stemmed, seeded, and chopped

1 small piece bay leaf (optional)

1 cup dry red wine

1 tablespoon red wine vinegar

1 cup Game Stock (page 263) or beef broth

1/2 cup pitted ripe black olives

Mix the flour, salt, and pepper together in a shallow dish. Dredge the meat in the seasoned flour and set aside.

Heat the oil in a large pot. Add the onion, garlic, and chile and sauté over medium-high heat for 3 to 5 minutes. Push the vegetables to one side of the pan. Add the meat and brown in the hot oil. Add the bay leaf, if using, red wine, red wine vinegar, and stock. Stir and cover. Simmer until the meat is tender, 2 1/2 to 3 hours. Stir in the olives just before serving and discard the bay leaf.

Soused Grouse with Butternut Squash Risotto *(pages 60, 277)*

Ostrich Satay with Peanut Dipping Sauce *(page 85)*

Grilled Quail Salad with Nectarines and Plums *(page 79)*

Grilled Wild Boar Chops with Juniper-Pepper Rub
with Sweet Potato, Arugula, and Bacon Hash *(pages 126, 275)*

Venison Osso Buco
with Mushrooms and Rigatoni *(page 130)*

MIXED GAME GRILL:
Double Venison Chop, Quail, and Rabbit Sausage
with Wildwood Fennel Slaw *(pages 147, 287)*

Rabbit Loins Stuffed with Prosciutto and Prunes
and Red Cabbage with Fuji Apples and Balsamic Vinegar *(pages 178, 271)*

Smoked Duck Hash (*page 234*)

STAGS' LEAP

Several years ago I had the good fortune of attending a dinner hosted by Carl Doumani, the owner of Stags' Leap Cellars, at his beautiful historic home in the Napa Valley. When I inquired about the origin of the name "Stags' Leap," he told me there were several old legends from the early 1900s about an albino deer who lived in the region. Hunters would come from as far away as San Francisco to try and bag this rare animal, but for years this elusive majestic stag proved smarter than they were. One of the legends was about a hunting party that had stumbled across the deer's hiding place. Although the deer was seriously wounded by one of the hunters, it was able to escape by leaping over a rocky bluff, never to be seen again. As we talked, I gazed up at the abrupt Napa hills behind his property, trying to imagine the scene he was describing. Sure enough, at the very top of the hill, there were two distinct rocky outcroppings that reminded me of the buffalo jumps used by early Americans before they had horses or guns.

The following day I found an article at the Napa library that had been written more than a decade before (September 7, 1985) by a local reporter, Louis Ezettie, for the *Napa Register.* He had interviewed an elderly Napa woman, whose stepfather used to hunt in vain for the albino stag: "The hunters combed the area for days. There was much talk about it, and as the mystery deepened, and time went by, the legend grew. Hunters and townfolk began to call the place 'Stags' Leap.' For several years stories circulated of people seeing the ghostly appearance of a white stag leaping across the lonely precipice at dusk or on a misty moonlit night."

VENISON CHILI WITH GOAT CHEESE

SERVES 4 TO 6

Stephan Pyles, renowned chef and owner of Star Canyon restaurant in Dallas, makes this hardy chili with dried chiles that he rehydrates and purees. The result is a rich and full-flavored dish that is enhanced with freshly toasted and ground cumin seeds and creamy fresh goat cheese.

2 tablespoons corn oil

1 onion, chopped

2 pounds venison or lean beef, well trimmed of fat and finely chopped

6 garlic cloves, finely chopped

4 tablespoons ancho chile puree (see page 9)

1 tablespoon chipotle chile puree (see page 9)

4 medium tomatoes, blanched, peeled, seeded, and chopped, or 1 (15-ounce) can diced tomatoes with juice

¹/₂ teaspoon ground toasted cumin seed (see page 11), or ¹/₂ teaspoon ground cumin

1¹/₂ teaspoons coarse salt

Freshly ground black pepper

4 ounces fresh goat cheese, crumbled

Heat the oil in a large heavy saucepan, add the onion, and brown for 5 minutes. Add the venison and garlic, and sauté over medium heat until the meat has browned, about 15 minutes. Add the chile purees, tomatoes, and cumin and cook for 15 minutes longer.

Pour in 1 quart of water and bring to a boil. Reduce the heat and simmer, stirring occasionally, for 1 to 1¹/₂ hours, or until the meat is perfectly tender and the chili is quite thick. Season with salt and pepper to taste.

Ladle about 1 cup per serving into individual bowls and garnish with the goat cheese.

Elk hunters homeward bound

OVEN-BAKED VENISON CHILI

SERVES 6

In this unusual recipe for chili, the venison and beans are slow-baked in the oven, seasoned with onion, garlic, and a piquant mixture of ground chiles. Buy the individual ground chile powders at specialty markets or at the grocery store. Look for them in the aisle with Mexican ingredients. If you can't find the ground chiles, substitute 2½ tablespoons commercial chili powder for the pasilla, California, and New Mexico ground chiles and the cumin. As with other bean recipes, this dish tastes best if it is made a day ahead and reheated.

½ pound pinto beans

1 large ham hock, about 1 pound

4 cups Game Stock (page 263), homemade chicken stock, or reduced-sodium chicken broth

1 large onion, peeled and diced

3 garlic cloves, coarsely chopped

½ pound venison or beef chuck steak, cut into small, bite-size pieces

1 (15-ounce) can chopped tomatoes with juice

2 teaspoons ground pasilla chile powder

1 teaspoon ground California chile powder

1 teaspoon ground New Mexico chile powder

2 teaspoons ground cumin

1 teaspoon dried oregano, crushed

1 teaspoon coarse salt

¼ pound smoked cheddar cheese, shredded

1 bunch fresh cilantro, stemmed

Soak the beans overnight in water to cover. Drain.

Preheat the oven to 300°F.

Put the presoaked and drained beans in a large pot with the ham hock. Pour in the stock. Bring to a boil, then reduce the heat and cook until the beans are tender, 35 to 40 minutes. Drain the beans, reserving the cooking liquid.

Put the cooked beans and ham hock in a large ovenproof pot. Add the onion, garlic, venison, and chopped tomatoes.

Mix the chile powders, cumin, oregano, and salt with the bean liquid and pour it over the beans. Cover the pot and bake for 2 hours. Remove the lid and bake for another hour, or until the liquid has thickened and become a rich reddish-brown color.

Serve in warm bowls, sprinkled with the smoked cheddar cheese and a few cilantro leaves.

Dinner-time for a group of city slickers at a Wyoming hunting camp

VENISON FLIPS

SERVES 4 TO 6

This recipe comes from a cookbook called *California Mission Recipes Adapted for Modern Usage*, written by Bess Cleveland in 1965. She says: "Because the Indians had always depended on wild game for food, the Fathers accepted the deer, bear, pheasant, quail, and other game the neophytes brought to the missions. However, the manner of their preparation at the missions was different than that of the Indian."

Today we can make this recipe in minutes with the help of a food processor. I have added fresh thyme to the original recipe for additional flavor.

1 small onion

1 1/2 pounds venison round steak or beef flank steak, well chilled and cut into 1-inch pieces

1/4 pound lean, hickory-smoked pepper bacon, cut into 1-inch pieces

1 egg

1/2 teaspoon chopped fresh thyme or 1/4 teaspoon dried, crushed

1 teaspoon coarse salt

1/4 teaspoon freshly ground black pepper

2 to 3 teaspoons olive oil

Pulse the onion in a food processor until it is coarsely chopped. Add the venison, bacon, egg, thyme, salt, and pepper in the bowl and pulse 10 to 12 more times until the mixture is homogenous.

Heat the oil in a large saucepan over medium-high heat. Shape the mixture into six 4-inch patties and fry for 2 minutes. "Flip," or turn over, and cook the other side. The flips are done when they are no longer pink in the center.

SKILLFUL HUNTERS

"They are very skillful hunters. To kill deer they put on the stuffed head of an already killed deer and then stalk close enough to shoot with an arrow and secure their game!"

California Indians by George Emanuels

A 1562 scene of three Native Americans deer hunting

BRANDING PARTY ELK POT

SERVES 12 TO 15 EXCEPTIONALLY HUNGRY RANCH-HANDS

Last year Kim and Kit Phelts, who own a small ranch in eastern Oregon near the Eagle Cap Wilderness area, decided to have a branding party. They hired a local blacksmith to hand-forge tripod stakes with dragon heads on top for their 10-gallon soup pot. On branding day they cooked elk stew with their neighbors, Kendrick and Leslie Moholt, and Kendrick's parents, Ray and Lorinda, who were visiting from Portland. Lorinda had just taken a class with renowned Chinese cooking teacher Nina Simonds, and it was Nina's inspiration that led to the creation of this incredibly flavorful dish.

The Phelts served the stew with big chunks of homemade bread to sop up the spicy broth in the shade of the cottonwood trees overlooking the pristine Wallowa Mountains, where large herds of wild elk roam.

4 tablespoons corn oil

3 onions, chopped coarsely

3 whole garlic bulbs, peeled and smashed

Twelve 1/4-inch slices ginger, smashed lightly

3 teaspoons Asian chile sauce or 1/4 teaspoon or more dried red pepper flakes

8 cinnamon sticks

1 tablespoon aniseed

2 quarts Game Stock (page 263) or beef stock

1 cup reduced-sodium soy sauce

6 pounds elk or other venison or beef stew meat, cut into 1-inch cubes

2 pounds fresh spinach leaves, stemmed

6 cups cooked flat noodles

In a large pot, heat the oil and add the onions, garlic, ginger, chile sauce, cinnamon, and aniseed. Stir-fry until fragrant, 3 to 4 minutes.

Add the stock, soy sauce, and 4 quarts of water and bring to a boil. Add the meat and simmer until it is tender, 2 to 2 1/2 hours. Skim the surface as needed. Remove the cinnamon sticks. Add the fresh spinach and stir until it is wilted.

Divide the noodles among the soup bowls and fill with the hot stew.

NOTE: To make this recipe for 4 servings use: 1 to 2 tablespoons oil, 1 onion, 1 whole garlic bulb, 4 slices ginger, 1 teaspoon hot chile sauce, 2 cinnamon sticks, 1 teaspoon aniseed, 2 cups Game Stock or beef stock, $\frac{1}{4}$ cup soy sauce, 1 quart water, 2 pounds elk stew meat, $\frac{1}{2}$ pound spinach leaves, and 2 cups cooked noodles. Follow the above instructions.

WILD CRACKER CATTLE

Florida's legendary wild cracker cattle, named after the "crack" of the conquistador's whip, were descendants of the Andalusian cattle the Spaniards brought to the New World to feed the garrisons. The herds roamed in Florida's wilderness areas, providing "exotic" game for the Native Americans. In the early 1700s, wild cracker cattle were seen ranging with bison in eastern Florida.

Wild cracker cattle

WILD GOAT WELLINGTON

SERVES 4

The late Dr. Terry Sanford created this dish for a group of dignitaries when he was president of Duke University. He wrapped goat meat in curry-flavored grits, then encased it in a biscuit wrapper. His elegant creation also works beautifully for both venison and pork loin. Instead of biscuit dough, I use store-bought puff pastry. Phyllo pastry is another good alternative.

Two steps in this recipe need to be done in advance. The meat must be browned, drained of any accumulated cooking juices, and left to cool to room temperature before it is encased in the grits and puff pastry. And, the grits need to be cooked and completely cooled before they are wrapped around the meat. Any heat from either the grits or meat would melt the layers of butter inside the puff pastry and keep it from rising.

The meat can be wrapped in the puff pastry up to 24 hours ahead of time, making this an ideal dish for entertaining.

> 1 pound young wild or farm-raised goat, venison, or pork loin
> 1 1/2 teaspoons coarse salt
> 1/2 teaspoon freshly ground black pepper
> 1 to 2 tablespoons olive oil
> 2 cups homemade chicken stock or reduced-sodium chicken broth
> 2 teaspoons curry powder
> 1/2 cup quick (not instant) hominy grits
> 1 sheet puff pastry, thawed according to the manufacturer's instructions
> 1 egg yolk, beaten

Season the meat with 1 teaspoon salt and the pepper. Heat the olive oil in a large skillet, add the meat, and brown on all sides. Let cool. Discard any cooking juices and pat the meat dry.

In a saucepan, heat the chicken stock to boiling with the curry powder. Stir in the grits and 1/2 teaspoon salt and cover the pan. Reduce the heat to simmer and cook, stirring occasionally, until the grits are quite thick, 8 to 10 minutes. Pour onto an ungreased dinner plate and flatten with the back of a spoon. Let cool completely.

Preheat the oven to 425°F. Cut a piece of parchment paper to fit on a cookie sheet. Lay a piece of plastic wrap or waxed paper, approximately 20 inches long, on the countertop in front of you. Remove the grits from the plate and lay them on the plastic wrap. Lay another piece of plastic wrap on top of the grits and, with a rolling pin, roll it out into a flat sheet large enough to wrap around the meat. Remove the top piece of plastic wrap and lay the loin in the middle of the sheet of grits. (If you are using pork, and there is a thin end, tuck it up under the meat so that the loin is approximately the same thickness throughout.) Pull up the sides of the plastic wrap and completely encase the meat in the grits. Leave the meat in the plastic wrap while you roll out the puff pastry.

Put the puff pastry sheet on a flat surface and roll it out so that it is large enough to wrap around the meat. Lay the grits-encased meat diagonally on the puff pastry sheet and remove the plastic wrap. Pull and stretch the puff pastry up over the meat, completely enclosing it. Pinch the edges together and seal with a dab of water on your fingers. Cut two small (about $1/4$-inch) holes in each end of the pastry to release the steam as it bakes.

Transfer the encased meat, seam side down, to the prepared baking sheet. Using a pastry brush, thoroughly glaze the pastry with the beaten egg yolk. Stick a meat thermometer in the center of the meat, and put the meat in the oven.

Bake for 30 minutes, or until the pastry is golden brown and the meat thermometer reads 148°F for goat or pork, 136°F for venison.

Rocky Mountain goat

SMALL AND
EXOTIC GAME

Alligator · Farm-Raised Alligator · Armadillo · Beaver · Farm-Raised Beaver

Frog · Kangaroo · Muskrat · Opossum · Rabbit and Hare · Farm-Raised Rabbit

Raccoon · Rattlesnake · Squirrel · Turtle · Farm-Raised Turtle

A hunter and his dog take a rest

GAME THAT WAS once common and consumed on a regular basis, such as beaver and turtle, for instance, is considered exotic game today. Small game animals, at one time plentiful in North America, played an important role in American history, not only for their pelts, but also as a reliable food source when large game was not readily available. Squirrels and raccoons kept many pioneer families from starving. Beaver was cherished by the Native Americans for the fatty flesh of its tail, and the sea turtle was cooked in a steaming pot of turtle soup by the colonists. But as the number of small game dwindled, so did their popularity, making them no more than culinary oddities, except for those who have them as their only source of meat.

Today the most common small game animals are rabbits and hares. The same rule applies to cooking them as to other game: The more tender domestic rabbits can be cooked by either the hot-and-fast or slow-

and-low cooking methods, while the leaner, and consequently tougher, wild rabbits and hares need slow-and-low moist heat.

Exotic game, on the other hand, includes a wide range of animals from the long slithery alligator to the small but mighty snapping turtle, and the best cooking method for each is discussed individually.

• ALLIGATOR •

The American alligator, indigenous to the southeastern United States, inhabits the coastal plain—from south Texas to the Florida Keys and up to North Carolina—and the rivers and marsh areas in southeast Oklahoma and south Arkansas. They are the largest reptile in North America, ranging from 6 to 12 feet in length.

Alligators live on the muddy banks of large bodies of water where they can bask in the sun and keep a watchful eye out for food. Their carnivorous diet includes small mammals, turtles, birds, fish, and an occasional deer or cow.

Before they owned guns, Seminole Indians in Florida caught alligators by jumping on their backs and spearing them. Small alligators were caught and kept in pens until they were big enough for eating. The meat was smoked over a smoldering fire of oak or hickory and then served with wild orange juice.

For many years alligators were heavily hunted for their skins but restrictions on hunting have allowed these giant reptiles to make a comeback. They were removed from the endangered species list in 1983 and limited hunts began in 1989.

Today, wildlife and land management programs regulate the farming and harvesting of alligators. In Florida, for example, approximately twelve thousand wild alligators are killed each year by nuisance hunters who are trained to dispose of these dangerous reptiles for property owners. The animals, averaging $8^1/_2$ feet in length, are taken to state-inspected and -licensed facilities where the meat is processed and sold commercially.

In wild alligators, the muscles that are used the most, the legs and some of the body meat under the jaw, are reddish and are often substituted for turtle meat or used for sausages, soups, and fritters. The sirloin, which is pure white meat and comes mostly from the tail next to the tenderloin, is the most tender cut, followed by the slightly pink tenderloin. Wild and farm-raised alligators are cooked using the same method.

• FARM-RAISED ALLIGATOR •

Alligators are farm-raised in enclosed areas where there is both water and land. They are fed a diet of red meat, chicken livers, and fish, and harvested when they are $4^1/_2$ feet long, at approximately 2 to 3 years.

Almost all alligator meat is sold frozen. A recent University of Florida study found that it can be safely frozen for 4 months without losing any of its qualities. Thaw the meat in the refrigerator and do not refreeze once it is thawed.

Alligator meat has only 3 percent fat per 3.6 ounce serving, and it is low in calories, too. The most tender cuts come from the tenderloin and sirloin. Unlike wild alligators, which have some red meat, farm-raised alligators are all white meat. Substitute alligator tenderloin and sirloin for delicate-tasting fish, such as fresh cod or monkfish.

Marinating alligator before cooking will tenderize it and add flavor, especially to the tougher leg meat. Use mild marinades so as not to mask the meat's flavor.

AVAILABILITY: Frozen year-round.

HOW TO BUY: 3 to 6 ounces per person. Cuts available are the sirloin and the tenderloin, which is slightly pinker than the sirloin, but the most tender and delicately flavored piece of meat.

BEST COOKING METHODS: Sauté the sirloins and tenderloins in butter or olive oil and season simply with salt and pepper and a squeeze of fresh lemon juice. The tougher cuts from the leg and body can be ground to make fritters or used in soups and gumbos. In the South, deep-frying is still the most popular cooking method.

ARMADILLO

Armadillos, sometimes referred to as "opossum on the half-shell," are members of the same family as sloths and anteaters. There are twenty species but only one in North America, the nine-banded armadillo, which ranges as far north as north Texas. These nocturnal animals eat insects, vegetation, and small mammals during the night and spend their days sleeping in their burrows.

Armadillo meat is light colored and tastes like pork. They are not sold commercially. Always wear rubber gloves when handling armadillo. They contract and carry leprosy. Never serve the meat rare or medium-rare.

BEST COOKING METHOD: Cut the meat into small pieces and sauté in butter.

BEAVER

Beavers and other furred game were the soft gold that first attracted French, Russian, and British explorers to the Northern Territories in the mid-sixteenth century. At one time these nocturnal animals ranged from northern Mexico to the Arctic Ocean, but overhunting has greatly diminished their numbers. Their pelts were in great demand for top hats, in vogue in Europe at the time, made from the beaver's cashmerelike hair under their thick fur. By the early 1800s, the beaver trade declined due to overhunting and the rising popularity of the silk top hat in Europe. At the same time, the advent of steamboats improved transportation on the Missouri and Santa Fe trails, and trade in bison hides took its place.

Today, while beavers have been eliminated from much of their original territory, they are being successfully reintroduced in many locations. These aquatic rodents weigh up to 60 pounds and live in creeks, ponds, and on the banks of small rivers. Their simple diet consists of tree bark and buds.

For centuries Native Americans trapped beavers in baskets for food (the fatty tail was highly prized) and their pelts. The baskets were eventually replaced with steel traps. Small numbers of beaver are still trapped.

Beaver meat is dark red with a strong flavor, and only young beaver, under 2 years old, should be cooked. A friend once told me that old beaver tastes like the underside of a Mexican saddle.

BEST COOKING METHODS: Follow the instructions for farm-raised beaver below.

⸰ FARM-RAISED BEAVER ⸰

AVAILABILITY: Frozen year-round.

HOW TO BUY: 3 to 6 ounces per person. Beavers are sold whole (5 to 8 pounds), legs, or saddles.

BEST COOKING METHOD: Soak beaver meat in salted water (1 quart water with 3 tablespoons coarse salt) for 1 hour before cooking. Drain and pat dry. Braise.

⸰ FROG ⸰

Frog's legs are widely eaten as a delicacy in both Europe and Asia, but that has never been the case in the United States, with the exception of a few Southern gulf states, where bull frogs flourish. In Louisiana and Florida, for instance, wild frog's legs are sold directly to restaurants and distributors, and every little country restaurant has them on their menus in the spring and summer when the frogs are plentiful. Every state has its own harvesting regulations for frogs, which can be obtained from each state's department of fish and wildlife.

Legs are the only edible part of a frog. The majority of frog's legs sold in the United States are imported from Southeast Asia and are sold frozen and skinned. Frog's legs are harvested in the United States in the spring and summer, when they are sold fresh in upscale grocery stores or fish markets.

Frog's legs have white meat with a delicate flavor that is, yes, similar to young chicken. To cook, thaw frozen legs overnight in the refrigerator. Do not refreeze. Serve smaller frog's legs as an appetizer, and large ones for an entrée.

AVAILABILITY: Frozen year-round; fresh in spring and summer in some parts of the country.

HOW TO BUY: 6 pairs per person for small frog's legs (6 to 8 per pound); 2 pairs per person for large frog's legs (4 to 6 per pound).

BEST COOKING METHOD: Dredge in seasoned flour and fry as you would chicken legs in butter or oil.

· KANGAROO ·

Kangaroos are the largest members of the marsupial family. They are indigenous to Australia and to the surrounding islands where they have been hunted for centuries for their hides and meat. As browsers, their diet consists of herbs and grasses, often competing with cattle and sheep for food.

Of the large kangaroos, the gray is the most common species harvested. Most of the meat from a kangaroo comes from its powerful hind legs, which enable the animal to leap more than 30 feet and run with speeds up to 30 miles per hour. Kangaroo meat is red and lean—with just 0.5 percent fat.

AVAILABILITY: Frozen year-round.

HOW TO BUY: 3 to 6 ounces per person. Cuts available are medallions, loins, bone-in leg, boneless leg, rump, French rack, and ground.

BEST COOKING METHODS: Sauté medallions, loins, and steaks to medium-rare. Stew or braise tougher cuts, such as the shoulder. Use in any venison recipe.

· MUSKRAT ·

Muskrats, named for their anal musk sacs, are semiaquatic rodents found throughout North America. They live in marshes and banks along water and are essentially vegetarian, eating aquatic plants and grasses, supplemented by mussels, crawfish, and fish. Known as "marsh rabbit" in some areas in the South and mid-Atlantic states, they are still sold seasonally in a few locations, such as Baltimore's famous Lexington Market from January through March.

AVAILABILITY: Limited.

HOW TO BUY: Muskrats are sold skinned and eviscerated with the head and tail removed. Buy 1 muskrat per person.

BEST COOKING METHOD: They have tough, dark meat that needs to be braised.

◦ OPOSSUM ◦

Opossums are one of the most primitive animals and the only marsupial in North America. They carry their immature young in their pouches until they are mature enough to be on their own. Originally opossums were only in the South, but they have gradually spread throughout most of the United States.

The Indians taught the colonists how to cook opossums and to hunt them in the fall and winter when the animals have a thick layer of fat under their skins. Opossums are still hunted and eaten in the South. They have dark meat that is traditionally roasted whole, accompanied by sweet potatoes—"possum 'n' taters."

Opossums are walking garbage disposals, eating almost anything that crosses their paths, from fruits, berries, insects, and small mammals to cultivated crops.

BEST COOKING METHODS: Roast or braise.

◦ RABBIT AND HARE ◦

Rabbits and hares, both native to both the Old and New Worlds, belong to the same family but have different characteristics. Hares are larger with longer hind legs and ears, necessary for their life in the open country where they must be on the alert and outrun their enemies to survive. Their young are born with hair and they can move around immediately after birth. Common hares in the United States are the snowshoe hare, the jackrabbit—both with white meat—and the introduced European hare with dark meat.

The wild Scottish blue hare, considered to be the same species as the Arctic hare in the Far North, is imported into the United States from the highlands of Scotland. It has dark meat that is well aged, perhaps too much so for most American palates.

Wild rabbits are born naked, blind, and helpless into a fur-lined nest. Unlike

A cross-country ski hunter and his bounty of snow-shoe hares

hares, they are not long-distance runners and live in bushy areas often near woody areas. Rabbits are prolific breeders with a gestation period of only 32 days. Their sheer numbers and fine-tasting meat make them America's most important small game animal.

The most common are the cottontail rabbits, with eastern cottontails, whose range covers the entire United States east of the Rocky Mountains, the most widely hunted small game animal. Both rabbits and hares eat a strict vegetarian diet and often compete with farmers and gardeners. Wild rabbits have flavorful white meat.

Most wild rabbits and hares carry tularemia, or rabbit disease, especially in warmer climates. Always wear rubber gloves when handling them and thoroughly cook the meat until it is well-done.

BEST COOKING METHODS: The lean meat of wild rabbit and hare needs to be marinated up to 24 hours and cooked with a moist heat, such as braising or stewing. Serve 1 pound per person.

⸰ FARM-RAISED RABBIT ⸰

Of all the game being farm-raised today, rabbits are the best buy and the most underutilized. Through genetic engineering, farm-raised rabbits have a greater ratio of meat to bone than wild rabbits. Their delicately textured white meat can be substituted in any recipe for chicken.

The most common farm-raised rabbits in the United States are the California and New Zealand whites, known for their high ratio of meat to bone and their fast growth rate. They are raised naturally, without hormones or antibiotics, and fed a diet of corn, soy, and wheat, supplemented with alfalfa.

Rabbits, sold at 9 to 12 weeks when they weigh 2 to 3½ pounds, are fryers. Their young age means that they will be more tender than the 5- to 6-month-old roasters. Both are sold whole or cut-up. To cut up a rabbit or hare, cut off the hind and fore legs at the joints. Cut the remaining saddle into two or four equal pieces.

AVAILABILITY: Fresh or frozen year-round.

HOW TO BUY: 3 to 6 ounces per person for boneless rabbit, 1 pound per person for bone-in. Fryers (2 to 3 pounds) and roasters (4 to 6 pounds) are sold whole and cut up into hindquarters, front quarters, bone-in saddle, boneless saddle, loins (4 to 6 per pound), and tenderloins (22 to 28 per pound). Ground rabbit is also available. Always buy hindquarters if they are available because they have more meat. Rabbits are often sold with their livers, which are large, sweet, and delicately flavored, perfect for pâtés.

BEST COOKING METHODS: Cook rabbit like chicken: Roast or grill fryers, braise the older roasters. Boned saddles are delicious stuffed and grilled. Loins and tenderloins are the most tender cuts and can be cooked like chicken breast: simply sautéed in butter and served with a sauce.

⸱ RACCOON ⸱

Raccoons, about the size of a small dog, live throughout the United States. They eat a varied diet from bird's eggs and frog's legs to nuts and fruits. They have long been valued for their fur and their meat was commonly eaten in colonial days. Today they are still hunted in the South.

BEST COOKING METHODS: Roast or braise.

⸱ RATTLESNAKE ⸱

Rattlesnakes are members of the pit viper family named for their tail that rattles when the snakes are threatened. All thirty species found throughout the United States feed on lizards and small mammals. They are the only animal in the United States that can be hunted and sold without restrictions.

Wild rattlesnakes are sold frozen, whole and skinned, through large meat distributors. Their meat is white and tastes like, yes, you guessed it, chicken.

AVAILABILITY: Frozen year-round.

HOW TO BUY: Only sold whole (1 to 3 pounds), skin off.

BEST COOKING METHOD: Cut the meat into bite-size pieces, dredge in seasoned flour or tempura batter, and deep-fry. Like all reptiles, rattlesnake have meat with a high percentage of water. Do not freeze it longer than 4 months and do not refreeze it once it has been thawed.

SQUIRREL

Although squirrels are not as common now as they once were in the diets of early Americans, they remain a popular small game animal in the Midwest, Northeast, and South. Of the various species, the two most commonly hunted are the eastern gray and the eastern fox squirrel, both tree squirrels that are found throughout the entire United States east of the Rocky Mountains. They eat a diet of nuts, fruits, fungi, and often the new layer of wood between the bark and the trunk.

Early settlers learned how to make stew from the Indians by cooking small game, such as squirrel and rabbit, with corn, tomatoes, and beans. Squirrel meat is white and tastes similar to chicken.

BEST COOKING METHODS: Substitute in any recipe for chicken.

TURTLE

Turtles appeared on earth more than two hundred million years ago, even predating dinosaurs, making them one of the oldest animals on the planet. Of the twelve families of turtles in the world, seven are indigenous to the United States and Canada.

All turtles, from the land-dwelling tortoises to the aquatic terrapins, have a hard outer shell with a toothless beak.

In American history, the sea turtle has always been prized for its meat. During the early nineteenth century, ships carried sea turtles from the Caribbean to Philadelphia three times a week. These 70-pound reptiles were auctioned off to local restaurants and taverns that specialized in turtle soup banquets. When supplies became short, cooks substituted the local marsh turtles.

Native Americans cut up the soft-shell turtle and cooked it in a pot but roasted other turtles right in their shells. Empty turtle shells were made into drums and rattles.

It is encouraging to note that turtle farmers throughout the world are discovering that the survival rate is high when farm-raised hatchlings are put back into the wild. In Iowa, for instance, the population of snapping turtles has actually increased thanks to the work of Fred Millard. For the past fifteen years Fred has been releasing eight to ten thousand hatchlings back into the wild. He recently released two hundred turtles in Oklahoma.

A snapping turtle

BEST COOKING METHODS: Braise or use for soups or stews.

FARM-RAISED TURTLE

The only family of turtles raised commercially for human consumption in the United States today is the indigenous snapping turtle, named for its method of biting. Both the common snapping turtle and the larger alligator snapping turtle have long been prized as food.

Snapping turtles, characterized by massive heads, long tails, and hooked jaws, are farm-raised in large 6-foot-deep ponds for 3 years and are fed a natural diet free of hormones and antibiotics. They are harvested at 10 to 12 pounds.

Turtle meat is composed of seven muscles, with both light and dark meat, like chicken, that are sold together. As with all reptiles, turtle meat has a high percentage of water in it. Do not freeze it longer than 4 months and do not refreeze it once it has been thawed.

AVAILABILITY: Sold frozen, semiboneless, and cut-up; good for stock.

HOW TO BUY: Sold in 5-pound tubs.

BEST COOKING METHODS: Braise or use for soups or stews.

BAKED GATOR FRITTERS

MAKES ABOUT 40 FRITTERS

If you want a dish that is an instant icebreaker at a party, this is it. Heather McPherson, food editor of the *Orlando Sentinel,* makes these tasty baked gator fritters when she entertains. They are golden brown, flecked with bits of red pepper and green onion, and packed with flavor. I like to serve them on a platter with an accompanying bowl of Thai sweet chili sauce—*tuong ot ngot*—to dunk them in. You can buy the sauce at Asian markets. Or, serve them with a spicy salsa, a splash of Tabasco, or a simple cocktail sauce.

The fritters can be made in advance and frozen in a plastic freezer bag for up to 30 days. Thaw them in the microwave using the medium-low setting, 30% power for 1 minute, then bake following the instructions below.

1 pound alligator tail meat, chopped

2 eggs, beaten

$1/2$ cup chopped red bell pepper

$1/2$ cup finely chopped scallions, including green tops

$1/2$ teaspoon coarse salt

2 garlic cloves, minced

1 cup dried bread crumbs

1 tablespoon grainy mustard

1 tablespoon ketchup or mild-flavored barbecue sauce

Tabasco

$1/4$ cup whole wheat flour

$1/4$ cup vegetable oil

Cocktail sauce or Thai sweet chili sauce

Preheat the oven to 350°F. Lightly grease 2 baking sheets. Pulse the alligator meat in a food processor until the meat is well ground and becomes almost puttylike in texture. Remove the meat to a bowl. Pick over and discard any tendons that remain.

Add the remaining ingredients, except the cocktail sauce, and mix thoroughly. Shape the mixture into small balls, about 1 inch in diameter, and arrange them on the baking sheets 1 or 2 inches apart.

Bake for 25 to 30 minutes and serve hot with cocktail sauce.

GATOR TAIL WITH SWAMP SAUCE

SERVES 9

*D*eep-frying is the most popular method of cooking alligator in the South. Bite-size pieces of alligator are marinated, deep-fried, and served with a spicy sauce.

Sherry Vinegar–Herb Marinade (page 245) or bottled Italian salad dressing

2 pounds alligator tail meat sirloin

2 eggs

2 cups milk

$1/4$ cup all-purpose flour

$1/2$ teaspoon coarse salt

$1/4$ teaspoon freshly ground black pepper

Peanut oil for deep-frying

SWAMP SAUCE

1 cup mayonnaise

3 tablespoons grainy mustard

1 tablespoon Worcestershire sauce

1 teaspoon whole oregano, crushed

3 garlic cloves, minced

Cayenne

Prepare the marinade. Remove all fat and sinew from the gator meat. Place the meat between 2 sheets of waxed paper and pound with a mallet to a thickness of $1/2$ inch. Cut the meat across the grain into 1-inch squares.

Marinate the meat in a shallow dish in the refrigerator overnight.

In a small bowl, whisk or blend together all the sauce ingredients, adding cayenne to taste. Set aside.

In a shallow dish beat the eggs with the milk. In another shallow dish, combine the flour, salt, and pepper. Remove the meat from the marinade. Dip the pieces of alligator in the egg mixture, then dredge into the seasoned flour. Set aside on a wire rack.

Heat the peanut oil to 350°F. Deep-fry the meat in batches until golden brown. Remove with a slotted spoon and drain on paper towels.

Serve hot with Swamp Sauce.

FRIED CURRIED FROG'S LEGS

SERVES 4

Frog's legs are most commonly cooked like chicken—simply dredged in flour and fried in oil and butter until they are crisp and golden brown. But Steven Raichlen—ex-Portlander who now lives in Miami—author of the IACP/Julia Child Award–winning *Miami Spice* cookbook, gives them a West Indian twist, seasoning the meat with curry powder and serving them with aioli, a garlicky mayonnaise enhanced with annatto, cilantro, and lime juice. Substitute chicken drumettes or drumsticks if frog's legs are unavailable.

I have included two different methods for cooking the frog's legs. The first is for deep-frying and the second is for sautéing; both work perfectly.

SUNSHINE AIOLI
1/4 cup canola oil
2 tablespoons annatto seeds
6 garlic cloves, minced
1/4 teaspoon coarse salt
1/4 teaspoon freshly ground black pepper
1/4 teaspoon cayenne
1 cup mayonnaise
2 tablespoons minced fresh cilantro
1 tablespoon fresh lime juice

1 tablespoon curry powder
1 teaspoon cayenne
1 teaspoon coarse salt
1 teaspoon freshly ground black pepper
1 1/2 pounds (6 pairs per person) small frog's legs (fresh preferred) or chicken drumettes
*   or drumsticks (if using chicken, remove the skin)*
1/2 cup all-purpose flour
1 egg, beaten
1/2 cup buttermilk
1 cup cracker crumbs
About 3 cups vegetable oil for frying or 2 tablespoons unsalted butter and 2 tablespoons
*   olive oil for sautéing*

First, make the aioli. Heat the oil in a small frying pan. Add the annatto seeds and cook over medium heat until the oil is orange and fragrant and the seeds begin to crackle, 3 to 4 minutes. Strain the oil into a clean jar and let cool.

In the bottom of a mixing bowl, mash the garlic and salt with a fork. Whisk in the pepper, cayenne, and mayonnaise. Whisk in the annatto oil in a thin stream, followed by the cilantro and lime juice. Set aside.

To prepare the frog's legs, combine the curry powder, cayenne, salt, and pepper in a mixing bowl and stir to mix. Remove half of the spice mixture and set aside. Add the frog's legs to the bowl. Toss and set aside for 15 minutes.

Combine the flour and reserved spice mixture in a shallow bowl and whisk to mix. Combine the egg and buttermilk in another bowl and whisk to mix. Place the cracker crumbs in a third bowl.

Using 2 forks, dip the frog's legs first in the flour mixture, then in the egg mixture, and finally in the cracker crumbs, shaking off the excess after each.

To deep-fry the frog's legs, pour the oil into a deep frying pan or electric skillet to a depth of 1 inch and heat to 350°F. Deep-fry the frog's legs until golden brown on the outside and opaque within, 1 to 2 minutes for small legs or 4 to 5 minutes for the larger ones, turning with a wire skimmer, and working in several batches so as not to crowd the pan. Drain on paper towels and serve with ramekins of Sunshine Aioli.

To sauté the frog's legs, heat a deep frying pan with 2 tablespoons butter and 2 tablespoons olive oil over medium-high heat until the butter is bubbling. Sauté the frog's legs following the instructions for deep-frying, but cook another minute or two longer.

RABBIT LOINS STUFFED WITH PROSCIUTTO AND PRUNES

SERVES 4

Rabbit loins are enhanced by the sweet, salty, and herbal-flavored ingredients in this recipe. The meat can be stuffed with the prunes and prosciutto up to 8 hours in advance, then rolled in the herbs just before baking, making this a perfect dish for entertaining.

12 pitted prunes
$^1/_4$ cup brandy
Four 4-ounce rabbit loins, $^3/_8$-inch thick
Coarse salt
Freshly ground black pepper
4 thin slices prosciutto
2 teaspoons olive oil
$^1/_2$ bunch arugula, coarse stems discarded, chopped, about $^1/_2$ cup
$^1/_4$ cup chopped fresh flat-leaf parsley
$^1/_4$ cup chopped fresh basil
1 large scallion, chopped

Preheat the oven to 350°F.

Combine the prunes and brandy in a small bowl and heat in the microwave on high for 30 seconds. Or, put them in a small pan over medium heat until the prunes are hot throughout. Remove from the heat and let macerate for 30 minutes. Remove the prunes from the brandy and cut 8 prunes in half lengthwise. Set aside 4 whole prunes.

Pat the loins dry with paper towels and season both sides with salt and pepper. Fold each piece of prosciutto in half lengthwise and place one slice on top of each rabbit loin. At the narrowest end of each loin, lay 4 prune halves, side by side, on top of the prosciutto. Starting at the narrowest end again, roll the loins pinwheel fashion and secure with toothpicks or wooden skewers. Brush the rolled loins with olive oil.

In a shallow dish, toss together the arugula, parsley, basil, and scallion. Coat each loin in the herbs and place in a lightly oiled baking dish.

Bake for 20 minutes. Put the reserved prunes on top of each rolled loin and bake for an additional 13 to 15 minutes, until the juices run clear. Serve hot on individual plates.

Braised Rabbit with Bing Cherries and Brandy

SERVES 4

If fresh cherries are not available, use high-quality frozen cherries now on the market. The slight sweetness of the fruit enhances the mild rabbit and creates a dusky red sauce that I season with fresh rosemary. Serve over steamed rice or hot noodles.

1 tablespoon unsalted butter

2 shallots, finely chopped

$^1/_4$ cup all-purpose flour

$^1/_2$ teaspoon coarse salt

$^1/_4$ teaspoon freshly ground black pepper

$1^1/_2$- to 2-pound rabbit, cut up, or rabbit hindquarters separated at the joint

1 tablespoon olive oil, or more as needed

1 cup Bing cherries, pitted and halved (if using frozen cherries, thaw and drain)

$^1/_4$ cup brandy or kirschwasser

$^1/_2$ cup homemade chicken stock or reduced-sodium chicken broth

1 teaspoon chopped fresh rosemary

Chopped fresh flat-leaf parsley

Melt the butter in a heavy skillet over medium-high heat. Add the shallots and sauté until they are soft and start to turn golden brown, 6 to 8 minutes.

In a shallow dish, combine the flour, salt, and pepper. Dredge the rabbit pieces in the flour mixture.

Push the shallots to one side of the pan and add the olive oil. Adding the larger pieces first, sauté the rabbit until the meat is golden brown. Add more oil if necessary to keep the pieces from sticking.

Sprinkle the cherries on top of the rabbit and pour the brandy over all. Holding the pan away from you, carefully light the brandy with a match. When the flame burns out, add the chicken stock and fresh rosemary. Cover and simmer for 45 minutes, until the rabbit is tender when pierced with a fork.

Transfer the rabbit to a plate and keep warm. Turn the heat to high and reduce the sauce to $^3/_4$ cup. Return the rabbit to the sauce and serve garnished with chopped parsley.

Rabbit Stew with Flumagina

SERVES 4

This unusual recipe for rabbit comes from Paula Naughton, who grew up in Montana where game was eaten almost every day. Both of her grandmothers were Italian, and they adapted their Old World recipes to New World ingredients. Here, rabbit is stewed with white wine and herbs and served with polenta and a dollop of flumagina, an onion sauce that Paula's grandmothers always served with polenta. As with all stews, this one develops more flavor when it is cooked in advance and reheated.

¹/₄ cup all-purpose flour

³/₄ to 1 teaspoon coarse salt

4 rabbit hindquarters, about 1¹/₄ pounds, leg and thigh separated

2 to 3 tablespoons extra virgin olive oil

2 to 3 garlic cloves, finely minced

1 cup finely chopped onion

¹/₂ cup finely chopped fresh flat-leaf parsley

1 cup finely chopped celery, leaves included

1 large carrot, grated

³/₄ teaspoon chopped fresh rosemary or ¹/₄ teaspoon dried

³/₄ teaspoon chopped fresh tarragon or ¹/₄ teaspoon dried

1 teaspoon chopped fresh basil leaves or ¹/₂ teaspoon dried

¹/₄ teaspoon freshly ground black pepper

1¹/₂ cups homemade chicken stock or reduced-sodium chicken broth

¹/₂ cup dry white wine

4 cups cooked Polenta (page 281)

FLUMAGINA

1 tablespoon unsalted butter

1 small garlic clove

¹/₂ small onion, chopped, about ¹/₄ cup

1 cup 2 percent or 4 percent cottage cheese (do not use nonfat cottage cheese)

Pinch of coarse salt (optional)

Blend the flour and salt together in a shallow dish and dredge the meat in the flour. Heat 2 tablespoons oil in a heavy saucepan over medium-high heat. Add the garlic and rabbit pieces. Cook until the rabbit is well browned. Transfer to a plate and set aside.

Add another tablespoon of oil to the pan, if necessary, and add the onion, parsley, celery, and carrot. Sauté until the onion starts to brown, about 5 minutes. Season with the rosemary, tarragon, basil, and pepper; pour in the stock and white wine. Return the rabbit pieces to the pan and cover. Bring to a boil, then reduce the heat and simmer until the meat is tender, 50 to 60 minutes.

To make the flumagina, melt the butter in a small skillet over medium heat. Add the garlic and onion and sauté until the onion just starts to soften, 3 to 4 minutes. Transfer to a food processor with the cottage cheese and puree until smooth. Season with salt, if necessary. Serve either at room temperature or chill and serve cold.

Make the polenta when the stew is done. Put a mound of polenta in a shallow soup bowl, and serve the stew over it. Add a dollop of flumagina and serve immediately.

TIME FOR RABBIT STEW

"May 20, 1870

"The weather is slowly warming up, and the garden and corn have sprouted. If I can keep the jackrabbits out of the garden, I will have a better stand. Last night they ate down a whole row of peas. I believe I'm ready for some rabbit stew."

Egg Gravy by Linda Hubalek

RABBIT TENDERLOIN
WITH GRAINY MUSTARD

SERVES 4

I have adapted this recipe from one given to me by Philippe Wagenfuhrer, executive sous chef at the Sheraton Grand's Grill Room Restaurant in Edinburgh, Scotland, who hunts rabbits with his pet ferret, which is not a common practice in the United States. The delicate sauce has just a hint of mustard with tarragon undertones, making it a perfect match for the mild-flavored rabbit. Because the individual loins vary in thickness, I roll them into pinwheel shapes, with the thin end in the center so they will cook evenly.

4 ounces (1 cup) dried bow tie pasta

1 1/2 tablespoons unsalted butter or olive oil

1 pound rabbit loins

Coarse salt and freshly ground black pepper

1 1/2 tablespoons chopped fresh tarragon

3 tablespoons extra virgin olive oil

1 shallot, chopped

1/2 cup coarsely chopped carrot

1/4 cup coarsely chopped celery

1 teaspoon chopped fresh thyme

3/4 cup homemade chicken stock or reduced-sodium chicken broth

1/4 cup white wine

1/2 pound mushrooms, sliced

1 teaspoon all-purpose flour

1 tablespoon cream

1 teaspoon grainy mustard

Bring 2 quarts of salted water to a boil. Add the pasta and cook for 3 minutes or until the pasta is al dente. Drain and toss with 1/2 tablespoon of butter. Set aside and keep warm.

Sprinkle the rabbit loins with salt, pepper, 1 tablespoon of the tarragon, and 1 tablespoon of the olive oil. Roll the loins up pinwheel fashion, putting the thinnest part of the loin in the middle, and secure with wood skewers (break off any of the skewer that sticks out from the meat) or toothpicks.

Heat 1 tablespoon oil in a large saucepan over medium-high heat. Add the shallot, carrot, celery, and thyme and sauté until the shallot starts to soften and turn brown, about 8 minutes. Add the chicken stock and white wine and continue cooking until the mixture is reduced by half, to approximately $1/2$ cup. Strain, discard the vegetables, and set the broth aside. (The broth can be made several days ahead.)

Preheat the grill or broiler. Brush the loins with a little olive oil and grill over medium heat, turning after 10 minutes, until the juices run clear, about 20 minutes. Put them on a warm plate and cover with foil to rest.

Melt the tablespoon of butter. Add the mushrooms and sauté until tender, about 8 minutes. Sprinkle the mushrooms with the flour and sauté for a few more minutes, stirring as they cook. Add the remaining tarragon, reserved broth, cream, and mustard. Stir, add the pasta, and season with salt and pepper, if necessary.

Divide the mushroom-pasta mixture among 4 warmed plates. Put 1 to 2 tenderloins in the center of each. Serve immediately.

TAOS RABBIT

SERVES 4 TO 6

Marcia Keegan is an award-winning photojournalist and author who lives in Santa Fe, New Mexico. For more than twenty years Marcia has passionately photographed local Pueblo and Navajo Indians, capturing their ancient customs on film. This recipe is from her book *Southwest Indian Cookbook* (Clear Light Publishers, 1987).

I have adapted this dish by adding black beans and substituting balsamic vinegar for the wine vinegar. Serve over polenta or rice.

> 3 tablespoons all-purpose flour
> 1½ teaspoons coarse salt
> 1 rabbit, about 1½ pounds, cut up, or 2 rabbit hindquarters, separated at the joint, or grouse, chukar partridge, or chicken
> 3 tablespoons olive oil
> 1 large onion, peeled and diced
> 2 garlic cloves, chopped
> 3½ cups homemade chicken stock or reduced-sodium chicken broth
> ¼ cup balsamic vinegar
> 1 to 2 teaspoons ground New Mexican red chile powder (see Note)
> 3 tablespoons cornmeal (blue or yellow)
> 1 (15-ounce) can black beans, drained
> Chopped fresh flat-leaf parsley or cilantro

Blend together the flour and ½ teaspoon of the salt. Dredge the rabbit pieces in the seasoned flour.

Heat 2 tablespoons of the oil in a Dutch oven over medium-high heat. Add the onion and sauté until it is soft and golden brown, about 8 minutes. Put the onion in a small bowl and set to one side. Add another tablespoon of oil to the pot, add the rabbit starting with the larger pieces first, and sauté until the meat is golden brown.

Return the onion to the pot with the rabbit and add the garlic, chicken stock, vinegar, and chile powder and simmer, covered, for 45 minutes. Remove the lid and stir in the cornmeal and black beans. Simmer for 10 minutes, until the sauce thickens. Taste and season with some or all of the remaining 1 teaspoon salt, if necessary. Spoon the rabbit and sauce into warm bowls.

Garnish with chopped parsley or cilantro.

THE NEW YORK RABBITS

Coney is the name used for Old World rabbits. When the Dutch settlers discovered the large population of rabbits on an island off the coast of New York they called it Konijn Eiland or "Rabbit Island."

BRAISED RABBIT WITH PRUNES AND PINOT NOIR

SERVES 4

As unusual as this dish sounds, it is a classic French recipe that is one of my favorites. The prunes, pinot noir, and seasonings cook down to create an intensely flavorful, rich brown sauce that I serve over wide noodles.

1 1/2 cups large pitted prunes, halved

3 cups pinot noir

1 to 2 tablespoons olive oil

2 tablespoons chopped shallot or onion

1 rabbit, about 2 1/2 pounds, cut into 6 to 8 pieces

Coarse salt and freshly ground black pepper

2 teaspoons chopped fresh rosemary

1 cup homemade chicken stock or reduced-sodium chicken broth

2 tablespoons balsamic vinegar

1/2 teaspoon coarse salt

4 cups cooked wide noodles

2 teaspoons soft butter or olive oil

Put the prunes and wine in a nonreactive bowl. Let sit at room temperature for 1 hour or microwave on high for 1 minute and let stand for 2 to 3 minutes, until the prunes are soft and plump.

Heat the olive oil in a large nonreactive skillet over medium-high heat. Add the shallot and sauté until it starts to soften and brown, 6 to 8 minutes.

While the shallot is cooking, season the rabbit pieces with salt and pepper. Add the meat to the shallot and sprinkle with 1 teaspoon of the chopped rosemary. Lightly brown the rabbit on all sides, then pour in the wine and prunes, stock, balsamic vinegar, and 1/2 teaspoon of salt. Bring the braising liquid to a boil, cover the pan, and reduce the heat to medium-low. Simmer for about 1 hour, or until the juices of the rabbit run clear.

Toss the noodles with the remaining 1 teaspoon of rosemary and butter or olive oil. Spoon the noodles into a large shallow pasta bowl or onto a platter with a lip. Arrange the rabbit pieces on top of the pasta and cover to keep warm.

Boil the sauce over high heat until it is reduced by half and slightly thickened. If the prunes are still in halves, gently mash them with the back of a spoon. It is okay if there are some bits of prune remaining. Adjust the seasoning and pour the sauce over the rabbit pieces. Serve at once.

THE SNOWSHOE DANCE

"Sioux and Chippeway snow shoes . . . are used in the deep snows of the winter, under the Indian's feet, to buoy him up as he runs in pursuit of his game. The hoops or frames of these are made of elastic wood, and the webbing, of strings of rawhide, which form such a resistance to the snow, as to carry them over without sinking into it; and enabling them to come up with their game, which is wallowing through the drifts, and easily overtaken. . . . The snow-shoe dance . . . is exceedingly picturesque, being danced with the snow shoes under the feet, at the falling of the first snow in the beginning of winter: when they sing a song of thanksgiving to the Great Spirit for sending them a return of snow, when they can run on their snow shoes in their valued hunts, and easily take the game for their food."

North American Indians by George Catlin, 1832

BRAISED RABBIT WITH MADEIRA

SERVES 4

The subtle flavor of fresh rabbit has an affinity for the richness of Madeira wine. The rabbit is coated with a layer of mustard before it is braised with fresh mushrooms, shallots, and garlic.

2 tablespoons unsalted butter, or substitute 1 tablespoon olive oil for 1 tablespoon of the butter

4 shallots, chopped

2 garlic cloves, coarsely chopped

$1/2$ pound fresh chanterelle mushrooms, sliced

3-pound rabbit, cut into 6 to 8 pieces (see page 171)

$1/4$ cup grainy mustard

Coarse salt and freshly ground black pepper

$1/4$ cup dry white wine

1 tablespoon chopped fresh tarragon

1 cup homemade chicken stock or reduced-sodium chicken broth

$1/4$ cup Madeira

$1/2$ cup half-and-half or cream

1 tablespoon chopped fresh flat-leaf parsley

In a large skillet, heat 1 tablespoon butter or oil over medium heat. Add the shallots, garlic, and mushrooms and sauté for 4 to 5 minutes, until the mushrooms begin to soften. Remove the mushrooms from the pan and set aside.

Coat the rabbit pieces with mustard, then sprinkle with salt and pepper. In the same skillet, melt the remaining 1 tablespoon butter and add the rabbit. Sauté until well browned over medium heat. Remove the rabbit pieces and deglaze the pan with the white wine, scraping the bottom as it cooks to release the caramelized bits stuck to the bottom of the pan.

Return the rabbit to the pan and add the mushrooms, tarragon, chicken stock, and Madeira. Simmer, covered, until the rabbit is tender and loose on the bone, about 50 minutes. Remove the rabbit pieces and the mushrooms from the pan. Discard the grease, then reduce the liquid by half. Add the half-and-half or cream and reduce again until the sauce is slightly thickened. Season with salt and pepper. Put the rabbit pieces and mushrooms back in the sauce to reheat and serve garnished with chopped parsley.

RABBIT CACCIATORE

SERVES 4

You can usually find rabbit cacciatore on the menu at Restaurant 301 in the Hotel Carter in Eureka, California. The proprietor, Mark Carter, inherited his passion for cooking and learned this recipe from his grandmother, Margarita Bassi, who emigrated from Italy. Serve the rabbit cacciatore over mounds of soft polenta.

1/3 cup dry white wine
1/2 ounce dried porcini mushrooms
1/4 cup all-purpose flour
1/2 teaspoon coarse salt
1/4 teaspoon freshly ground black pepper
2 1/2 pounds rabbit, cut into 6 to 8 pieces
1 tablespoon olive oil
1 tablespoon unsalted butter
1 heaping teaspoon chopped fresh rosemary or 1/2 teaspoon dried
1 teaspoon Italian seasoning
2 garlic cloves, minced
Pinch of sugar
1 (15-ounce) can tomato sauce
Polenta (page 281)

Pour the wine in a small bowl and heat in the microwave on high for 10 seconds. Put the mushrooms in the warm wine to rehydrate for 30 minutes.

In another bowl, blend the flour, salt, and pepper together. Dredge the rabbit pieces in the seasoned flour.

Heat the olive oil and butter in a large nonreactive skillet. Add the rabbit pieces and sauté over medium heat on both sides. When they are golden brown, add the mushrooms, rosemary, Italian seasoning, garlic, sugar, and tomato sauce. Cover and simmer for 30 minutes. Remove the lid and simmer for 20 to 30 more minutes, until the rabbit is tender when pierced with a fork.

To serve, put a mound of polenta on a warmed dinner plate and indent the mound with the back of large serving spoon. Lay a piece of rabbit on the side of the polenta and ladle a spoonful of sauce over all. Repeat with the other 3 dinner plates and serve immediately.

CURRIED RABBIT SOUP WITH ASPARAGUS

SERVES 6

David Nelson is the corporate chef and vice president of sales for Prairie Harvest, a company in Spearfish, South Dakota, that sells wild game (see Mail-Order Sources, page 294). This soup is one of his favorite game recipes.

1¹/₂ cups homemade chicken stock or reduced-sodium chicken broth

1 ounce dried morels

5 ounces fresh asparagus, trimmed

2¹/₂ tablespoons butter

1 pound rabbit loin, sliced into ¹/₃-inch medallions

1 small white onion, quartered and minced

2 teaspoons yellow or green curry paste (see Note)

1 (14-ounce) can unsweetened coconut milk

1³/₄ cups half-and-half

2 tablespoons all-purpose flour

2 pinches of saffron threads

Bring the chicken stock to a boil. Add the mushrooms and stir to soften for 2 minutes. Cover and remove from the heat to rehydrate for 30 minutes.

Bring ¹/₂ cup water to a boil in a shallow skillet and add the asparagus. Cook 2 minutes for pencil-thin asparagus and 4 minutes for thicker spears. Remove the asparagus from the liquid and run under gently running cold water until cooled. Cut the stalks into 3- to 4-inch pieces and set aside.

Drain the mushrooms, reserving the liquid. Cut the morels crosswise into rings, about ¹/₃ inch thick. Rinse them under cool running water to remove any remaining dirt particles and set aside.

Melt ¹/₂ tablespoon of the butter in a large saucepan over medium heat. Add the rabbit and onion and sauté until the onion starts to soften, about 8 minutes. Stir in the curry paste and cook for an additional 2 minutes.

Add the coconut milk, half-and-half, and reserved mushroom soaking liquid and bring to a slow boil. Stir from time to time to avoid scorching.

Melt the remaining 2 tablespoons of butter in a small pan over medium heat. Stir in the flour with a whisk. Cook the roux for 3 to 4 minutes, stirring constantly. When done, the roux will be lightly browned and have a nutty aroma.

Stir $1/2$ cup of the soup into the roux. When it is smooth, stir the mixture into the soup until it is slightly thickened.

Stir the saffron threads into the soup. Remove from the heat and add the reserved morel rings and asparagus and serve.

NOTE: Yellow or green curry paste can be purchased in most major supermarkets or specialty food shops.

BRUNSWICK STEW

Reverend Forest Porter, the pastor at the church in Staunton, Virginia, was born in Brunswick County, Virginia, and has eaten one version or another of Brunswick stew his entire life. His wife, Ruth, a distant relative of my family, makes Brunswick stew every year with the women from the church to raise money for the annual bazaar.

"There are lots of Brunswick Stew recipes from Virginia to Georgia," Ruth told me. "Most include beef, but the old-time recipes included squirrel and Lord knows what else. In the South-side Virginia (below the James River) lots of Brunswick stews are made in the outdoors in large kettles. They stir it all day until it is all mashed together, then they call it 'muddle.'"

THAI GREEN CURRY TURTLE SOUP

SERVES 4 AS AN ENTRÉE

Green curry paste, a combination of ground green chiles, onion, garlic, spices, and condiments, is made commercially in Thailand. It's available in Asian markets and supermarkets and will keep for up to a year in the refrigerator. Adam Zwerling, chef for Nicky USA, Inc., a distributor of game birds and meats in Portland, Oregon, uses it for his rich and spicy Thai green curry turtle soup, which he serves over fragrant basmati rice, making it a complete meal in itself.

While the recipe calls for turtle, wild fowl, large or small game, or domestic birds or meats can be substituted.

2 tablespoons oil

1 tablespoon green curry paste

1 pound boned turtle meat, picked over for bones and cartilage, finely diced

1 1/2 cups diced Japanese eggplant

1 tablespoon finely sliced lemongrass

2 garlic cloves, minced

1 small jalapeño, seeded and diced

1 tablespoon minced ginger

1/2 cup homemade chicken stock or reduced-sodium chicken broth

1 (14-ounce) can unsweetened coconut milk

1 cup fresh or frozen petite green peas

1/2 cup (1 2/3-ounce can) baby Chinese corn, drained

1/3 cup chopped fresh basil or 1/4 cup chopped fresh cilantro

4 cups cooked basmati or jasmine rice, hot

Warm 4 soup bowls.

Heat the oil in a large wok or skillet over medium-high heat. Add the curry paste and stir constantly for 1 to 2 minutes, then add the meat and eggplant. Stir-fry for another 3 minutes, and add the lemongrass, garlic, jalapeño, and ginger. Cook for 2 to 3 more minutes while pushing the ingredients around with a wooden spoon.

Deglaze with the chicken stock and pour in the coconut milk. Simmer for 8 to 10 more minutes, then stir in the peas, corn, and basil.

Put a mound of rice in the center of each bowl and ladle the soup over the rice.

GAME SAUSAGE, PÂTÉ, AND OTHER CHARCUTERIE

* * *

Making elk sausage the old-fashioned way

THE UNIQUE FLAVOR of game produces superior sausages, pâté, terrines, and other charcuterie that could easily fill the pages of an entire book. I have included a small selection of my favorite recipes, from fresh duck sausages with coconut milk and cilantro to a simple game terrine that I frequently prepare.

Of all the game dishes I have cooked, I enjoy making game sausages the most. They are not difficult once you have the basic equipment and essential ingredients on hand.

When I make large quantities of sausage, I grind the meat using the grinding attachment for my electric mixer or an old-fashioned meat grinder, Universal No. 333 with a $3/16$-inch blade. For smaller batches I chop the meat in the food processor fitted with the steel blade. Although the food processor doesn't produce ground meat with a consistently smooth texture, or remove tendons and tough membranes, it is adequate for grinding small amounts of game meat.

Because venison is so lean, when making venison sausage, I combine it with fatty pork butt to add moisture, using a ratio of one-third venison to two-thirds pork butt. Or, you can use one-third venison, one-third pork shoulder, and one-third pork fat. Whichever ratio you use, always start with well-chilled meat and work quickly to keep the fat from becoming warm and soft, which will cause an inconsistent grind.

If the meat is to be stuffed into casings, you will need a stuffer spout. These are made to fit on both a meat grinder with a screw handle and an electric meat grinder. Stuffer spouts are available at kitchenware shops and come in several sizes—$1/4$-inch diameter for lambs' casings, $1/2$-inch for hogs' casings—depending on what size casing is used.

I prefer the smaller, more tender lambs' casings used commercially for pork links, but these can be difficult to find. I buy them at a local butcher supply house (look under "Meat Processors' Equipment and Supplies" in the *Yellow Pages*) and share them with friends because they have a short shelf life of only 30 to 40 days. They are sold with one or two hanks per bag, and each hank holds 35 pounds of sausage meat. The diameter of these sausages will be about the size of a dime, and a stuffer spout with a $1/4$-inch diameter is required.

I also use salt-packed hogs' casings, which keep for a year if refrigerated. They are sold in 1-pound containers with enough casings for approximately 25 pounds of sausage meat. The diameter of these casings is about the width of a quarter and a stuffer spout with a $1/2$-inch diameter is required.

Once the sausage is made, I divide it into 1-pound portions. I wrap the sausage, with or without casings, in plastic wrap and then double-wrap it in freezer paper. The sausage will keep in the freezer for 6 months without deteriorating in quality.

To cook link sausages, prick each sausage with a fork or metal cake tester. Put them in a frying pan with enough cold water to cover and turn the heat to medium-high. Simmer the sausages for 3 or 4 minutes to release excess fat. Pour off the water and continue cooking the sausages over moderate heat until they are brown on the outside and the juices run clear when poked with a fork.

To grill sausages, it isn't necessary to cook them in water first. Simply prick the sausages and grill them over medium heat, turning them as they cook.

GERMAN-STYLE VENISON SAUSAGE

MAKES 3 POUNDS OF SAUSAGE OR 12 PATTIES

A friend gave me this recipe more than twenty years ago when he returned from a business trip to Chicago. He had stopped at a deli to buy sausage on the way to the airport and the friendly butcher wrote this recipe on the outside of the package. I have been making it ever since with venison. Reminiscent of the beer sausages served in German taverns, it is best when accompanied by a tall glass of ice-cold beer.

4 to 5 pieces salt-packed hogs' casings (optional)
1 pound venison stew meat, cut into 1-inch cubes, well chilled
2 pounds fatty pork butt, cut into 1-inch cubes, well chilled
2 tablespoons coarse salt
3 garlic cloves
2 teaspoons ground allspice
1¹/₂ teaspoons freshly ground black pepper
2 teaspoons paprika
1 tablespoon oil

If you are making links rather than patties, soak the casings in warm water for 15 minutes to make them soft and pliable. Then, holding each one up to the faucet, let water run through it to remove excess salt and to check for leaks.

Using the coarse (³/₁₆-inch) blade of a meat grinder, grind the venison and pork together. Combine with the salt, garlic, allspice, pepper, and paprika and mix.

If you are using a food processor, fit the machine with the steel blade. With the machine running, drop the garlic through the feed tube to chop. Put the venison, pork, salt, allspice, pepper, and paprika in a large bowl and toss. Put half the mixture in the food processor and pulse 8 to 10 times, until the meat is coarsely chopped. Transfer to a large bowl and repeat for the other half. Combine the 2 batches.

Heat the oil over medium heat in a small skillet. Fry a small patty of sausage and taste it to see if the seasonings are adequate. Add more if necessary.

If stuffing into casings, remove the plate and blade from the meat grinder and attach the stuffer spout. Run the sausage mixture through the meat grinder until it reaches the outside end of the stuffer spout. Tie a knot in the free end of the casing. (If you tie a knot in the casing before the meat is run through the grinder, air will be trapped in the casing, causing it to blow up like a balloon.) Continue stuffing the mixture into the casing. Tie with string or twist the sausages at 3-inch intervals. If you twist the sausages, alternate the direction of the twisting: that is, twist the first sausage 4 turns to the right and the second sausage 4 turns to the left, and so on. This will keep the links from coming undone.

If you prefer, shape the sausage meat into patties.

Fry the sausages or patties on all sides until they are done in the center, about 10 minutes.

Store any uncooked sausage double-wrapped in freezer paper in the freezer. For the best eating, cook within 3 months.

Columbia River elk drawing

Venison Sausage with Wild Rice and Porcini Mushrooms

MAKES ABOUT 3½ POUNDS

The earthy flavor of porcini mushrooms is a natural paired with venison. To give the sausage an interesting texture, I add the chopped mushrooms and wild rice after the other ingredients have been run through the meat grinder.

1 pound venison, cut into 2-inch cubes, well chilled

2 pounds pork butt, cut into 2-inch cubes, well chilled

1 small onion, quartered

2 tablespoons coarse salt

2 teaspoons freshly ground pepper

2 teaspoons stemmed chopped fresh thyme

2 teaspoons stemmed chopped fresh rosemary

8 ounces fresh porcini mushrooms, chopped, or 2 ounces dried porcini, reconstituted (page 11), drained (save liquid if you are not using the beef broth) and chopped

1 cup cooked wild rice

¼ cup beef broth or water from reconstituted mushrooms, strained

1 tablespoon vegetable oil

If you are making links rather than patties, soak the casings in warm water for 15 minutes to make them soft and pliable. Then, holding each one up to the faucet, let water run through it to remove excess salt and to check for leaks.

Using the coarse (³/₁₆-inch) blade of a meat grinder, grind the venison, pork butt, and onion. Season with salt, pepper, thyme, and rosemary. Add the chopped mushrooms, wild rice, and broth. Stir until blended.

If you are using a food processor, fit the machine with the steel blade. With the machine running, drop the onion through the feed tube to chop. Put the onion in a large bowl with the venison and pork and toss to mix. Put half the mixture in the food processor and pulse 8 or 10 times, until the meat is coarsely chopped. Transfer to a large bowl and repeat for the other half. Combine the 2 batches and add the salt, pepper, thyme, rosemary, mushrooms, wild rice, and broth. Stir until blended.

Heat the oil over medium heat in a small skillet. Fry a small patty of sausage until done. Taste to see if the seasonings are adequate. Add more seasonings, if necessary.

If stuffing into casings, remove the plate and blade from the meat grinder and attach the stuffer spout. Run the sausage mixture through the meat grinder until it reaches the outside end of the stuffer spout. Tie a knot in the free end of the casing. (If you tie a knot in the casing before the meat is run through the grinder, air will be trapped in the casing, causing it to blow up like a balloon.) Continue stuffing the mixture into the casing. Tie with string or twist the sausage at 3-inch intervals. If you twist the sausages, alternate the direction of the twisting: that is, twist the first sausage 4 turns to the right and the second sausage 4 turns to the left, and so on. This will keep the links from coming undone.

If you prefer, shape the sausage meat into patties.

Fry the sausages or patties on all sides until they are done in the center, about 10 minutes.

Store any uncooked sausage double-wrapped in freezer paper in the freezer. For the best eating, cook within 3 months.

An American elk

THREE-WAVE VENISON
CHILE SAUSAGE

MAKES 3 POUNDS OR 12 VENISON PATTIES

When you take a bite of this spicy sausage, flavors from the chiles—the pasillas and ground paprika—hit your palate in waves. Paprika is made from the pimiento chile, and it is sold as both hot and sweet in specialty markets. If you cannot find hot paprika, substitute cayenne.

4 to 5 pieces salt-packed hogs' casings (optional)

8 ounces fresh pasilla chiles

1 pound venison stew meat, cut into 2-inch cubes, well chilled

2 pounds pork butt, cut into 2-inch cubes, well chilled

1 tablespoon toasted cumin seeds (see page 11)

1 tablespoon ground cumin

1 teaspoon hot paprika or ¹/₂ teaspoon cayenne

1 teaspoon sweet paprika

1 tablespoon coarse salt

1 teaspoon freshly ground black pepper

1 tablespoon olive oil

If you are making links rather than patties, soak the casings in warm water for 15 minutes to make them soft and pliable. Then, holding each one up to the faucet, let water run through it to remove excess salt and to check for leaks.

Grill or roast the chiles. Then place in a tightly closed plastic bag to steam for 15 minutes. Pull off their thin outside skin. Discard the stem, seeds, and any white membrane inside.

Using the coarse (³/₁₆-inch) blade of a meat grinder, grind the venison and pork together with the chiles. Season with the cumin seeds, cumin, paprikas, salt, and pepper.

If you are using a food processor, fit the machine with the steel blade. Working with half the meat at a time, pulse 8 or 10 times, until the meat is coarsely chopped. Transfer to a large bowl and repeat for the other half. Combine the 2 batches and season with the cumin seeds, cumin, paprikas, salt, and pepper.

Heat the oil over medium heat in a small skillet. Fry a small patty of sausage until done. Taste to see if the seasonings are adequate. Add more seasonings, if necessary.

If stuffing into casings, remove the plate and blade from the meat grinder and attach the stuffer spout. Run the sausage mixture through the meat grinder until it reaches the outside end of the stuffer spout. Tie a knot in the free end of the casing. (If you tie a knot in the casing before the meat is run through the grinder, air will be trapped in the casing, causing it to blow up like a balloon.) Continue stuffing the mixture into the casing. Tie with string or twist the sausage at 3-inch intervals. If you twist the sausages, alternate the direction of the twisting: that is, twist the first sausage 4 turns to the right and the second sausage 4 turns to the left, and so on. This will keep the links from coming undone.

If you prefer, shape the sausage meat into patties.

Fry the sausages or patties on all sides until they are done in the center, about 10 minutes.

Store any uncooked sausage double-wrapped in freezer paper in the freezer. For the best eating, cook within 3 months.

TWO DIPS AND A FLIRT

May 9, 1805

Lewis selected a fat buffalo and saved "the necessary materials for making what our wright-hand cook Charbono called the boudin blanc; this white pudding we all esteem one of the gretest delicacies of the forrest." Lewis wrote a long detailed recipe on the subject of Charbonneau's method of making the sausage. The recipe ended, "It is then baptised in the missouri with two dips and a flirt, and bobbed into the kettle; from whence after it be well boiled it is taken and fryed with bears oil untill it becomes brown, when it is ready to esswage the pangs of a keen appetit or such as travelers in the wilderness are seldom at loss for."

Undaunted Courage: Meriwether Lewis, Thomas Jefferson, and the Opening of the American West by Stephen E. Ambrose

WARTIME VENISON-POTATO SAUSAGE

MAKES 3 POUNDS

Kaspar Donier, the chef-owner of Kaspar's restaurant in Seattle, Washington, grew up in Switzerland, and during World War II his mother made this sausage with two of the few ingredients that were readily available: venison and potatoes. It is a flavorful, soft-textured sausage with very little fat.

4 to 5 pieces salt-packed hogs' casings (optional)
1 1/2 pounds venison stew meat, cut into 1-inch cubes, well chilled
1 1/2 pounds baking potatoes, peeled, boiled, and drained
1 small onion, quartered
3 garlic cloves
2 tablespoons all-purpose flour
1 tablespoon ground sage
1 tablespoon coarse salt
2 teaspoons freshly ground black pepper
1/4 cup red wine
1 tablespoon olive oil

If you are making links rather than patties, soak the casings in warm water for 15 minutes to make them soft and pliable. Then, holding each one up to the faucet, let water run through it to remove excess salt and to check for leaks.

Using the coarse (3/16-inch) blade of a meat grinder, grind the venison, potatoes, onion, and garlic. Sprinkle with flour, then add the sage, salt, pepper, and wine. Stir until well mixed.

If you are using a food processor, fit the machine with the steel blade. With the machine running, drop the onion and garlic through the feed tube and process until well chopped. Combine the venison and potatoes in a large bowl. Working with half the meat mixture at a time, pulse 8 or 10 times, until the meat is coarsely chopped. Transfer to a large bowl and repeat for the other half. Combine the 2 batches and sprinkle with the flour. Add the sage, salt, pepper, and wine and mix well.

Heat the oil over medium heat in a small skillet. Fry a small patty of sausage until done. Taste to see if the seasonings are adequate. Add more seasonings, if necessary.

If stuffing into casings, remove the plate and blade from the meat grinder and attach the stuffer spout. Run the sausage mixture through the meat grinder until it reaches the outside end of the stuffer spout. Tie a knot in the free end of the casing. (If you tie a knot in the casing before the meat is run through the grinder, air will be trapped in the casing, causing it to blow up like a balloon.) Continue stuffing the mixture into the casing. Tie with string or twist the sausage at 3-inch intervals. If you twist the sausages, alternate the direction of the twisting: that is, twist the first sausage 4 turns to the right and the second sausage 4 turns to the left, and so on. This will keep the links from coming undone.

If you prefer, shape the sausage meat into patties.

Fry the sausages or patties on all sides until they are done in the center, about 10 minutes.

Store any uncooked sausage double-wrapped in freezer paper in the freezer. For the best eating, cook within 3 months.

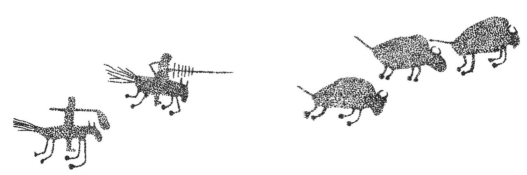

A rock painting near the Snake River
in Idaho of Indian buffalo hunters

Duck Sausage with Cilantro, Ginger, and Coconut Milk

MAKES 2 POUNDS

This is a dense, rich duck sausage that can also be made with pheasant or chicken. If using chicken, use both boneless chicken breasts and thighs. The thighs add just enough fat and moisture to keep the sausage from becoming too dry.

> *4 to 5 pieces salt-packed hogs' casings (optional)*
>
> *1 pound boneless duck or pheasant breast meat, skin and fat removed, cut into 2-inch pieces, well chilled*
>
> *1 pound boneless chicken thighs, skin and fat removed, cut into 2-inch pieces, well chilled*
>
> *1 teaspoon grated fresh ginger*
>
> *2 inches lemongrass, outside leaves removed*
>
> *1 large shallot*
>
> *1 jalapeño pepper, stemmed, seeded, and inside membranes removed*
>
> *1 bunch fresh cilantro, stems discarded*
>
> *1 tablespoon coarse salt*
>
> *$1/4$ cup canned unsweetened coconut milk*
>
> *2 to 3 teaspoons olive oil*

If you are making links rather than patties, soak the casings in warm water for 15 minutes to make them soft and pliable. Then, holding each one up to the faucet, let water run through it to remove excess salt and to check for leaks.

Using the coarse ($3/16$-inch) blade of a meat grinder, grind the duck, chicken, ginger, lemongrass, shallot, jalapeño, and cilantro. Season with salt and pour in the coconut milk. Stir until well mixed.

If you are using a food processor, fit the machine with the steel blade. Add the lemongrass, shallot, and jalapeño and process until coarsely chopped. Add the duck, chicken, ginger, cilantro, and salt and pulse 8 or 10 times, until the meat is coarsely chopped. Pour in the coconut milk and process until the mixture is homogenous.

Heat the oil over medium heat in a small skillet. Fry a small patty of sausage until done. Taste to see if the seasonings are adequate. Add more seasonings, if necessary.

If stuffing into casings, remove the plate and blade from the meat grinder and attach the stuffer spout. Run the sausage mixture through the meat grinder until it reaches the outside end of the stuffer spout. Tie a knot in the free end of the casing. (If you tie a knot in the casing before the meat is run through the grinder, air will be trapped in the casing, causing it to blow up like a balloon.) Continue stuffing the mixture into the casing. Tie with string or twist the sausage at 3-inch intervals. If you twist the sausages, alternate the direction of the twisting: that is, twist the first sausage 4 turns to the right and the second sausage 4 turns to the left, and so on. This will keep the links from coming undone.

If you prefer, shape the sausage meat into patties.

Fry the sausages or patties on all sides until they are done in the center, about 10 minutes.

Store any uncooked sausage double-wrapped in freezer paper in the freezer. For the best eating, cook within 3 months.

Life on a white Pekin duck farm

Duck Sausage Raviolis with Golden Ginger Plum Sauce

4 APPETIZER SERVINGS

Wonton wrappers are convenient for making quick raviolis, without having to make pasta dough. They are sold fresh and frozen at Chinese markets and need only to be cooked in boiling water for a few minutes. Always buy the fresh ones if they are available. Otherwise thaw the frozen wrappers before using.

12 wonton wrappers

*³/₄ cup (12 tablespoons, 1 per wonton wrapper) uncooked Duck Sausage with Cilantro,
    Ginger, and Coconut Milk (page 204)*

GOLDEN GINGER PLUM SAUCE
¹/₂ cup golden plum sauce (available in supermarkets)
¹/₂ teaspoon ground ginger

Boil the wonton wrappers, 6 at a time, in a large pot of boiling water for 2 to 3 minutes. Transfer with a slotted spoon to a bowl of cool water.

Drain the wrappers and lay them on a flat surface. Place 1 tablespoon of uncooked duck sausage in the middle of each and fold all sides of the wrapper into the middle—using an envelope fold—completely enclosing the sausage meat.

Steam the raviolis on a rack in a covered pan over simmering water for 5 minutes, until the sausage is cooked. Serve hot.

To make the sauce, combine the plum sauce and ginger in a small bowl. Microwave for 1 minute on high. Serve a scant teaspoon spooned over each duck sausage ravioli.

NOTE: These can be made ahead of time if they are tightly covered in the refrigerator or frozen in a single layer on a cookie sheet. The recipe can be doubled or tripled. They will keep frozen for up to 2 weeks. To cook them frozen, steam for 15 minutes.

DUCK PROSCIUTTO WITH CARAMELIZED PEARS

SERVES 4

Every once in a while I discover a recipe that makes me wonder how I ever lived without it, and this is one of them. It comes from *The Splendid Table*, the award-winning cookbook on Emilia-Romagna by Lynne Rossetto Kasper. She sautés fresh Bosc pears in butter with a pinch of sugar and serves them hot from the pan accompanied by thin slices of prosciutto. I substitute duck prosciutto—cured and dried duck breast meat, which is intensely rich and flavorful—that I buy from a specialty market, instead of the usual pork prosciutto. I serve it as a first course.

2 large ripe Bosc pears

1/2 lemon

3 tablespoons unsalted butter

1/2 teaspoon sugar

Generous pinch of freshly ground black pepper

8 thin slices duck prosciutto, at room temperature

4 sprigs fresh mint

Warm 4 salad plates in a low (200°F) oven. Peel and core the pears, then cut them in half. Cut each half into 4 wedges and rub them with lemon juice to keep them from discoloring.

Melt the butter in a sauté pan over medium-high heat. Arrange the pears in 1 layer and sprinkle with the sugar. Cook over high heat for 3 minutes, turning gently after 1 1/2 minutes with two wooden spatulas.

Fan the pears out on each heated plate. Sprinkle lightly with the pepper. Arrange 2 slices of prosciutto over, underneath, or tucked alongside the pear wedges. Serve garnished with a sprig of mint.

PÂTÉ WITH APPLES AND SHALLOTS

MAKES 1 CUP

Do not shy away from rabbit liver, for it is sweet and delectable. You will need 2 livers for this recipe. They often come in packages with cut-up rabbit. Substitute chicken or wild or domestic goose livers in place of the rabbit liver if you prefer.

2 tablespoons unsalted butter

1 shallot, coarsely chopped

1/2 small tart apple, peeled, cored, and chopped

5 ounces domestic rabbit, chicken, or goose livers

Pinch or two of coarse salt and freshly ground white pepper

2 tablespoons apple brandy or brandy

2 to 4 tablespoons heavy cream

1 sprig fresh flat-leaf parsley

Melt 1 tablespoon of butter in a medium skillet. Add the shallot and sauté until soft and lightly browned. Add the chopped apple and cook for 3 to 4 minutes. Transfer the mixture to a food processor fitted with a steel blade.

Add the remaining tablespoon butter to the pan, and cook and turn the livers until they are browned on the outside, but still pink on the inside, 2 to 3 minutes. Season with salt and pepper. Pour in the apple brandy and cook until it evaporates.

Transfer the liver mixture to the food processor. Add 2 tablespoons heavy cream and blend the mixture until it is smooth, adding more cream if the mixture is too thick. Pack the pâté in a ramekin or small crock and chill for 30 minutes or up to 2 days before serving.

Garnish with a parsley sprig and serve with thin slices of French bread or crackers.

POTTED GAME IN A BREAD BOWL

Before refrigeration, cooked meats were preserved in pots under a layer of fat. The old-fashioned practice of serving potted meats in hollowed-out breads was popular during Queen Victoria's reign. I've added a contemporary twist to this classic. Leftover game is pureed with butter and brandy, making a savory appetizer. If I use just 4 tablespoons of butter, the potted game will be thick and dense but still tasty. Adding another 2 to 4 tablespoons makes it easier to spread, and it will serve more. How I make it depends on the number of guests I'm serving and how decadent I am feeling.

If you are using leftover smoked game, be sure that it is hot-smoked, which ensures that the meat has been thoroughly cooked, since it is not cooked again before it is served.

1 cup cooked or hot-smoked game meat, skinned and boned, or 1 smoked duck breast

4 to 8 tablespoons cold butter

2 tablespoons chopped fresh chives or scallions

2 tablespoons brandy

1/2 teaspoon coarse salt

Freshly ground black pepper

1 small round loaf French bread

Put all of the ingredients, except the bread, in a food processor fitted with a steel blade. Process until smooth. Adjust the seasonings, if necessary.

Slice 1/2 inch off the top of the bread and set aside. With your fingers, remove about 1 cup of the bread, leaving the crust. Fill the hollowed-out bread with the pâté and replace the top slice of bread slightly askew.

Serve with a small butter knife and let guests pull off pieces of the bread to spread with the pâté.

NOTE: The pâté can be made a day or two in advance, but put it in the bread just before serving, or serve it in a ramekin with crackers.

GAME TERRINE WITH ROASTED SHALLOT MUSTARD

SERVES 16

Greg Higgins, chef/owner of Higgins Restaurant and Bar in Portland, Oregon, makes some of the best terrines I have ever eaten. He uses a combination of game and domestic meats to add interesting flavors and textures. When served, the terrine slices are a mosaic of color with the snow-white chicken and rabbit meat next to dark chunks of duck and bits of dried apricots and chopped hazelnuts. Other game can be substituted, such as goose for the duck or pheasant for the rabbit. This terrine serves at least 16 people as a first course or more as part of a buffet, making it a great dish for entertaining. Best of all, it can be prepared 5 days in advance.

One caveat: When the terrine comes out of the oven, it will look watery with meat juices. Do not drain it. Once the terrine is chilled most of the liquid will solidify.

2 heaping teaspoons coarse salt

1/2 teaspoon ground allspice

1/2 teaspoon ground coriander

1/2 teaspoon freshly ground white pepper

10 ounces skinless, boneless rabbit hindquarter, cut into 3/4-inch cubes

10 ounces skinless, boneless duck breast, cut into 3/4-inch cubes

10 ounces skinless, boneless chicken breast cut into 3/4-inch cubes

1 medium onion, cut into 1/2-inch slices

6 bay leaves

2 cups dry white wine

1 pound fresh ground pork

1 tablespoon minced garlic

2 tablespoons minced shallots

1/2 cup dried bread crumbs

1/2 cup heavy cream

1/2 cup diced dried apricots

1/2 cup chopped toasted hazelnuts (see page 11)

1/3 cup brandy

Roasted Shallot Mustard Sauce (page 212)

Combine the salt, allspice, coriander, and white pepper in a small bowl. Put the rabbit, duck, and chicken in a medium bowl and season with 2 level teaspoons of the salt mixture, reserving the rest. Add the onion, bay leaves, and wine and stir to mix. Marinate for 4 to 6 hours in the refrigerator. Drain and discard the wine, onion, and bay leaves.

Preheat the oven to 375°F. Prepare a $3^1/_2 \times 11 \times 2$-inch terrine mold by lining with clean cheesecloth, rinsed but damp. Leave an inch or two extra over the sides to be used later to enclose the terrine. Have ready a 9×13-inch pan to use as a water bath for the terrine.

Combine the ground pork with the garlic, shallots, bread crumbs, cream, apricots, hazelnuts, brandy, and the remaining salt mixture. Add the marinated meats and, working quickly so that the mixture does not get warm, fill the terrine. Be careful to avoid any gaps or air pockets. Smooth the top of the terrine and enclose in the cheesecloth. Cover the terrine with foil, then cover with the lid.

Put the terrine in the 9×13-inch pan and put in the oven. Fill the water pan with water until it reaches one-third of the way up the terrine.

Bake for $1^1/_4$ hours or until the juices run clear when the terrine is poked with a knife. Cool in the refrigerator for 8 hours or overnight.

Unmold, remove the cheesecloth, and cut into $1/_2$-inch slices. Serve with Roasted Shallot Mustard Sauce.

ROASTED SHALLOT MUSTARD SAUCE

MAKES ABOUT 2 CUPS

8 ounces shallots
2 tablespoons extra virgin olive oil
1/4 cup aged sherry vinegar
1 cup grainy mustard
Coarse salt (optional)

Preheat the oven to 400°F.

Place the shallots in a small roasting pan and drizzle with olive oil. Roast for 20 to 30 minutes, stirring occasionally, until they are well caramelized. Put the shallots, vinegar, and mustard in a food processor or blender and puree until smooth. Season with salt, if necessary.

Serve at room temperature or directly from the refrigerator. Store in the refrigerator for up to 1 month.

AN ABUNDANCE OF GAME

"We have an abundance of game, fine turkies, one of which we had roasted for dinner today, prairie chickens, hares, and they say we are to have bear meat soon. Three were seen this morning by the teamster, and we passed in el camino [the road] the carcass of one seeming to have been killed yesterday. I must look sharp when I ramble about through these woods, or I will get myself into a nice hugging scape with Mr. Bruen."

Down the Santa Fe Trail
The Diary of Susan Shelby Magoffin, 1846–1847

GAME PIES AND TURNOVERS

* * *

Iowa Wild pigeons as far as the eye can see in the 1800s

A RUSTIC GAME PIE, filled to the brim with a juicy filling and encased in a flaky pastry crust, is a comforting dish. During medieval days these savory pastries were common fare in Europe. It was the British colonists who brought the tradition to the New World. Every tavern in early America offered a pigeon or another type of game pie to weary travelers.

Meat pies can be prepared in advance and served warm from the oven or chilled and packed in a picnic basket. But best of all, game pies make a little bit of meat go a long way.

The cook has a variety of options to choose from for the crust besides the classic pie pastry, giving each individual game pie distinction. One of the most familiar is a mashed potato crust. Mashed potatoes are the topping on shepherd's pie, a dish of ground meat and vegetables baked in a rich gravy. Puff pastry and phyllo dough are both convenient because they are available commercially. Biscuit dough makes a good topping, too.

HAUNCH PIE

SERVES 6

This humble pie is at the top of my favorite list of comfort foods. Most of us know it as shepherd's pie, an old English dish that was popular in colonial America. Last year, a British friend of mine, Susan Franklin, brought this recipe back from a restaurant in Salisbury, England, The Haunch of Venison, which is named after a cut of meat, the haunch, which includes an animal's loin and hindquarters. Built in 1320, the restaurant continues to specialize in venison dishes. The chef, Rupert Willocks, makes the traditional mashed potato and chopped cabbage topping, better known as "bubble and squeak."

1 to 2 tablespoons olive oil

1 garlic clove, finely chopped

1 onion, chopped

1 carrot, peeled and coarsely chopped

1 celery stalk, chopped

2 pounds ground venison round steak, venison hamburger, or beef ground round (see Note)

2 teaspoons coarse salt

1 teaspoon freshly ground black pepper

1/2 cup dry red wine

1 cup beer

3 tablespoons butter

2 tablespoons all-purpose flour

1 1/2 cups beef broth

4 tablespoons tomato paste

2 1/2 cups chopped cabbage

1/2 recipe for Buttermilk Mashed Potatoes with Garlic Chives (page 272) without the chives (or use the chives but omit the cabbage)

3 tablespoons grated Parmigiano-Reggiano

In a large nonreactive saucepan, heat the olive oil over medium heat. Add the garlic, onion, carrot, and celery and sauté until the onion starts to brown, about 8 minutes.

Add the ground venison, salt, pepper, wine, and beer and stir well. Simmer, uncovered, until the liquid has cooked down by half, 45 to 60 minutes.

Ten minutes before the filling is done, melt 2 tablespoons butter over medium heat in a small saucepan and stir in the flour. Cook for 3 minutes, stirring constantly, then stir in the beef broth and tomato paste. When the sauce has thickened, pour it into the venison mixture and stir until blended. Transfer the pie filling to a shallow 3-quart baking dish.

Preheat the oven to 375°F. Melt the remaining tablespoon butter in a large skillet over medium heat. Add the cabbage and sauté until it is wilted and cooked, about 3 minutes. Fold the cabbage into the mashed potatoes. With a spoon, put mounds of the potato on the pie, starting first with the perimeter of the dish, then filling in the remainder to cover all of it. Smooth the topping with the back of the spoon—it doesn't have to be perfect—and sprinkle with the cheese. Bake for 30 minutes until the top of the pie is golden brown.

Serve at once, hot from the oven.

NOTE: If you are using venison hamburger or beef ground round, heat the olive oil over medium heat in a large nonreactive saucepan. Sauté the garlic, onion, and carrot for 3 to 4 minutes, until the onion starts to turn translucent. Add the venison hamburger or ground round, cook until brown, about 4 minutes, and season with the salt and pepper. Discard any fat that may have accumulated. Pour in the red wine and beer, stir to mix, and cook, uncovered, until the liquid has been reduced by half, 45 to 60 minutes.

GAME PIE PASTRY

I like this pastry recipe because it makes enough for two double-crusted pies, plus a single crust. Keep it double-wrapped in plastic wrap in the refrigerator for up to a week or for up to 3 months in the freezer.

5 cups all-purpose flour

2 teaspoons baking powder

2 teaspoons salt

2¹/₂ cups shortening

1 egg

1 tablespoon white vinegar

Combine the flour, baking powder, salt, and shortening in the bowl of an electric mixer.

Break the egg in a measuring cup and add the vinegar. Whisk with a fork. Fill with cold water not quite to the 1-cup line.

Turn the mixer on and gradually add the liquid. Blend until the mixture forms a ball. On a floured surface, knead the pastry three or four times until smooth.

Store the pastry tightly wrapped in plastic wrap up to a week in the refrigerator or for up to 3 months in the freezer. To store in the freezer, divide the dough into 5 balls, wrap in plastic, then put into plastic freezer storage bags.

NOTE: To make in a food processor, combine the flour, baking powder, salt, and shortening in a food processor. Break the egg in a measuring cup and add the vinegar. Whisk with a fork. Fill with cold water not quite to the 1-cup line.

With the motor on, gradually add the liquid. Continue processing until the mixture forms a ball. Add more flour if necessary. Knead on a floured surface as above.

Rabbit and Artichoke Pie

SERVES 4

The rich, creamy texture of this pie highlights the delicate flavor of the rabbit tenderloin. I bake it in a 2½-quart au gratin dish, but a 9-inch deep-dish pie pan works, too. If you wish to elaborate, decorate the top of the pie with pastry cut out in the shape of a rabbit, moistened with a little beaten egg so that it will adhere to the pastry top.

2 tablespoons unsalted butter

2 tablespoons all-purpose flour

1½ cups 2 percent milk

¼ cup dry white wine

1½ pounds boneless rabbit tenderloin, pheasant, or chicken, cut into bite-size pieces

1 (9-ounce) package frozen artichoke hearts, thawed, or 1 (14-ounce) can artichoke
    hearts, drained and cut in half

1 teaspoon coarse salt

½ teaspoon freshly ground black pepper

4 ounces freshly grated Parmigiano-Reggiano, about 1 cup

1 recipe Game Pie Pastry, chilled (page 217)

2 tablespoons heavy cream

Preheat the oven to 400°F.

Melt the butter over moderate heat in a small saucepan. Stir in the flour and cook for 2 to 3 minutes, stirring constantly. Stir in the milk and wine and cook, stirring constantly with a wire whisk, until a smooth sauce has formed. Set aside to cool.

Put the rabbit meat and artichoke hearts in an ovenproof baking dish or pie pan just large enough for the pieces to fit snugly. Season with the salt and pepper. Cover with the cooled sauce and sprinkle with the cheese.

Roll out the pastry just large enough to cover the pie dish and place it on top of the pie. Crimp the edges and cut 2 slits in the crust to allow the steam to escape. Brush generously with the cream.

Bake the pie for 35 to 40 minutes, until the top is golden brown and juices bubble. Serve at once, hot from the oven.

PHEASANT AND CABBAGE PIE

SERVES 4

Make this savory pie with any wild or domestic fowl, including chicken or duck. For a different flavor, use smoked fowl, such as duck or pheasant.

2 strips smoked meaty bacon, diced

1/2 medium onion, diced

1 pound pheasant meat, skinned, boned, and cut into bite-size pieces

8 ounces kielbasa, cut into 1/2-inch pieces

4 cups shredded green cabbage (1 small head)

1/2 cup homemade chicken stock or reduced-sodium chicken broth

1 tablespoon chopped fresh tarragon

1 teaspoon coarse salt

Freshly ground black pepper

1 recipe Game Pie Pastry, chilled (page 217)

2 tablespoons heavy cream

Preheat the oven to 400°F.

In a large skillet, fry the bacon over medium heat for 3 to 4 minutes, until the bacon starts to brown. Pour off the fat, but leave the bacon in the pan. Add the onion and sauté for 5 more minutes, until the pieces start to turn golden brown. Add the pheasant, sausage, cabbage, and chicken stock. Cover and cook for 10 more minutes. Season with the tarragon, salt, and pepper and let cool.

Put the filling in a 9-inch deep-dish pie pan or 2 1/2-quart au gratin dish.

Roll out the pastry to cover the pie. Place over the pie. Crimp the edges and cut 2 slits in the pastry to release the steam as it bakes. Brush generously with the cream.

Bake the pie in the preheated oven for 30 to 35 minutes, until the crust is golden brown and the juices bubble.

Serve at once, hot from the oven.

ANACONDA GAME PASTIES

MAKES 1 DOZEN

everal years ago, I attended my nephew's wedding in Anaconda, Montana. Lyle married the daughter of a local family whose relatives have lived in this small company town since the 1800s. The founder of Montana's copper industry, Marcus Daly, paid the passage for both of Molly's great-grandparents from Ireland in return for their labor at the town's copper smelter.

The McLain family still makes venison pasties—a hardy meat turnover—from a recipe passed down by Molly's Irish great-grandmother. She, like the other wives in this company town, used to wrap the turnovers in newspaper for her husband to carry to work in his pocket. This cherished family recipe is an invisible bond that will always connect the Old World with the New. I have given the recipe my own spin, in particular, by substituting buffalo for the venison.

1 to 2 teaspoons butter

1/4 cup chopped onion

1 cup sliced shiitake mushrooms (a little more than 2 ounces)

1/2 pound lean ground buffalo, venison, or beef

4 ounces smoked pork loin, trimmed and diced

1 teaspoon toasted cumin seeds (page 11)

1 teaspoon ground cumin

1/2 teaspoon coarse salt

1/4 teaspoon freshly ground black pepper

1/3 recipe Game Pie Pastry (page 217)

Preheat the oven to 375°F.

In a small skillet, melt the butter over medium heat. Add the onion and mushrooms and sauté until they start to soften, about 5 minutes. Remove from the heat and let cool.

Meanwhile, mix the ground meat with the pork loin, cumin seeds, cumin, salt, and pepper. Add the onions and mushrooms and mix well.

Roll out the pastry to an 1/8-inch thickness. With a 3 3/4-inch round biscuit cutter make 12 circles.

Shape a golf-ball-size portion of the meat mixture into an oval shape, approximately 2$^1/_2$ inches by 1$^1/_2$ inches, to fit on one half of a pastry circle. With your fingers, moisten the edges of the pastry with water. Fold the remaining half of the pastry over the top of the meat and seal the edges by pushing them together. Repeat for the other 11 pasties. Arrange the pasties on a baking sheet without touching.

Bake for 30 minutes, or until the pastry is golden brown and the meat is cooked throughout. Serve hot or at room temperature.

A GAME WARDEN'S HEARTY APPETITE

My godfather, Art Ford, is eighty-six, and he loves to tell the story about the game warden who used to call on his family's ranch in northern California during the Depression to "check on things."

"He'd regularly show up at eleven o'clock," Art told me, "and, of course, we always invited him to stay for lunch. Times were tough and the only meat my mother cooked was deer. That old game warden ate twice as much as the rest of us, and he never said a word."

VENISON-MUSHROOM TURNOVERS

MAKES 14

A ny of the recipes listed in the sausage chapter will work for these bite-size turnovers. I sometimes make them with slivers of smoked duck, instead of sausage, to serve with Bing Cherry Marmalade (page 258).

Make the turnovers several weeks in advance if you like. Freeze them on cookie sheets, then store them in self-sealing plastic bags in the freezer. They will keep frozen up to 1 month. Bake the frozen turnovers on a cookie sheet in a 450°F oven for 15 minutes, or until they are golden around the edges.

> *8 tablespoons cold unsalted butter, cut into small pieces*
> *3 ounces Neufchâtel or cream cheese, cut into small cubes*
> *1 cup all-purpose flour*
> *1/3 cup uncooked Venison Sausage with Wild Rice and Porcini Mushrooms (page 198)*

To make the pastry, place the butter, cream cheese, and flour in a food processor. Process the ingredients only until the dough begins to form a ball. Form the pastry into a ball, flatten slightly, and place in a plastic bag. Chill in the freezer for 20 minutes, or in the refrigerator for 1 hour.

Preheat the oven to 450°F.

Roll out the pastry on a floured board to a 1/8-inch thickness and cut into circles with a 2 1/2-inch round biscuit cutter.

Place a teaspoon of the sausage mixture in the middle of each circle. Fold the pastry over the sausage, creating a semicircle. Crimp the edges together with your fingers.

Transfer the turnovers to an ungreased cookie sheet, and bake in the preheated oven for 5 minutes, or until slightly browned. Turn them over and bake for another 3 to 5 minutes to brown both sides. Cool on racks until they are cool enough to touch.

Serve warm or at room temperature.

HOMEMADE MINCEMEAT

MAKES 4 QUARTS (USE 2½ CUPS PER PIE)

The first time I tasted a wedge of homemade mincemeat pie I couldn't believe how good it was compared to store-bought; I've been making my own ever since. I use butter, though, preferring its rich flavor to the traditional suet. Serve warm mincemeat over frozen vanilla yogurt for a simple Christmas Eve dessert.

¼ cup unsalted butter

2 pounds venison scraps or beef round steak, finely chopped

10 Golden Delicious apples, about 5 pounds, peeled, cored, and coarsely chopped

2 pounds raisins

2 cups brown sugar

2 teaspoons ground cinnamon

1 teaspoon freshly grated nutmeg

1 teaspoon ground cloves

1 teaspoon ground allspice

1½ teaspoons coarse salt

¼ cup grated orange rind (optional)

Apple cider to cover, about 2½ quarts

1 cup apple brandy (optional)

Melt the butter in a large 5-quart pot. Add the remaining ingredients, except the brandy, and cook slowly until the flavors meld, about 1 hour. Cool and add the brandy, if desired. Use at once or ladle the mixture into freezer containers, label, and freeze for up to 3 months.

HOMEMADE MINCEMEAT PIE

1 recipe Game Pie Pastry (page 217)

2½ cups Homemade Mincemeat (see above)

2 tablespoons heavy cream

SCOTCH BUTTER SAUCE

8 tablespoons unsalted butter

⅓ cup heavy cream

3 cups confectioners' sugar

3 tablespoons Scotch

Preheat the oven to 425°F.

Roll out 1 ball of the pastry and fit into a 9-inch pie pan. Pour the mincemeat into the pastry-lined pan.

Roll out the remaining ball of the pastry and transfer to cover the pie. Flute the edges and cut steam vents. Brush the top of the pie with the cream. Bake for 40 to 45 minutes, until the pastry is golden brown.

To make the sauce, melt the butter over low heat in a saucepan. Stir in the cream, sugar, and whisky and beat until the mixture is smooth and has a creamy consistency.

Serve the pie warm with 2 to 3 tablespoons of the Scotch Butter Sauce spooned over each slice.

CHILDHOOD MEMORIES

My longtime friend Mary Ellen Jensen grew up in Superior, Wisconsin, where her father was the general roadmaster for the Great Northern Railroad, which later became Burlington Northern. "Employees frequently brought Dad game from the Mesabi Range where they hunted on the weekends. Our pantry always had plenty of jars of homemade mincemeat—it was eaten year-round in our house," she told me.

SMOKED GAME

Florida Timucuan Indians smoking their game

SMELLING THE PUNGENT aroma of meat as it smokes over smoldering embers evokes for me a sense of accomplishment, the same feeling I get when making blackberry jam or baking bread from scratch. I am sure my feelings stem from knowing how good it's going to taste, but sometimes I wonder if they are a genetic carryover from days when game was smoked out of necessity to preserve it for leaner times.

We still practice this time-honored tradition of smoking meat because it enhances the unique flavor of game. While smoking food—in this case, game—takes time, it is a satisfyingly simple process that involves two steps: The meat is first cured by either a dry rub of salt and spices or a wet cure using a brine. For a dry cure, the meat is rubbed with a salt and spice mixture and is left to cure in the refrigerator for 4 to 8 hours. As the salt draws the liquid out of the meat, it also penetrates the meat and brings out its flavor. The salt also discourages the growth of harmful bacteria. Sugar is sometimes added to a dry cure for flavor, but too much causes a sweet aftertaste, so use it judiciously.

For a wet cure, the meat is submerged in a highly concentrated salt solution (in England grains of salt were called "corn," thus corned beef) with spices, and the same principle applies. The salt permeates the food while drawing out the liquid, inhibiting microbial growth. The wet-cure method has the advantage of more evenly covering the meat. The length of time meats are cured depends upon their thickness. For example, a buffalo roast would take 3 to 4 days for corned buffalo, while thin strips for buffalo jerky would take 2 to 3 hours. After the meat is cured, it is then rinsed in fresh water and air-dried.

After the allotted curing time, the game is smoked over a smoldering fire. The meat absorbs more than two hundred chemicals as the drifting vapors curl around it, adding flavor, retarding oxidation, and inhibiting the growth of unwanted bacteria.

When I smoke food outside I use a small electric smoker called a Little Chief made in Oregon. It operates between 150° and 200°F. To determine the temperature of your smoker, check it with an oven thermometer. If the smoker is electric, consult the manufacturer's instructions.

If you don't have a smoker, you can adapt a grill with a cover to smoke meat. Put 2 cups of presoaked and drained chips directly on the charcoal. The meat will be smoked as it cooks (hot smoking), or you can smoke the meat indirectly by burning the briquettes off to one side with the smoldering chips and placing the meat on the other side with a drip pan underneath.

To smoke game indoors, you will need a small roaster or a wok with a rack, or a broiler pan. Cover the bottom of the roaster with a layer of wood chips, and put the rack in the pan. Season the meat with a rub and lay it on top of the rack. Cover the pan with a lid or a foil tent to trap the smoke inside. Heat a burner to high and when it is red hot, put the pan on the burner just until the chips start to smoke. It will take less than a minute. NEVER leave it unattended. Remove the pan from the heat and turn the burner off. Turn on your fan for any escaping smoke. Let the pan sit for 4 to 5 minutes, then remove the meat and finish cooking.

This method produces a light smoke that I have used for everything from quail to buffalo steaks. The secret is to smoke the food without cooking it. The farther away the food is from the heat source, the better it is.

A new smoking product for easy smoking without curing comes from Finland. It is a disposable foil bag lined on the inside with wood chips covered with foil punctured with little holes. The meat goes into the bag, it is then sealed, and put in a 500°F oven for

25 to 40 minutes. The meat is smoked while it cooks. Whole game birds, such as guinea hens work with great success. They turn out lightly smoked, moist, and delicious.

The best fuel for smoking comes from hardwood trees. It is interesting to note that every region of the U.S. prides itself on food smoked with the wood indigenous to their area. In the West it is alder, in the Southwest mesquite, hickory and pecan in the South, maple in the Northeast, and hardwood from fruit trees in the Midwest. Wood from evergreen trees, such as pine, is not commonly used because it can produce a resinous flavor.

Innovative chefs, like Jerry Traunfeld at the Herb Farm Restaurant at the foothills of the Cascade Mountains outside of Seattle, often use the woody stems of basil and sage plants for smoking, while chefs in the Pacific Northwest wine country use dried grape clippings. In the South, pecan shells are often mixed with the wood chips to add a sweet, unique flavor. Which fuel to use is a matter of preference that can only be determined by trial and error.

The wood can be used in almost any form, but chips and shavings are the most popular and commonly available. They are sold commercially at outdoor stores, hardware stores, and upscale supermarkets. Soaking the chips in water for 30 minutes and draining them before adding them to hot coals ensures that they will smolder, producing thick smoke, instead of burn. In Scotland, game is smoked over ground aged whiskey barrels, so if you want to experiment, try soaking your chips next time in half water and half inexpensive Scotch. Or, as they do in the South, moisten pecan shells with bourbon.

There are two methods of smoking, using either hot or cold smoke. Hot smoking, or smoke cooking, means that the food is smoked at temperatures from 120°F to 225°F, until the food is thoroughly cooked. The smoke imparts a savory flavor and cooks the meat throughout. Hot-smoked food is perishable and needs to be stored in the refrigerator.

Cold smoking means that the temperature inside the electric smoker or covered grill, where the meat is pushed to one side away from the direct heat, is below 120°F, requiring the meat to be cooked after it is smoked.

To determine how long meat should be smoked, use an instant-read thermometer. Venison should be cooked to an internal temperature of 136°F and game birds to 170°F. After the initial smoking of 3 to 4 hours, wrap the game in foil and bake in a 350°F oven until the meat reaches the required internal temperature.

If you don't want to smoke your own game, there is a good selection available commercially—pheasant, duck, magret, and quail, to name a few.

WET CURE

To prepare 3 pounds of game meat or birds for smoking using a wet cure, combine $\frac{1}{2}$ cup coarse salt with 1 quart water in a 9 × 13-inch glass dish. Put the game in the brine and cover with plastic wrap. Cure for 3 to 4 hours in the refrigerator, turning every half hour. Pour the brine off the meat and fill the dish with cold tap water. Repeat two more times, until the meat is completely rinsed, then transfer the pieces to a rack to air-dry. Smoke with either hot or cold smoke.

DRY CURE

Choose any rub recipe starting on page 241. Pat the game dry and thoroughly massage the rub into the flesh, using 1 teaspoon dry rub per pound of meat or $\frac{1}{2}$ teaspoon per pound for birds. Cover with plastic wrap and leave in the refrigerator for 1 to 3 hours. Smoke with either hot or cold smoke.

CHINESE SMOKED WILD DUCK

SERVES 6 TO 8

Wild ducks turn a rich mahogany brown when they are marinated in this honey-flavored soy sauce and then smoked. To serve, I put them on a cutting board with a knife and let guests slice their own pieces. Accompany with a small bowl of tangy Chinese mustard or Roasted Shallot Mustard Sauce (page 212) on the side.

2 medium-size mallards, about 2½ pounds each, quartered
4 garlic cloves
4 scallions, chopped
⅓ cup honey
⅓ cup reduced-sodium soy sauce
½ teaspoon dry mustard

Pat each duck dry with paper towels and rub with a sliced clove of garlic. Put the ducks in a shallow dish.

Finely chop the remaining garlic and combine with the scallions, honey, soy sauce, and mustard in a small pan over low heat. When the sauce is warm, pour it over the ducks and marinate for 30 minutes.

Drain the ducks and let dry on a rack.

To hot smoke the ducks in your covered barbecue grill, light the fire and soak 2 cups of chips in water. When the fire is hot, drain the chips and sprinkle half of them over the hot coals. Put the grate over the coals and lay the ducks on top, skin side up. Close the lid. Add the remainder of the chips after 10 minutes, or when the first batch quits smoking. Turn the ducks over, close the lid, and continue cooking until the ducks reach an internal temperature of 170°F. The total cooking time should be about 25 minutes.

NOTE: To cold smoke the ducks, place them in a commercial smoker and cold smoke for 3 to 4 hours at 150° to 200°F. Finish cooking them in a 325°F oven, until the ducks reach an internal temperature of 170°F.

VENISON JERKY

The word "jerky" is derived from the Spanish *charqui*, referring to thin strips of dried meat, historically dried in the sun as a means of preservation. Nowadays we use driers or electric smokers to dry the meat, but the results are still the same: Jerky is uniquely flavorful and still popular today.

Recent studies by William E. Keene, an Oregon Health Division epidemiologist, have linked some venison jerky with E. coli 0157:H7, a food-borne bacterium that can cause serious illness. This is the first time it has been documented that the disease can be transmitted to humans by animals other than beef.

The reason this occurs is because jerky is commonly dried at low temperatures, ranging from 90°F to 200°F. In order to be safe, the outside of the meat must be cooked to 160°F to destroy any contamination from E. coli. Many dehydraters and home smokers simply do not get hot enough to destroy this deadly bacterium. The following method for making jerky is recommended by the Oregon State University Extension Service and ensures that any E. coli bacteria will be destroyed.

Although any sauce can be used, here's the one I prefer. The meat is dipped into the boiling sauce to kill any bacteria, then the meat is dried.

1 pound venison round steak
1 cup reduced-sodium soy sauce
3 tablespoons Worcestershire sauce
4 garlic cloves, minced
2 teaspoons freshly ground black pepper
2 teaspoons cracked black peppercorns

Freeze the meat first to make it easier to slice, then partially thaw and slice it across the grain into 1 × 5-inch strips, 1/4 inch thick.

Combine the soy sauce, Worcestershire sauce, garlic, and ground and cracked pepper in a small saucepan. Bring to a full rolling boil. Add a few meat strips and return to a rolling boil. Remove the meat from the hot marinade and lay on a rack to air dry so that the pieces are not touching. Repeat until all the meat strips are cooked.

Dehydrate in a dehydrator or smoker until the thin strips are brown, dry, and hard. It will take approximately 8 hours at 150°F to 200°F. Store the jerky in a covered jar or plastic bag. It will keep indefinitely in a cool place, and it freezes well.

NOTE: Do not soak the meat in the marinade overnight. If there is bacteria on the meat it could spread the next day when the meat is drained, and the marinade would contaminate anything it comes in contact with.

ORANGE-AND-ALLSPICE-CURED SMOKED RABBIT

SERVES 2

This recipe comes from Rodger Babel, the talented chef at Restaurant 301 at the Hotel Carter in Eureka, California.

CURE

3 tablespoons ground allspice

1 tablespoon black peppercorns

2 tablespoons brown sugar

5 tablespoons coarse salt

1 blood orange or navel orange, juice and zest

1 small rabbit, boned and quartered (you will use only the loins and hind legs—reserve
the remainder for other purposes, such as stock), about 2¹/₂ pounds, or 4 loins

1 navel orange, juice and zest

3 large rosemary branches

¹/₄ cup brandy

Combine all of the dry ingredients for the cure. Stir in the orange juice and zest. Add the rabbit pieces and toss to coat. Refrigerate for 3 hours, turning the meat occasionally.

Remove the rabbit pieces from the cure and rinse twice in cold water. Pat dry with paper towels and refrigerate in a single layer, uncovered, on a sheet pan overnight.

Two hours before smoking, soak 1 cup apple wood chips in the navel orange juice, rosemary, and brandy.

In a large roaster with a rack, place 3 cups apple wood chips in one half of the roaster. Place the portion of the roaster containing the wood chips on a burner over the highest heat. When the chips begin to smolder, add the soaked wood chips and the rosemary branches. Cover the roaster and reduce the heat to medium-high.

When the chips are smoking heavily, turn off the flame. In the portion of the roaster not containing any wood chips, place the cured rabbit pieces on a wire rack. Replace the cover and leave the rabbit pieces in the roaster until the smoke subsides. Repeat the entire process once more, which will give the rabbit a moderate level of smoke flavor. Finish the rabbit in a preheated 350°F oven, uncovered, for 5 to 7 minutes. Chill, slice, and serve.

Smoked Duck Hash

Serve this unusual hash for brunch with a poached egg on top or for dinner accompanied by a green salad.

1 pound unpeeled Yukon Gold potatoes, shredded

6 ounces smoked duck, goose, pheasant, or chicken breast, diced

1 shallot, finely chopped

1/2 teaspoon coarse salt

1/4 teaspoon freshly ground black pepper

2 tablespoons chopped fresh thyme

2 tablespoons olive oil, plus 2 teaspoons

1/2 cup regular or low-fat sour cream

1 teaspoon ground horseradish

Chopped fresh flat-leaf parsley

Toss the potatoes, duck, shallot, salt, pepper, and thyme together.

Heat 1 tablespoon oil in a large nonstick skillet over medium-high heat. When the oil is hot, loosely arrange half the potato-duck mixture over the bottom of the pan. Don't press down the potatoes; the air between the potatoes keeps the center from becoming soggy. Cook the hash without turning until the bottom of the potatoes is a dark golden brown, about 5 minutes. Drizzle the remaining teaspoon of oil over the uncooked side of the potatoes.

Shake the pan to loosen the hash and flip over, or, if you're not so daring, turn the hash over with a pancake turner. If the hash falls apart, just push it back together and gently pat it down. Reduce the heat to medium and cook for another 5 minutes, until the potatoes are done and dark golden brown on the bottom. Keep warm in a 200°F oven.

Repeat for the other half of the hash.

Stir together the sour cream and horseradish. Divide the hash among 4 plates and serve each with a dollop of the sauce. Garnish with chopped parsley.

PAPPARDELLE WITH SMOKED DUCK AND WILD MUSHROOMS

SERVES 4

In this dish, pappardelle, an extra-wide pasta traditionally used in Italy with wild hare, is paired with smoked duck for a simple yet satisfying meal. It can be purchased at upscale grocery stores and Italian markets. If pappardelle is not available, substitute fettuccine.

1/4 cup Madeira

1/5 ounce dried porcini mushrooms

2 tablespoons unsalted butter

1/4 pound (about 1 1/2 cups) fresh shiitake mushrooms, stems discarded and caps sliced

1 tablespoon plus a pinch coarse salt

3/4 pound pappardelle

1 tablespoon olive oil

1 shallot, finely chopped

1 carrot, diced

1/2 celery stalk, diced

1/2 pound smoked boneless and skinless duck, goose, or chicken breast, diced

2 teaspoons chopped fresh rosemary

1 cup homemade chicken stock or reduced-sodium chicken broth

1/2 cup freshly grated Parmigiano-Reggiano

Chopped fresh flat-leaf parsley

Pour the wine in a bowl and heat in the microwave on high for 10 seconds. Put the porcini mushrooms in the warm wine to rehydrate for 30 minutes. Drain, reserving the wine, and coarsely chop the mushrooms. Set aside in a large bowl.

In a large skillet, melt 1 tablespoon butter over medium-high heat. Add the shiitake mushrooms and sauté until they start to soften, about 5 minutes. Season with a pinch of salt and transfer to the bowl with the porcini mushrooms. Set aside.

Meanwhile bring 5 quarts of water to a boil in a large pot with the remaining 1 tablespoon salt. Drop in the pasta, stir, and cook until the pasta is *al dente,* 7 to 8 minutes. Drain and toss with the remaining tablespoon butter. Cover and keep warm.

In the same pan that the mushrooms were cooked in, heat 1 tablespoon olive oil over medium heat. Add the shallot, carrot, and celery and sauté until they start to soften and are lightly brown, 5 to 7 minutes. Add the duck, rosemary, and reserved Madeira. Cook until the Madeira is almost completely evaporated. Add all the mushrooms and the chicken stock and cook until the stock is reduced by half.

Toss the pasta with the duck-mushroom mixture and the freshly grated cheese. Garnish with chopped parsley and serve.

> Cut game birds in half for grilling, in 4 to 6 pieces for braising, and leave them whole for roasting.

SMOKED MAGRET WITH BING CHERRY MARMALADE

SERVES 4 AS A FIRST COURSE

A magret is the breast of a duck raised to produce foie gras. When this rich meat is smoked, it gains an earthy complexity. I use it for a multitude of recipes, including this one that I like to serve as a first course. If you like, substitute a handful of fresh raspberries for the marmalade.

> *2½ tablespoons extra virgin olive oil*
> *1 teaspoon fresh lime juice*
> *Pinch of coarse salt*
> *Freshly ground black pepper*
> *3 ounces mixed salad greens*
> *4 ounces smoked magret duck breast, thinly sliced and trimmed of any fat*
> *Bing Cherry Marmalade (page 259)*

Whisk together the oil and lime juice and season with salt and pepper. Put the salad greens in a bowl and toss with the dressing. Divide the greens among 4 salad plates. Lay a few slices of duck breast on each plate next to the greens. Put a dollop of cherry marmalade next to the duck slices and serve immediately.

SMOKED DUCK AND TOASTED HAZELNUT SALAD

SERVES 4

imilar to chicken salad, this duck salad is something I often serve for a light summer lunch. I put the salad on the table with thin slices of bread, and we each make our own open-faced sandwiches. Both smoked magret and muscovy duck breast are available commercially, or substitute smoked pheasant, poussin, quail, turkey, or chicken.

8 ounces (about 1 1/2 cups) smoked duck, skin and fat removed, finely diced
1/2 cup finely diced celery
1/2 cup finely chopped scallions, including the green stem
1/4 cup roasted and chopped hazelnuts (see page 11)
1 to 2 tablespoons mayonnaise
Coarse salt and freshly ground black pepper
1 baguette, cut into 1/2-inch slices

Mix the duck, celery, scallions, and hazelnuts with the mayonnaise. Season with salt, if necessary, and pepper. Serve on sliced bread.

PIRATE GAME DINNERS

In Hispaniola (now Haiti and Santo Domingo), homeless men lived off herds of stray cattle. When these men became pirates, they were called buccaneers, a name probably derived from the wooden grate, the *boucan,* on which they smoked their wild beef.

SMOKED DUCK SALAD WITH JONAGOLD APPLES AND TOASTED HAZELNUTS

SERVES 4

I prepare this Waldorf-style salad in the fall when the markets have fresh crops of apples and hazelnuts. I use Jonagolds early in the season when they are crisp and juicy, and Fujis later in the fall.

1 crisp Jonagold or Fuji apple, cored and diced

3 teaspoons fresh lemon juice

8 ounces (about 1¹/₂ cups) smoked duck (either magret or muscovy), pheasant, poussin, or chicken breast, skinless and with fat removed, diced

¹/₂ cup diced celery

¹/₄ cup roasted and chopped hazelnuts (see page 11)

¹/₂ cup chopped scallions, including the green stems

¹/₄ cup mayonnaise

Coarse salt (optional)

2 tablespoons hazelnut or olive oil

6 to 8 ounces mesclun, about 8 cups

4 sprigs fresh flat-leaf parsley

Freshly ground black pepper

Toss the apple pieces with 1 teaspoon of lemon juice. Add the duck, celery, hazelnuts, and scallions and mix with the mayonnaise. Season with a pinch of salt, if necessary.

Whisk together the hazelnut oil and the remaining 2 teaspoons of lemon juice and toss with the mesclun. Divide the greens among 4 salad plates. Put a mound of the duck salad on top of the greens in the center of each. Garnish each with a sprig of parsley. Serve seasoned with pepper.

Smoked Poussin, Papaya, and Blueberry Salad

SERVES 4

In the summer I prepare our evening meal in the morning before my kitchen gets too hot. More often than not, I serve simple salads that are easy yet satisfying, like the following recipe. I buy the birds already smoked and pair them with the rich pungent flavor of toasted hazelnuts and the sweet bite of fresh blueberries. Substitute raspberries or sweet cherries if blueberries are not available.

2 smoked poussin, skinned, meat removed from the bone and chopped into bite-size
    pieces, or ³/₄ pound smoked turkey or duck, cubed, about 2¹/₂ cups
¹/₂ cup chopped Walla Walla or other sweet onion
¹/₄ cup mayonnaise
2 tablespoons fresh lime juice
1 tablespoon chopped fresh flat-leaf parsley
Coarse salt and freshly ground black pepper
¹/₄ cup chopped toasted hazelnuts, plus 1 tablespoon (see page 11)
1¹/₄ cups fresh blueberries, raspberries, or sweet cherries
2 papayas
4 lettuce leaves

In a medium bowl, toss together the smoked poussin, onion, mayonnaise, 1 tablespoon lime juice, and the parsley. Season the mixture with salt, if necessary, and pepper. (The salad can be prepared up to 1 day in advance up to this point.)

Carefully fold in ¹/₄ cup hazelnuts and 1 cup blueberries just before serving. (If the blueberries get crushed, you will have violet poussin.)

Cut the papayas in half lengthwise and remove the seeds. Arrange a lettuce leaf on each plate and put a papaya half, cut side up, on top of each leaf. Sprinkle the remaining 1 tablespoon lime juice over the papaya halves and fill with the smoked poussin salad. Sprinkle a pinch or two of the remaining hazelnuts on top of each salad. Garnish with the reserved berries and serve.

VIETNAMESE SMOKED PHEASANT SOUP

SERVES 4

I particularly like this recipe, given to me by David Nelson—corporate chef for Prairie Harvest, a large distributor of wild game meats—because it is so versatile. Make it with any smoked and boned game. If you make it with red meat use game or beef stock instead of chicken stock.

2 ounces cellophane noodles

5 cups homemade chicken stock

1 yellow onion, thickly sliced

2 slices ginger, 1/2 inch thick

1 tablespoon fish sauce

1 1/2 garlic cloves, quartered

2 star anise

3/4 teaspoon whole cloves

1 pinch red pepper flakes (preferably Thai)

1 carrot, julienned

1/2 pound smoked pheasant, sliced against the grain

4 romaine leaves, thinly sliced

1 scallion, thinly sliced

4 lemon wedges

Bring 3 cups of water to a boil in a large pot and add the noodles. Remove from the heat and allow the noodles to soften for 25 minutes. Strain and rinse the noodles under cold running water. Cut them into 2-inch pieces. Set aside.

Combine the stock, onion, ginger, fish sauce, garlic, star anise, and whole cloves in a large pot and bring to a boil. Reduce the heat to a simmer and cook for 30 minutes. Strain out the solids and return the broth to the stove.

Bring the broth to a boil, add the pepper flakes and carrot, and cook for 2 minutes. Remove from the heat and stir in the sliced meat to reheat in the hot broth. Add the softened noodles.

Place the romaine, scallion, and lemon wedges on the table in separate bowls. Serve the smoked pheasant and noodle broth in large soup bowls. Your guests can top their soup with the lettuce and scallion and squeeze in the lemon juice.

MARINADES AND RUBS

Indians trading game for goods at an 1874 Hudson Bay outpost

MANY GAME COOKS follow the European custom of marinating game. Although most game tastes good without additional ingredients, acid-based marinades add flavor and help tenderize the meat. My rule of thumb is to marinate wild game more often and longer than farm-raised game.

Marinades are made up of a combination of the following: an acid, an oil, herbs, spices, and sometimes a sweetener, such as molasses or honey. Seasonings, of course, add flavor, but the other components do much more.

Acids—wine, vinegar, citrus juice, fruit juice, milk, buttermilk, or yogurt—tenderize the surface of game meat by breaking down the outside layer of tissue. Oils act as a moisturizer, while sugar adds additional flavor by caramelizing the outside of the meat as it cooks.

Never use a marinade in which meat has been sitting as a sauce unless you boil it for at least 3 minutes. Boiling kills any bacteria that may have been present on the meat. I prefer to avoid the danger of a contaminated marinade by doubling the recipe. I set aside half the recipe for the sauce and use the remaining half for marinating the meat.

To marinate game, pat the pieces dry with paper towels. Put the meat or joints and the marinade in a shallow nonreactive dish, such as a 9 × 13-inch baking dish, or a large plastic self-sealing bag. If you are using the latter, remove all the air from the bag before sealing it. To rotate the meat, just flip the bag over. Use approximately $1/2$ cup marinade for every pound of meat, and always marinate the meat in the refrigerator.

How long to marinate game depends upon the type of game—wild or farm-raised—and how it is cut. Marinate wild game, which is exceptionally lean, for 2 to 3 hours for stew meat or steaks and 8 to 24 hours for larger cuts. The more tender farm-raised game can be marinated for flavor but it is not necessary. Avoid marinating it too long or it will become soft-textured.

Remember, marinades are forgiving, so be creative and try something new, such as using one of the many flavored oils or vinegars now available. Oils with emulsifiers penetrate meat faster and deeper than olive or vegetable oils. Read the label to see if they are present.

Rubs, a blend of spices that enhances the special taste of game, are applied after the meat has marinated. Remove the meat from the marinade and pat dry. While there are many commercial spice mixtures that can be used as rubs, they are never as good as when they are made from scratch. Always start with fresh spices and roast them first to bring out their flavors. After roasting, I grind them in an inexpensive coffee grinder that I keep just for that purpose but you can grind them in a food processor. Use a salt shaker for sprinkling the rub on the meat. Store any leftover rub that has not come into contact with raw meat in a small airtight jar in the refrigerator.

To use a rub, pat the meat dry with paper towels and brush with a mild flavored oil. How much rub to use will depend on how intensely flavored you want the meat to be and your cooking method. As a general rule, use 1 to 2 tablespoons rub per pound of meat, $1/3$ cup rub for a 4-pound duck, and $1/2$ cup rub for a side of buffalo ribs. If you are roasting or sautéing game and plan to make a sauce in the same pan by reducing the cooking liquids, use only a small amount of rub on the game meat. Too much rub can ruin a sauce by making it too salty. Massage the mixture into the flesh, coating completely. Cover the meat and store in the refrigerator for 1 to 24 hours.

ORANGE, SOY, AND HONEY MARINADE

MAKES 1 CUP

 Use this marinade for game birds, especially ratites (ostrich, emu, and rhea), and small game animals, such as rabbit.

3 tablespoons olive oil

1/2 cup fresh orange juice

2 tablespoons fresh lime juice

3 tablespoons reduced-sodium soy sauce

1/4 cup honey

2 tablespoons chopped fresh cilantro

1 whole orange, peeled and sliced

In a small bowl, stir together the oil, orange juice, lime juice, soy sauce, and honey. Microwave on high for 2 minutes.

Sprinkle the meat with the chopped cilantro and orange slices after it has been added to the marinade. Marinate for 1 to 3 hours, turning frequently.

NOTE: Before adding the meat to the marinade, pat dry with paper towels and rub with salt and pepper.

INNOVATIVE COOKING

When the pilgrims arrived in the New World, overnight hunts were sometimes necessary to feed their large numbers. On occasion, they used their swords as skewers for roasting their game over their blazing campfires.

SHERRY VINEGAR–HERB MARINADE

MAKES ½ CUP

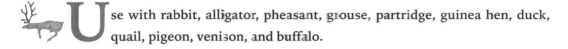se with rabbit, alligator, pheasant, grouse, partridge, guinea hen, duck, quail, pigeon, venison, and buffalo.

½ cup olive oil

3 tablespoons sherry vinegar

2 garlic cloves, coarsely chopped

2 teaspoons chopped fresh thyme or 1 teaspoon dried

2 teaspoons chopped fresh rosemary or 1 teaspoon dried

½ teaspoon coarse salt

½ teaspoon freshly ground black pepper

Whisk together all the ingredients in a glass bowl. Marinate the birds or meat for 1 to 3 hours, turning frequently.

RED WINE MARINADE

MAKES ½ CUP

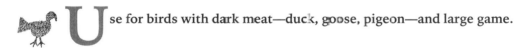se for birds with dark meat—duck, goose, pigeon—and large game.

¼ cup dry red wine

¼ cup extra virgin olive oil

1 teaspoon chopped fresh thyme or ½ teaspoon dried, crushed

1 teaspoon chopped fresh rosemary or ½ teaspoon dried, crushed

½ teaspoon coarse salt

½ teaspoon freshly ground black pepper

Whisk together all the ingredients in a glass bowl. Marinate the birds or meat for 1 to 3 hours, turning frequently.

White Wine Marinade

MAKES ¹/₂ CUP

Use for game with a delicate flavor—guinea fowl, poussin, grouse, quail—and small game, such as rabbit.

¹/₄ *cup dry white wine*
¹/₄ *cup extra virgin olive oil*
1 tablespoon coarse grainy mustard
1 shallot, coarsely chopped
1 tablespoon chopped fresh tarragon or 1¹/₂ teaspoons dried
1 teaspoon coarse salt
¹/₂ *teaspoon freshly ground black pepper*

Whisk together all the ingredients in a glass bowl. Marinate the birds or meat for 1 to 3 hours, turning frequently.

Ground Porcini Rub

MAKES ABOUT ¹/₃ CUP

Although porcini and other dried mushroom rubs are commercially available, it's easy to make your own. Use for venison, buffalo, ostrich, duck, squab, and quail.

¹/₄ *ounce dried porcini mushrooms*
1 tablespoon coarse salt
2 teaspoons freshly ground black pepper

Put the dried mushrooms in a food processor with a steel blade and process until finely ground. It does not have to be perfectly smooth. Stir together with the coarse salt and pepper. Store in an airtight jar.

SPICY TEXAS RUB

Use for all game when you want bold flavors. It is especially good on venison, buffalo, and quail.

1 tablespoon freshly ground cumin
1 tablespoon ground New Mexican chile pepper (medium)
1 tablespoon ground pasilla chile pepper
2 tablespoons coarse salt

Combine all the ingredients in a small bowl and blend. Store in an airtight jar.

NOTE: To make your own ground cumin first dry roast 1 tablespoon whole cumin seeds over high heat until they start to brown and pop. Grind in an inexpensive electric coffee grinder used just for spices.

CORIANDER-FENNEL RUB

MAKES A SCANT ¹⁄₃ CUP

This rub can be used on all game, but it is exceptionally good on quail, partridge, grouse, pheasant, and rabbit.

1 tablespoon fennel seeds
1 tablespoon coriander seeds
1 tablespoon coarse salt
2 teaspoons freshly ground black pepper

Put the fennel and coriander seeds in a small pan over high heat and toast for 2 to 3 minutes, until the seeds turn a deep golden brown. Put the seeds in a food processor fitted with a steel blade and process until finely ground. It does not have to be perfectly smooth. Stir together with the salt and pepper. Store in an airtight jar.

JUNIPER-PEPPER RUB

MAKES A HEAPING $1/3$ CUP

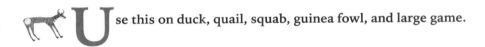Use for grouse, partridge, quail, pheasant, duck, and large game.

4 tablespoons dried juniper berries
2 tablespoons coarse salt
2 teaspoons freshly ground black pepper

Put the juniper berries in a small pan over high heat and toast for 2 to 3 minutes, until they become very fragrant. Transfer the berries to a food processor fitted with a steel blade and process until finely ground. It does not have to be perfectly smooth. Stir together with the salt and pepper. Store in an airtight jar.

SZECHUAN AND GREEN PEPPERCORN RUB

MAKES ABOUT $1/3$ CUP

Use this on duck, quail, squab, guinea fowl, and large game.

2 tablespoons freeze-dried green peppercorns
2 tablespoons Szechuan peppercorns
1 tablespoon coarse salt

Put the green and Szechuan peppercorns in a small pan over high heat and toast for 2 to 3 minutes, until they become very fragrant. Transfer the peppercorns to a food processor fitted with a steel blade and process until finely ground. It does not have to be perfectly smooth. Stir together with the coarse salt. Store in an airtight jar.

SAFFRON-GINGER RUB

MAKES 1 1/2 TABLESPOONS

Use for game birds and small game.

1/2 teaspoon saffron threads (2 good pinches)
2 teaspoons ground ginger
1/4 teaspoon turmeric
1 teaspoon coarse salt

Put the saffron threads in a small pan over high heat and toast for 2 to 3 minutes, until they become very fragrant and dark red. Transfer them to a small bowl and, when they are cool enough to touch, crush them to a powder with your fingers. Add the ginger, turmeric, and salt and stir to blend. Store in an airtight jar.

SAVORY HERB AND PEPPERCORN RUB

MAKES ABOUT 1/2 CUP

Use for duck, quail, grouse, partridge, guinea hen, and small, large, and exotic game.

2 tablespoons freeze-dried green peppercorns
2 tablespoons white peppercorns
2 teaspoons dried rosemary
2 teaspoons dried thyme
1 heaping tablespoon coarse salt

Put the green and white peppercorns, rosemary, and thyme in a small pan over high heat and toast for 2 to 3 minutes, until the peppercorns become very fragrant. Transfer the mixture to a food processor fitted with a steel blade and process until finely ground. It does not have to be perfectly smooth. Stir together with the coarse salt. Store in an airtight jar.

SONG OF THE HUNTER'S WIFE

To help her husband in his hunting exploits, a Tewa Indian (one of the Pueblo Indian tribes) wife would make a path with cotton thread leading to her house. Afterwards she would go inside and sing this song:

Now comes the deer up to our house
He brings the needed food of life,
While we give needed food to him.

We love you! So come now hither,
On the road that we have laid!
Come hither to our house where we
May love you! Eat now this little!

"Song of the Hunter's Wife" from *San Cristóbal* by Christina Singleton Mednick

SAUCES

Two young hunters bag their limit

FOR MANY OF the dishes in this book, the instructions for making the sauce are included with the recipe, because some of the best game sauces are made in the same pan the game was cooked in. These simple sauces are easy to make and can be used for both wild and farm-raised game.

Remove the cooked—sautéed, roasted, or broiled—game meat or bird and discard the fat, but save the cooking juices. Put the pan back on the stove over medium-high heat. Pour in 1 cup chicken stock (for all game) or game or beef broth (for large game) and cook over high heat, scraping the bottom and sides of the pan to release the caramelized cooking particles, until the sauce is reduced by half. Season with salt. Never season before reducing the sauce or it will be too salty. For more flavor, substitute ½ cup wine (white for white meat, red for dark meat) for half the stock. Or, instead of wine, add 3 tablespoons Scotch or bourbon after the sauce has been reduced.

A slightly different method, and equally as good, is the one I use for Breast of Wood Pigeon with Mushrooms (page 75). The breast meat is taken off the carcass and the carcass is sautéed with vegetables to make the sauce—basically you are making a quick stock. The breast meat is sautéed and then sauced just before serving. For hunters this is an excellent reason to save more than just the breast meat from wild birds.

Commercial demi-glace, a highly reduced (so reduced it is solid) sauce made from half brown stock and half brown sauce, has just recently become available in some up-scale grocery stores. Use it to make game sauces according to the manufacturers' instructions. A demi-glace will add complexity and a depth of flavor to a sauce that usually only comes from a restaurant kitchen.

Fruits and game meat have an affinity for each other and another way to enhance a sauce is to add fruit to it. Throwing a handful of fresh berries into the sauce a minute or two before serving gives the fruit just enough time to become slightly warm without disintegrating. High-quality dried fruit can also be used, and it is not necessary to reconstitute it first. I particularly like to use dried sweet cherries and sweetened dried cranberries. Sprinkle the dried fruit in the sauce 5 minutes before serving to give it time to rehydrate.

Aside from sauces, a tablespoon or two of a fruit relish or tangy onions that have been simmered with blackberry jelly and red wine, like the Sweet Onion Jam on page 269, are perfect accompaniments for game dishes.

A GOOD SAUCE MAKER

Whenever Jim Ferguson buys farm-raised game, he always orders enough meat with bones in it so he can make a good stock for his game sauces.

"The quality of a kitchen—at home, the Homestead, or any other establishment—is greatly revealed by its sauces."

Dining at The Homestead by Jim Ferguson, Eleanor Ferguson and Albert Schnarwyler

RED CURRANT SAUCE

Use either homemade chicken stock or reduced-sodium commercial chicken broth for this recipe. Most regular commercial chicken stocks would be too salty when they are reduced twice, as this recipe calls for. Use this sauce with any game bird.

4 cups homemade chicken stock or reduced-sodium chicken broth
1 pint fresh or frozen red currants, cranberries, huckleberries, blueberries, raspberries, or blackberries
1 shallot, finely chopped
About 3 tablespoons crème de cassis
Coarse salt

Reduce the chicken stock to 2 cups over high heat.

If you are using frozen berries, thaw on a single layer on a paper towel for 20 minutes. Then puree the fruit in a food processor and add to the chicken stock with the shallot. Reduce the stock to 1 cup and add the crème de cassis. Season with salt to taste, and serve hot.

NOTE: The amount of crème de cassis you add depends upon the tartness of the fruit you are using. Add less for sweeter fruits, such as huckleberries, blueberries, raspberries, and blackberries.

LADY FIONA'S APPLE AND RED CURRANT SAUCE

MAKES 4 CUPS

Lady Fiona Elworthy and her husband, Sir Peter, raise deer and elk on their farm near Timaru, on the South Island of New Zealand. They graciously cooked a Cervena venison dinner for me one night while I was visiting and she served this wonderful sauce to accompany the meat. Lady Fiona used black currants but her preference is for the red ones because the color of the sauce is more appealing. Either works perfectly.

6 tart apples, such as Gravenstein or Granny Smith, peeled, cored, and cut into eighths
2 tablespoons honey
1 heaping cup red or black currants, rinsed

Put the apples and honey in a saucepan with 2 cups water and bring to a boil. Reduce the heat to medium and cook until the apples are tender, about 15 minutes.

Drain and coarsely mash the apples with a potato masher, then drop in the currants and simmer slowly until the currants are hot, 3 to 4 minutes. Don't boil the mixture or the currants will lose their attractive round shape.

Serve warm or at room temperature to accompany game dishes.

SPICY CRAB APPLES IN CABERNET SAUVIGNON

MAKES 3 QUARTS

Katie Sutton, chef at the Hess Collection in the Napa Valley, created this recipe for spiced crab apples to serve with smoked turkey. One bite gives you the perfect combination of sweet, sour, and spicy all at the same time. These apples go particularly well with both game birds and wild boar. I have also substituted Seckel pears in place of the crab apples. I cook the pears until they are fork tender and let them cool in the spicy liquid. They can be served immediately or kept covered in the refrigerator for up to a month.

2^1/$_2$ *quarts crab apples*
1 bottle Cabernet Sauvignon
3 cups sugar
3 cups cider vinegar
4 cinnamon sticks
1 tablespoon whole cloves
1 tablespoon allspice berries
1 whole nutmeg

Rinse the crab apples and pierce the skin repeatedly to prevent bursting.

Combine the wine, sugar, vinegar, and spices in a large pot. Bring to a boil, then reduce the heat and add some crab apples, simmering in 4 small batches until the crab apples are hot throughout, but still firm to the touch, about 10 minutes. Remove the apples with a slotted spoon and place in a large bowl. Continue until all the apples are partially cooked and removed to the bowl.

Return the liquid to a rolling boil for 5 minutes, then pour over the crab apples and let stand overnight.

Pack the apples into hot, sterilized jars to within ^{1}/$_2$ inch of the top. Return the syrup to the pot and bring to a boil. Strain and pour into the jars to cover the apples, leaving ^{1}/$_4$ inch head space. Close the jars with sterilized lids and rings. Process in a boiling water bath for 15 minutes according to the lid manufacturer's instructions.

Store in a cool, dark place for at least 3 to 4 weeks for optimum flavor and texture.

SPICY CRANBERRY-PEAR RELISH

MAKES ABOUT 7 PINTS

This is a modified version of Katie Sutton's cranberry-pear relish that she served to accompany a smoked turkey dinner in the Napa Valley several years ago. This relish is so good that it is hard to stop eating it. I make it to give as gifts during the holidays. It will keep for 1 week in the refrigerator. Cut the recipe in half for a smaller quantity.

2 tablespoons canola oil

1 cup chopped onions

2 to 3 jalapeños, seeded and minced

3 tablespoons minced fresh ginger

2 garlic cloves, minced

1 cup cider vinegar

1 cup dry red wine

2 cups brown sugar

1 tablespoon freshly ground black pepper

2 teaspoons ground cinnamon

1 teaspoon ground allspice

1 teaspoon ground coriander

1 teaspoon ground cloves

$1/2$ teaspoon ground nutmeg

6 cups fresh cranberries (two 12-ounce bags)

6 medium pears, peeled and cut into $1/2$-inch dice

1 cup golden raisins

$3/4$ cup maple syrup

In a large stainless steel pot, heat the oil over medium heat. Add the onions, jalapeños, ginger, and garlic and sauté until translucent. Add the vinegar, wine, brown sugar, pepper, cinnamon, allspice, coriander, cloves, and nutmeg. Simmer, stirring occasionally, until syrupy, about 20 minutes.

Stir in the cranberries, pears, raisins, and maple syrup; simmer for 20 more minutes. (If a lot of liquid remains in the mix, strain it off into a small saucepan, bring to a boil, reduce, then add back to the fruit mixture.) Serve hot, cold, or warm.

Store in the refrigerator for 1 week.

HERB SAUCE

MAKES ABOUT 2 CUPS

his tangy herb sauce explodes with flavors that complement the richness of grilled red meat. Try it with venison, buffalo, ostrich, or boar. It can be used as a marinade, as a basting sauce, and as an accompaniment at the dinner table. To use as a marinade, pour half the sauce in a shallow dish with the game, reserving the second half. Marinate the meat covered with plastic wrap in the refrigerator for 1 to 3 hours, turning occasionally. Discard the marinade, grill the game, and serve with the reserved sauce.

2 garlic cloves, finely chopped
1 cup fresh flat-leaf parsley leaves (about 1/2 bunch)
2 tablespoons minced fresh chives or 1 tablespoon dried
2 tablespoons fresh oregano leaves or 2 teaspoons dried, crushed
1/2 cup packed fresh basil leaves (about 1/2 bunch)
1/4 teaspoon coarse salt
1/2 cup extra virgin olive oil
3 tablespoons white wine vinegar

Mince the garlic, parsley, chives, oregano, and basil leaves. Whisk with the remaining ingredients.

Or, combine the garlic, parsley, chives, oregano, basil, and salt in a food processor. Pulse for 8 to 10 times to chop the herbs. With the machine running, pour in the oil and vinegar and process for 1 minute, or until the herbs are finely chopped and the mixture is well blended.

Store in a covered jar in the refrigerator. It will keep for up to 5 days.

BREAKFAST IN THE OREGON TERRITORY

"1826, October, Towards the Umpqua River

"After resting a short time, Mackay made us some fine steaks, and roasted a shoulder of doe for breakfast, with an infusion of Mentha borealis sweetened with a small portion of sugar. The meal laid out on the clean mossy foliage of Gaultheria Shallon in lieu of a plate and our tea in a large wooden dish hewn out of the solid and supporting it with spoons made from the horns of mountain sheep or Mouton Gris of the voyageurs."

Journal Kept by David Douglas During his Travels in North America, 1823–1827

BING CHERRY MARMALADE

MAKES ½ CUP

Other fruits can be successfully substituted for the cherries in this recipe. Try fresh plums, figs, blueberries, or mango. Use as an accompaniment for grilled or smoked game.

1 teaspoon olive oil
½ cup chopped yellow onion
1 teaspoon minced garlic
1 tablespoon minced peeled fresh ginger
1 cup pitted Bing cherries, coarsely chopped (do not drain if using frozen cherries)
Coarse salt

In a medium saucepan, heat the oil over medium heat. Add the onion, garlic, and ginger and sauté until the onion starts to wilt, about 6 minutes. Mix in the cherries and continue cooking for several minutes, until the cherries start to soften. Season with a pinch of salt. Serve at room temperature.

CHIPOTLE MAYONNAISE

MAKES 1 CUP

Chipotles are smoked jalapeños. They are notoriously hot, so use them judiciously.

Store any leftover mayonnaise in a covered jar in the refrigerator. Use as a spread for buffalo pot roast sandwiches (page 120) or grilled buffalo steak sandwiches (page 114).

1/2 teaspoon chipotle puree (see Note)
1 cup commercial mayonnaise

Stir the chipotle puree into the mayonnaise and store in a covered container in the refrigerator until needed.

NOTE: Pureed chipotles in adobo sauce, whole chipotles in adobo sauce, and dried chipotles can be purchased at markets that carry a good assortment of Mexican ingredients. To make chipotle puree, roast 1 chipotle in a dry pan over high heat for 2 to 3 minutes. When it is cool enough to handle, put on rubber gloves and remove the stem, seeds, and membranes. Soak in 1/2 cup warm water for 10 minutes. Remove and puree in a food processor. Add a little of the soaking water to make a thick puree that is the consistency of tomato paste.

Store in a covered jar in the refrigerator for 1 week.

DUCKY'S PORT SAUCE

MAKES ABOUT 1 CUP

Ducky is Dan Duckhorn, owner of Duckhorn Vineyards in St. Helena, California. His delightful Port sauce has an intense, complex fruity flavor without being overly sweet—a perfect match for both wild and domestic ducks. To use this recipe with roast ducks, separate the cooking juices from the fat after the bird is cooked and add the cooking juices to the sauce.

2 cups Port, preferably Tawny

¹/₂ cup orange juice

1¹/₂ tablespoons fresh lemon juice

1 garlic clove, crushed

³/₄ teaspoon Worcestershire sauce

2 cups homemade beef stock or canned beef broth

1 heaping teaspoon peach chutney

2 heaping teaspoons blackberry jelly

1 thin slice red onion

¹/₄ cup unsalted butter, frozen

In a 2-quart saucepan, bring the Port to a simmer, then add the orange and lemon juices. Cook for 15 minutes over medium heat.

Stir in the garlic, Worcestershire sauce, stock, chutney, jelly, and onion. Turn the heat to medium-low and reduce the sauce by half. Strain and continue cooking until the sauce turns dark brown and has a syruplike consistency. You will have about ¹/₂ cup sauce. Whisk in the frozen butter in small pieces.

WARM CRANBERRY-ORANGE COMPOTE

MAKES 1 QUART

Stephan Pyles, chef and owner of Star Canyon restaurant in Dallas, Texas, serves this intensely flavorful warm cranberry-orange sauce with a variety of game dishes. It's delicious with game birds, especially wild turkey, and with grilled or roasted large game. I use it as a thick glaze for Roast Leg of Wild Boar (page 127).

Juice of 2 large oranges
1 cup sugar
1 pound fresh cranberries
Zest of 1 orange
1/2 cup toasted pecans
1 tablespoon chopped mint
2 tablespoons Grand Marnier or other orange liqueur

In a small saucepan, bring the orange juice and sugar to a boil. Add the cranberries and orange zest, reduce the heat, and simmer for about 5 minutes, or until the cranberries burst their skins. Remove from the heat and stir in the pecans, mint, and Grand Marnier. Serve warm. It will keep for up to 1 week in the refrigerator.

TURKEY FEATHERS

Large flocks of wild turkeys have inhabited the Jemez Mountains of New Mexico for more than 2,500 years. The Anasazi—the early Navajo Indians, who lived in the area as early as 750 B.C.—hunted for turkeys during the winter months when the birds moved to the lower elevation to avoid the harsh winter weather in the mountains. By A.D. 600 the birds were domesticated, not for food, but for their feathers. Some feathers were woven into blankets, while those from the tail and wing were highly prized for their use in ceremonies and with sacred objects.

GAME STOCK

Game stock is the foundation for any great game sauce. I brown the game bones with the carrots and onions in the oven to intensify their flavor and color before simmering them with herbs and spices.

2 carrots, cut into 3-inch lengths

1 onion, cut into eighths

5 pounds venison bones

3 sprigs fresh thyme

6 sprigs fresh parsley

1 celery stalk

5 peppercorns

4 juniper berries (optional)

Preheat the oven to 400°F.

Put the carrots, onion, and game bones on a baking sheet and roast for 15 minutes, shaking the pan every few minutes, until the bones are brown. Transfer all the ingredients to a large pot. Pour 1 cup water onto the baking sheet and scrape with a spatula to release the caramelized cooking particles. Add to the pot with the bones and vegetables.

Tie the thyme and parsley together with the celery stalk and add it to the pot with the peppercorns and juniper berries. Cover with 5 quarts cold water and turn the heat to high. Just before it boils, reduce the heat to a simmer, and cook for 4 hours. Set aside to cool.

Strain out the solids and discard them. Store the cooled stock covered in the refrigerator for up to 5 days or put in plastic freezer containers and freeze for up to 3 months.

NOTE: Never use game bones that have a strong gamy odor or your stock will be strong and gamy, too.

CHICKEN STOCK

MAKES ABOUT 3 QUARTS

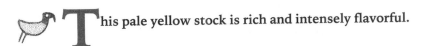This is a basic recipe that can also be used for wild birds, such as geese. For smaller wild birds, add 2 to 4 chicken wings for more flavor.

3 sprigs fresh thyme
6 sprigs fresh parsley
1 celery stalk
3 chicken necks
Wing tips
3 chicken carcasses or 1 goose carcass
1 onion, quartered

Tie the thyme and parsley together with the celery stalk and put it in a large pot.

With a cleaver, cut the necks in half and add them to the pot with the remaining ingredients. Cover with 4 quarts cold water and turn the heat to high. Just before it boils, reduce the heat to a simmer, and cook for 3 to 4 hours. Add more water if necessary to keep the bones covered. Set aside to cool. Strain out the solids and discard them.

Store the stock covered in the refrigerator for up to 5 days or in the freezer for up to 3 months.

BLACK CHICKEN STOCK

MAKES 3 CUPS

This pale yellow stock is rich and intensely flavorful.

1 black chicken
¹/₂ onion, quartered
¹/₂ teaspoon coarse salt

Remove the bird's head and feet and discard. Quarter the chicken and put it in a pot with the onion and 1 quart of water. Bring to a boil over high heat. Lower heat and simmer for 30 minutes. Cool. Strain and season with salt. Store the stock covered in the refrigerator for up to 5 days or in the freezer for up to 3 months.

SIDES AND SALADS

* * *

The cover of *The American Sportsman,* 1851

AME BIRDS AND meats are so good by themselves they do not need fancy accompaniments. The basic rule is to serve more assertive flavors with stronger-tasting game, which is game with dark meat, and milder flavors with delicate game birds with white meat. Well-seasoned starches, like mashed potatoes, sweet potato hash, and creamy polenta, complement all game dishes.

For vegetables, I like old standbys with new twists, like sautéed cabbage with bacon and wild rice or a baked wild mushroom gratin. Or, I sauté a mixture of fresh arugula and spinach in a little oil seasoned with a clove of garlic. The vivid green brightens the plate and makes a good "nest" for game birds or sausages.

Fruits are colorful, too, and their flavors complement almost all game dishes. They can be grilled, baked with chile-flavored honey, made into a sauce, pickled, or combined with rice or bread for a savory dressing, or stuffing, as the dish is called in some parts of the country. For safety reasons, it is best to cook dressings in a separate dish rather than stuffed inside the bird. If you do stuff the bird, always cook it until the internal temperature of the stuffing reaches 165°F.

Choosing what accompaniments to serve depends upon the type of game you are cooking and what fruit or vegetables are available. In the summer I grill quail and serve them on a bed of greens sprinkled with fresh raspberries, but in the winter, when a more hearty dinner is in order, I sauté the quail and serve them with red cabbage and apples.

Determine what game you will be serving, then let the bounty of the seasons guide you.

WILD MUSHROOM GRATIN

SERVES 4

The subtle woodsy flavors of fresh mushrooms evoke the outdoors, making this dish a perfect match for sautéed quail, roast game birds, or grilled game meats, such as venison, buffalo, or ostrich.

2 teaspoons olive oil

1 shallot, chopped

1 tablespoon unsalted butter

1½ pounds mushrooms, such as chanterelles, portobellos, shiitakes, and meadow mushrooms, stems removed and sliced

Coarse salt and freshly ground black pepper

1 teaspoon chopped fresh rosemary or ½ teaspoon dried, crushed

2 tablespoons all-purpose flour

½ cup half-and-half

1 cup grated Fontina cheese, about 4 ounces

Preheat the oven to 350°F. Butter a shallow 1-quart baking dish.

Heat the oil in a sauté pan over medium heat and add the shallot. Sauté until it starts to soften and brown, about 5 minutes. Remove from the pan and set aside. In the same pan, melt the butter and add the mushrooms. Sauté for 5 minutes. Season with salt and pepper and gently toss the mushrooms with the rosemary and flour. Continue to cook for 3 more minutes, then pour in the half-and-half. Stir to blend.

Transfer the mixture to the buttered baking dish and sprinkle with the grated cheese. Bake for 10 minutes, or until the cheese melts.

Serve at once, hot from the oven.

SWEET ONION JAM

SERVES 4

This deep ruby-red onion jam is both sweet and sour with an intense, complex flavor—perfect to accompany dark game meat and birds.

1 to 2 tablespoons olive oil

4 cups (about 1 pound) thinly sliced red onions

3 tablespoons brown sugar

$1/4$ cup red wine vinegar

$1/2$ cup red wine

$1/4$ cup blackberry jelly

Heat the oil in a large saucepan over medium-high heat. Add the onions and sauté with the sugar until they are a light caramel color, about 15 minutes. Stir in the vinegar, wine, and jelly. Cover and simmer for 30 minutes. Remove the lid and cook for another 15 to 20 minutes, until the mixture is thick with little remaining liquid.

Serve hot or at room temperature.

HOMEMADE BUTTER

"The women had finished with the peeling of the chile and Doña Paula was calling her family to supper. The smell of roasting kid was all over the place. In the middle of the table was a pile of beautiful round tortillas, a bowl of green chile and another one with homemade butter which Doña Paula had just made. That morning she had skimmed the evening's milk and saved the thick cream which she beat with a spoon until it turned into yellow butter to spread on the flat round bread."

The Good Life: New Mexico Traditions and Food by Fabiola Cabeza de Beca Gilbert

SAUTÉED CABBAGE WITH APPLE-SMOKED BACON AND WILD RICE

MAKES ENOUGH TO STUFF 2 MALLARDS OR SERVE 2 TO 3 AS AN ACCOMPANIMENT

Serve this simple but savory cabbage dish with any roasted, grilled, or sautéed game birds or meat. In Scotland it was served with roast grouse. It also makes a tasty stuffing for game birds. Just be sure to let it cool completely before spooning it into their cavities. To be safe, the internal temperature of the stuffing must reach 165°F at the end of the roasting time.

2 slices apple-smoked bacon
1/3 cup chopped onion
2 1/2 cups finely chopped cabbage
1/2 cup cooked wild rice
1 tablespoon minced flat-leaf parsley
1 teaspoon fresh lemon juice
1/4 teaspoon coarse salt

In a large nonstick skillet, fry the bacon over medium-high heat until crisp. Transfer the bacon to a plate lined with a paper towel and discard the grease, but do not wash the pan. Crumble the bacon when it is cool enough to handle. Set aside.

Sauté the onion in the same pan until it starts to soften, about 5 minutes, then add the cabbage, and turn the heat to low. Stir the mixture as it cooks for another 10 minutes, until the cabbage is wilted and the onion is lightly browned.

Add the bacon, wild rice, parsley, lemon juice, and salt, and cook for another minute or two, until the rice is hot. Serve hot as a side dish.

RED CABBAGE WITH FUJI APPLES AND BALSAMIC VINEGAR

SERVES 4

The assertive flavor, soft crunch, and bright color of red cabbage with apples makes this dish an appealing accompaniment for game. The balsamic vinegar adds a pleasing, slightly sweet flavor that has more depth and complexity than red wine vinegar. Serve it with grilled or roasted game with red meat, such as venison, buffalo, boar, or ostrich.

> 1 1/2 tablespoons olive oil
> 1 onion, peeled and chopped
> 6 cups thinly sliced red cabbage
> 2 Fuji or other crisp, tart apples, unpeeled, but cored and thinly sliced into bite-size pieces
> 2 tablespoons balsamic vinegar
> 2 tablespoons red wine vinegar
> 1 teaspoon coarse salt

Heat the oil in a large skillet over medium heat and add the onion and cabbage. Sauté until the onion is soft, about 5 minutes. Add the apples, 1/2 cup water, the vinegars, and salt and cook for an additional 20 minutes, or until the cabbage is just barely tender. Serve hot.

OLD-FASHIONED BAROMETERS

Dolf Hatfield grew up in New Mexico next to the Mescalero Apache Indian reservation. As a child he learned how to determine a change in the weather by the Apaches' ancient custom of observing the rise and fall of bear oil in a deer bladder, which worked as a barometer. When the oil rose with high pressure, the weather would be fair, and when it fell with low pressure, it indicated stormy weather ahead.

BUTTERMILK MASHED POTATOES
WITH GARLIC CHIVES

SERVES 8

Buttermilk adds a rich and tangy flavor to these creamy mashed potatoes, which are seasoned with flecks of chives. I use garlic chives, which I grow in my garden for their punchy, garlicky flavor and snowy white blossoms, but plain chives will work as well.

Boil the potatoes just until they are tender, then drain immediately. Overcooking causes them to become watery and less flavorful. The amount of buttermilk you add will vary, depending on how thick or thin you like your potatoes, but remember—the more you use, the better they taste.

I also make fried potato patties with this same recipe. Chill the mashed potatoes in the refrigerator for several hours or overnight. Shape into patties and fry in a nonstick skillet in 2 to 3 tablespoons vegetable oil or half oil and half butter. For the best results turn them only once, when they are a deep golden brown on the bottom.

Serve with roasted or grilled game birds or large game.

6 medium baking potatoes, about 3¹/₂ pounds, peeled and cut into thirds
6 tablespoons unsalted butter
¹/₂ to 1 cup buttermilk
1¹/₂ teaspoons coarse salt
1¹/₂ tablespoons fresh garlic chives or dried chopped chives

Put the potatoes in a pot and barely cover with cold water. Bring to a boil and cook until the potatoes are tender when pierced with a fork, about 20 minutes. Drain. Mash with a portable electric mixer or by hand with a potato masher for 1 minute. Add the butter, buttermilk, and salt and continue mashing until the potatoes are smooth. Stir in the garlic chives and serve immediately.

NOTE: For a variation, microwave 4 slices of meaty smoked bacon in the microwave until crisp. Crumble and blend the bits into the mashed potatoes.

POTATO, CELERIAC, AND APPLE PUREE

SERVES 4

Celeriac is a type of celery raised specifically for its root, which has a pungent, earthy flavor similar to celery but not as strong. It adds a pleasant, complex flavor when combined with apples and potatoes. Serve with grilled duck or venison.

1 pound celeriac, peeled and quartered
2 tart green apples, peeled, cored, and quartered (see Note)
1 teaspoon sugar
1 teaspoon fresh lemon juice
Pulp from 1 large baked potato (discard skin)
3/4 teaspoon coarse salt or to taste

Put the celeriac in a small saucepan and cover with salted water. Cover and boil until tender, about 35 minutes. Drain and transfer to a food processor fitted with a steel blade, along with the potato pulp.

Combine the apples and sugar in a small saucepan and add 1/4 cup of water. Cover and simmer until tender. Drain and stir in the lemon juice. Pour the cooked apples into the bowl with the celeriac and potato pulp. Pulse 10 to 12 times until almost smooth. Do not overprocess or the potatoes will become gluey. If you do not have a food processor, transfer the cooked celeriac, apples, and potato pulp to a medium bowl and mash until almost smooth.

Season with salt to taste. Transfer the puree to a saucepan and reheat. Serve hot.

NOTE: Use 1 cup commercial applesauce and omit the sugar.

Stuffed Baked Potatoes with Porcini Mushrooms

SERVES 4

The earthy flavor of porcini mushrooms adds a richness to these restuffed potatoes, making them hearty companions to accompany roasted or grilled venison or buffalo.

3 baking potatoes

1 cup homemade chicken stock or reduced-sodium chicken broth

1/2 ounce dried porcini mushrooms

1 teaspoon each coarse salt and freshly ground black pepper

1/2 cup freshly grated Parmigiano-Reggiano

2 tablespoons unsalted butter

Paprika

Bake the potatoes in a 350°F oven for 1 hour, or until tender.

While the potatoes are baking, pour the stock into a small bowl and heat in the microwave on high for 10 seconds. Put the mushrooms in the warm stock to rehydrate for 30 minutes. Drain, reserving the stock, and coarsely chop the mushrooms. Set aside.

When the potatoes are done, cut them in half and remove the flesh with a spoon (a grapefruit spoon works great) to a medium bowl. Be careful not to destroy the skins. Add the stock and mushrooms, salt, pepper, Parmigiano-Reggiano, and butter. Beat with a mixer or fork until smooth. Adjust seasoning if necessary.

Spoon the potatoes back into 4 of the potato skin halves, heaping the mixture well above the skins. Sprinkle with paprika.

Reheat in the oven for 10 to 15 minutes or in the microwave, covered, for 2 minutes. Serve hot.

SWEET POTATO, ARUGULA, AND BACON HASH

SERVES 4 TO 6

This is an exceptionally colorful dish when it is made with a combination of yellow sweet potatoes and ruby red yams. I use two sweet potatoes to one yam because the yams are softer and do not hold their shape as well when they are fried. The yams and potatoes can be baked several days in advance, making this an easy recipe to assemble at the last minute. Serve it with any grilled or roasted game with dark meat, such as venison, buffalo, ostrich, quail, ducks, geese, or turkey.

2 pounds sweet potatoes and/or yams
4 strips thick-sliced smoked meaty bacon
1 medium onion, chopped
Pinch of sugar
1 bunch arugula (about 4 ounces), stemmed and chopped
1/2 teaspoon salt
Freshly ground black pepper

Preheat the oven to 400°F.

Pierce the sweet potatoes with a knife to keep them from exploding while they are baking. Bake for about 50 minutes, or microwave on high for 13 minutes, until the flesh is tender when poked with a knife. Peel and discard the skins. Cut the flesh into 1/2-inch cubes and set aside.

Fry the bacon until crisp in a large nonstick skillet and drain on paper towels. Let cool, then coarsely chop and set aside.

Pour off the bacon grease but leave a teaspoon or so in the pan. Return the pan to the burner and add the onion, sprinkled with a pinch of sugar. Sauté until the onion starts to brown around the edges, about 10 minutes. Add the potatoes and yams, bacon, and arugula to the pan and toss to mix. Season with salt and pepper and cook for 3 more minutes, until the arugula has wilted and the hash is hot.

Serve hot on a warm platter or shallow bowl.

New Potatoes with Capers and Garlic

MAKES 4 TO 6 SERVINGS

I first ate these savory potatoes in the high country of New Zealand at the mountain hut of Jim and Anna Guild. We took time out from touring their deer farm to stop for lunch. Jim sautéed a venison tenderloin in a cast-iron frying pan tucked in the corner of the fireplace while Anna put the accompaniments she had packed in the "chilly bin" (cooler) on the table. At first glance I thought the potatoes were marinated hard-boiled eggs but on closer inspection I realized they were tiny white potatoes. I also use small red potatoes. If they are larger than an inch in diameter, I cut the potatoes into quarters. It's a good recipe that goes well with venison. The potatoes can be prepared up to 2 days in advance.

2 pounds tiny new potatoes, unpeeled
1 ounce (half of a 2-ounce can) anchovies, drained and finely chopped (optional)
1 tablespoon capers, chopped
1 tablespoon chopped flat-leaf parsley
1 garlic clove, coarsely chopped
Zest of 1 lemon
1 teaspoon fresh lemon juice
3 tablespoons extra virgin olive oil
Freshly ground black pepper
Coarse salt

Put the potatoes in a steamer basket and rinse under cold water. Steam the potatoes in a covered pot until they are tender, about 30 minutes. Transfer to a bowl and stir in the anchovies, if you are using them, capers, parsley, garlic, lemon zest, lemon juice, and olive oil and toss with the potatoes. Sprinkle with pepper and salt, too, if you do not add the anchovies. Leave at room temperature until the potatoes are cool. Cover and store in the refrigerator until 1 hour before serving. Serve at room temperature.

BUTTERNUT SQUASH RISOTTO

SERVES 4

Chef-owner Tom Douglas of the Dahlia Lounge in Seattle serves this with his Slow-Roasted Duckling with Red Currant Sauce (page 45). The creamy texture, rich flavor, and bright colors make it a good accompaniment for venison and game birds. The recipe calls for imported Parmigiano-Reggiano cheese. Other Parmesan cheeses can be used, but some tend to be very salty. Don't add salt to the risotto until after all the cheese has been stirred in and you have tasted it.

1 large butternut squash, halved lengthwise and seeds removed
¹/₄ cup unsalted butter, at room temperature
2 cups Arborio rice
2 garlic cloves, minced
7 to 8 cups homemade chicken stock or reduced-sodium chicken broth
1 cup freshly grated Parmigiano-Reggiano
2 tablespoons chopped mixed fresh herbs (such as rosemary, oregano, and thyme)
Coarse salt and freshly ground black pepper

Preheat the oven to 400°F.

Put the squash cut side down in a baking dish and bake for 45 minutes, or until the squash is tender when it is pierced with a fork. Or, wrap the halves in plastic wrap and roast on high in the microwave for 7 minutes a pound, or until the squash is tender. When the squash is cool enough to handle, cut off the skin and dice. You will need about 2 cups.

Melt 2 tablespoons butter over medium heat. Add the rice and garlic and stir until the grains are coated with butter. Pour in a ladleful of chicken stock and cook until the rice has absorbed almost all the stock. Add more stock, a cup at a time, adding more when the rice has absorbed almost all of the stock already in the pan. Stir frequently.

When the rice is cooked to the al dente stage, about 14 minutes, add the remaining 2 tablespoons butter, the squash, cheese, and herbs. Add enough chicken stock to make the risotto soupy and creamy in consistency. Season to taste with salt and pepper.

Orzo Baked with Summer Vegetables

SERVES 8

When I don't have orzo on hand, I make this recipe with basmati rice. It's a colorful dish that takes advantage of the summer's rich bounty.

1 teaspoon plus a pinch coarse salt

8 ounces orzo, uncooked

3 to 4 teaspoons olive oil

1 large Walla Walla or other sweet onion, halved and cut into ¹/₄-inch slices

1 red bell pepper, cut lengthwise into ¹/₄-inch slices

1 yellow bell pepper, cut lengthwise into ¹/₄-inch slices

2 medium zucchini, cut lengthwise in ¹/₄-inch slices

1 cup half-and-half

1 teaspoon plus a pinch coarse salt

¹/₂ pound Gruyère cheese, shredded

1 cup lightly packed fresh basil leaves, chopped

Preheat the oven to 350°F. Lightly grease a 9 × 13-inch glass baking dish.

Bring 3 quarts of water to a rolling boil with a pinch of salt. Pour the pasta into the water and return to a boil. Cook, uncovered, until the pasta is tender, 9 to 11 minutes. Drain well and transfer to the baking dish.

In a large skillet, heat 2 teaspoons olive oil over medium heat and sauté the onion slices until they are golden, about 12 minutes. Transfer the onion slices to the baking dish.

In the same pan, heat the remaining 1 to 2 teaspoons olive oil. Sauté the peppers and zucchini until they begin to soften, 4 to 5 minutes. Transfer to the baking dish and toss with the pasta and sautéed onions.

Stir the salt into the half-and-half and pour over all. Bake for 15 minutes uncovered, then sprinkle with the cheese and bake until the cheese melts, 3 to 5 more minutes.

Remove the dish from the oven and sprinkle with the chopped basil. Serve immediately.

BHUTANESE RED RICE

SERVES 4

Bhutanese red rice is imported from the Kingdom of Bhutan where it is grown at 8,000 feet in the Himalayan Mountains. It has not been polished to white like many types of rice, but still has its nutritious bran coating, which adds a rich, nutty flavor and a lovely reddish-brown color. This ancient variety of rice has a softer texture than most brown rices and cooks in just 20 minutes. You can buy Bhutanese red rice in specialty food shops or by mail order (see page 294). Substitute basmati or half brown and half wild rice if it is not available. Serve with grilled or sautéed rabbit, frog's legs, or game birds.

1 cup Bhutanese red or basmati rice

1 tablespoon unsalted butter

1 teaspoon minced fresh ginger

1/2 cup sliced scallions

1 1/2 cups homemade chicken stock or reduced-sodium chicken broth

1/2 teaspoon coarse salt

1 cup diced mango

1/2 cup chopped fresh cilantro

2 teaspoons fresh lime juice

Rinse and drain the rice in a strainer.

Melt the butter over medium heat in a 1-quart saucepan. Add the ginger and scallions and sauté for 5 minutes, or until the scallions start to soften. Stir in the rice, chicken stock, and salt, and bring the mixture to a boil. Cover the pan and reduce the heat to simmer. Cook for 20 minutes, or until the rice is tender. Remove from the heat and let stand, covered, for 10 minutes.

Microwave the mango pieces on high for 40 seconds. Stir the mango, cilantro, and fresh lime juice into the rice. Serve at once.

WILD RICE, CRANBERRY, AND PECAN DRESSING

SERVES 8

This dressing makes enough for an 8-pound turkey.

1 cup sugar
12-ounce package fresh cranberries
4 tablespoons unsalted butter
1 large onion, finely chopped
2 large celery stalks, finely chopped
2 cups wild rice, well rinsed
2¹/₂ cups homemade chicken stock or reduced-sodium chicken broth
1¹/₂ teaspoons coarse salt
1 tablespoon chopped fresh thyme or 1 teaspoon dried, crushed
¹/₂ teaspoon freshly ground black pepper
1 cup coarsely chopped pecans, toasted

In a medium saucepan, combine the sugar with 1 cup of water over medium heat. Bring to a simmer, stirring constantly until the sugar is dissolved. Add the cranberries and cook just until all the cranberries are popped, about 3 minutes. Using a slotted spoon, transfer the cranberries to a bowl, leaving the cranberry syrup in the saucepan. Use the syrup for making Kir Royales (see page 87) if you wish.

In a large saucepan, melt the butter and add the onion and celery. Sauté until soft, about 4 minutes. Add the rice, stock, 2¹/₂ cups water, the salt, thyme, and pepper. Bring to a boil, reduce the heat to low, cover, and simmer until the rice is tender but chewy, about 45 minutes. Remove from the heat and let stand, covered, for 15 minutes (drain off any excess liquid). Add the toasted pecans and cranberries to the wild rice mixture and toss. Use either as a turkey stuffing or bake separately.

To bake separately, preheat the oven to 350°F. Place the dressing in a buttered 9 × 13-inch baking dish and bake, covered with foil, for 30 to 40 minutes, until the dressing is heated throughout. Serve hot.

POLENTA

SERVES 6

Semolina is finely ground durum or other hard wheat that is used in pasta making. In this recipe, it is mixed with the cornmeal to make a softer-textured polenta. If you wish, substitute another $1/2$ cup cornmeal in its place. Polenta is the perfect accompaniment to roast quail, other game birds, and grilled venison.

4 cups homemade chicken stock or reduced-sodium chicken broth

$1/2$ teaspoon coarse salt

$1/2$ cup cornmeal

$1/2$ cup semolina

$1/2$ cup freshly grated Parmigiano-Reggiano

2 tablespoons unsalted butter

Heat the chicken stock and salt in a 2-quart saucepan over medium heat until almost boiling. Reduce the heat to a simmer, mix together the cornmeal and semolina, and slowly stir it into the hot stock, stirring constantly with a wire whisk. To avoid lumps, continue stirring until all the polenta has been added and the mixture begins to thicken, 24 to 25 minutes. Remove from the heat and stir in the cheese and butter. Season with salt, if necessary.

NOTE: For the Quail Roasted in Polenta (page 84), immediately pour the polenta into the prepared baking dish.

GARLIC CUSTARD ON A BED OF GREENS

SERVES 4

The subtle garlic nuance in this savory custard recipe comes from infusing half-and-half with fresh garlic. I bake the custards in individual ramekins and serve them warm on mixed greens that have been tossed with a light vinaigrette. I accompany this dish with mild-flavored upland game birds, such as pheasant or partridge, and, to complete the meal, I grill slices of mango (page 283).

CUSTARDS

1¹/₂ cups half-and-half

3 garlic cloves

2 eggs

1 egg yolk

³/₄ teaspoon coarse salt

GREENS

¹/₄ pound mesclun

1 tablespoon extra virgin olive oil

1 teaspoon balsamic vinegar

Pinch of coarse salt

Preheat the oven to 325°F. Lightly grease 4 ramekins or custard cups. Put the ramekins in a shallow pan (an 8 × 8-inch cake pan, for instance) and set aside.

Pour the half-and-half into a small saucepan. Crush the garlic cloves with the back of a knife and remove the skin. Put the garlic in the half-and-half and heat it to almost boiling. Remove the pan from the heat and let cool to room temperature.

Beat the eggs and yolk together with the salt, then whisk into the half-and-half. Strain into the ramekins and put the pan with the ramekins in the oven. Pour enough hot water into the pan to come up halfway on the sides of the ramekins. Bake for 45 minutes, or until a knife inserted in the center comes out clean. Use a pot holder and carefully remove the ramekins from the hot water. Set aside while you prepare the greens.

Put the greens in a small bowl and toss with the olive oil, vinegar, and salt. Divide the salad equally among 4 dinner plates.

Unmold the custard by carefully running a thin knife around the sides of the ramekins. Unmold onto the greens and serve immediately.

GRILLED FRUIT

SERVES 4

Fruits—especially nectarines, plums, peaches, and mangoes—are particularly good grill mates with rabbit, game birds, and wild boar. Not only does their warm texture and juicy, sweet flavor cut through the richness of the game, but the fruit adds a welcome splash of color to the plate. It is not necessary to skin the fruit before grilling. The skin on the nectarines and plums can be eaten but not the mango's—it is too stringy—just scoop the pulp out with your fork.

2 tablespoons fresh lime juice
2 teaspoons honey
Pinch of cayenne
2 nectarines, halved and pitted
4 plums, halved and pitted, or 1 mango, cut off the pit vertically

Stir together the lime juice, honey, and cayenne. Lightly score the flesh of the fruit. Put the fruit on the grill, cut side down, for 2 to 3 minutes. Turn the fruit over and brush with the honey-lime mixture. Grill for 2 to 3 more minutes, until the fruit is hot. Serve hot or at room temperature.

BAKED PEARS WITH CHIMAYO CHILE HONEY

SERVES 4

My good friend Zanne Stewart, the columnist of *Gourmet* magazine's "Forbidden Pleasures" and the magazine's executive food editor, shared her recipe for chile honey, which can be used on everything from apples to garlic to an unusual peanut butter sandwich. What makes the honey so special is the dusky red chile powder ground from New Mexican red chiles, which are grown near the town of Chimayo in the foothills of the Sangre de Cristo Mountains. This chile powder is sold as New Mexican red chile in markets (or to mail-order it, see page 294).

Serve these spicy pears to accompany grilled or roasted game, such as duck, quail, guinea hen, venison, buffalo, or boar. I make them a day in advance and serve them at room temperature to accompany smoked game birds.

1 cup clover honey
1 tablespoon powdered New Mexican red chile
2 Bosc pears, peeled, cored, and cut lengthwise into quarters

Preheat the oven to 400°F.

Heat the honey and chile powder in a small, heavy saucepan over medium-low heat. Bring to a simmer, stirring, then remove from the heat to infuse until cool.

Put the pear quarters in a small baking dish. Roast for 25 minutes, or until they are just barely tender. Turn the pieces over and drizzle with a tablespoon of the chile honey. Cook for 5 more minutes, or until the pieces are completely tender when pierced with a fork.

Store leftover honey in a jar at room temperature. It will keep for 3 months.

VARIATION: In the summer, grill quarters of fresh plums, nectarines, and mangoes with the chile honey. Cut the fruit in half and remove their pits. Grill the fruit cut side down over medium coals for 5 minutes. Turn the fruit over and brush with the chile honey. If the chile honey is too stiff to brush it on, gently heat it over low heat, or drizzle it on from the back of a spoon. Cook for 2 to 3 more minutes, until the fruit is hot throughout.

AVOCADO AND ASIAN PEAR SALAD

SERVES 4

Asian pears are juicy and crunchy, a direct contrast to the buttery texture of avocado. In this recipe I arrange them side by side on crisp butter lettuce and then sprinkle with chopped hazelnuts and drizzle with a honey-lime juice dressing.

1 head butter lettuce

1 small avocado, peeled, pitted, and sliced vertically into 1/8-inch slices

1/2 large Asian pear, peeled and sliced into 1/8-inch slices

2 tablespoons olive oil

2 teaspoons fresh lime juice

1 teaspoon honey

2 tablespoons chopped and roasted hazelnuts

Separate the lettuce leaves, rinse, and pat dry. Arrange them in a circle in a single layer on a large plate, covering the entire bottom.

Make a concentric circle of alternate slices of avocado and pear apple.

Whisk the olive oil, lime juice, and honey together and pour it over the slices of avocado and pear apple.

Sprinkle with the chopped hazelnuts.

CHOPPED CITRUS SALAD

SERVES 4

I love this colorful salad because its tangy citrus flavors refresh the palate without being overly filling. Make it a day or two in advance if you wish, but add the cilantro just before serving.

1 orange, peeled and segmented

1 grapefruit, peeled, segmented, and fruit removed from its membrane

$1/2$ English cucumber, cut into quarters and chopped

$1/4$ cup chopped red bell pepper

$1/4$ cup chopped red onion

1 tablespoon extra virgin olive oil

1 teaspoon champagne vinegar

4 sprigs fresh cilantro, stemmed and chopped

Cut the fruit segments into $1/2$-inch pieces and put them in a bowl with the cucumber, red pepper, and onion. Whisk the olive oil and champagne vinegar together and toss. Just before serving, sprinkle the cilantro over the fruit and toss.

NOTE: To make a citrus gazpacho, add 6 ounces grapefruit juice to the salad. Serve in soup bowls for a first course before a game dinner.

WILDWOOD FENNEL SLAW

SERVES 6 TO 8

This unusual fennel slaw that Cory Schreiber serves at his popular Wildwood restaurant in Portland, Oregon is one of my treasured recipes to pair with game. The acidic bite from the vinegar cuts the richness of any game it is served with. I have made it with savoy and Napa cabbage: Both worked beautifully. Serve it with any grilled or roasted game birds such as quail or squab, or with grilled game meat like wild boar, venison, or buffalo. I like to leave the fennel seeds whole—they add a pleasant woodsy aftertaste.

1 small head cabbage (preferably savoy)
1 small fennel bulb
2 carrots, peeled and grated
1 red onion, sliced very thinly
1/4 cup mayonnaise
1/4 cup chopped fennel fronds
1/4 cup red wine vinegar
1 tablespoon fennel seeds, toasted and ground (see page 11)
3/4 teaspoon coarse salt
Freshly ground black pepper

Remove the tough outer leaves of the cabbage and fennel, and slice them very thinly, discarding their cores. Combine in a large bowl and mix with the carrots and onion. Add the remaining ingredients and toss.

Let sit in the refrigerator for 1 hour to allow the flavors to blend.

Serve chilled.

AMERICAN GAME TIME LINE

12,000 years ago The Ancient Ones, the ancestors of Native Americans, follow the mammoths, musk-oxen, and other large game animals over the Trans-Bering land bridge connecting northeastern Siberia and Alaska.

10,000 years ago Pleistocene megafauna become extinct, including camelops, mammoths, mastodons, and horses; the remaining animals include our modern bison, elk, deer, moose, etc.

7,000 years ago Northern Hemisphere goes through a drying period; game populations decrease due to lack of food; hunters focus on smaller game, antelope, rabbits, marmots; and there is an increased emphasis on plant foods. It is the beginning of New World domestication of corn, beans, and squash in northern Mexico.

4,000 years ago Most Native Americans are still hunters and gatherers, but many groups start seasonal village life. Beginning of farming in what is now the southwestern and southeastern United States, and some groups invent pottery. In the west, the Plains Indians and those in the Great Basin are still hunter-gatherers while coastal inhabitants survive on fishing and hunting.

3,000 years ago Northern Hemisphere experiences a return to a wetter climate, more like today's. Gradual increase in bison, elk, and deer on the Great Plains. Hunters begin to refocus efforts on bison hunting.

1,000 years ago Little Ice Age. Climate becomes wetter, causing grass to grow abundantly on the Great Plains. Height of bison hunting in North America. There are communal bison kills through the Great Plains from Alberta to Texas, and even across the Rockies into Idaho, Washington, and Utah. The early Americans are expert hunters and rely on game for the substance and source of their spiritual life. The supply of game seems limitless.

1492 Columbus introduces horses, cattle, and pigs to North America.

1535 First fur traders in North America arrive from France and establish outposts on the banks of the St. Lawrence. In western North America there is an intensification of a communal hunting pattern that includes antelope, bison, mountain sheep, rabbits, and crickets.

1620 The Pilgrims found Plymouth Colony. Game is the sole source of their existence until domestic herds increase and crops start producing.

1650 The horse is introduced to the Native Americans in the Great Plains. Hunting is suddenly easier, and they develop their entire culture around the bison. With the settling of the East Coast, many Indian tribes—Cheyenne, Arapaho, and Dakota (Sioux)—give up their agricultural village life and move onto the plains to become nomadic bison hunters. They follow the large herds as the bison migrate throughout the region.

1670 Hudson Bay Company builds outposts in North America under the patronage of Prince Rupert to seek a passageway to the Pacific and to establish a profitable business. It engages in the fur trade for the next two hundred years.

1781 Shortly after the American Revolution, early lawmakers rule that the land belongs to all the people, guaranteeing the privilege of hunting and fishing to all Americans, unlike in Europe, where the land and all the game that is on it belongs to the aristocracy.

1823 Hudson Bay Company builds outposts in the Oregon Territory to collect beaver furs to sell in Europe for their booming hat industry.

1843 Railroads open up the West and, as the land is settled, game animal populations rapidly decrease. The small fur trade comes to an end from overhunting and a declining market—Europeans begin to wear silk hats instead of fur. Hunters turn their attention to the bison, which becomes the target of massive decimation. Hides, and sometimes only the tongue, are shipped back to the East Coast while the rest of the animal goes to waste.

1869 First Transcontinental Railroad is completed.

1871 U.S. Bureau of Fisheries is established.

1872 First legislation is passed to set aside land for preservation. Yellowstone National Park is made America's first national park. Created mainly to protect the geysers and hot springs, it is not until 1894 that Congress passes a game protection law to fine game poachers.

1885 U.S. Bureau of Biological Survey is established.

1888 Boone and Crockett Club is founded by Theodore Roosevelt to fight for the military protection of the public forests and named after two of his heroes, Daniel Boone and

Davy Crockett. It consists of one hundred scientists, politicians, and military men who are all hunters themselves. With the closing of the frontier by the end of the nineteenth century, hunting becomes a sport rather than a way of life for survival, but market hunters are still shooting birds by the thousands.

1893 Only three hundred buffalo exist in the United States—down from an estimated 60 million in early America.

1904 Theodore Roosevelt creates fifty-one game refuges and becomes the first president to set aside national parcels of land for the protection of game.

1905 Theodore Roosevelt establishes the U.S. Forest Service, which sets aside large parcels of forest land to help preserve our forests and herds of large game animals. American Bison Society is established to stock preserves and parks with buffalo.

1908 The National Bison Range is created in northern Montana.

1914 Last passenger pigeon dies.

1918 Migratory Bird Act is established between the United States and Canada, and later Mexico. This international treaty limits hunting of migratory birds and protects their breeding grounds, migration routes, and wintering areas.

Game disappears from menus due to scarcity and changing game laws.

1930 Aldo Leopold pioneers the concept of ecology, the interrelation of organisms and their environment. In three decades, a critical problem had emerged on the game refuges. The herds and flocks of animals multiplied at such fast rates that they overpopulated and the animals began to starve. Leopold realized that while wolves and other predators benefited the large game herds by culling out the weak and disabled, there were too many animals for the food available. His ideas helped inspire the management organizations that safeguard the delicate balance in the survival of our wildlife today.

In addition, two federal laws are passed to benefit migratory birds in the 1930s. One places a tax on hunting licenses and ammunition, while the other, the Duck Stamp Law, requires all duck hunters over the age of sixteen to purchase a duck stamp every year. Revenues generated from these taxes go toward the purchase, maintenance, and improvement of wildlife refuge areas. (Buying an annual duck stamp is a good way for nonhunters to contribute to wildlife refuges.)

1937 Formation of Ducks Unlimited, Inc.

1939 Both the Bureau of Fisheries and Bureau of Biological Surveys are transferred to the Department of the Interior.

1940 Bureau of Fisheries and Bureau of Biological Surveys are combined into one bureau and named the Fish and Wildlife Service.

1956 The Fish and Wildlife Service is renamed the U.S. Fish and Wildlife Service.

1966 Formation of the National Buffalo Association.

1970 The Bureau of Commercial Fisheries is separated from the Bureau of Biological Surveys and sent back to the Department of Commerce. The bureau is renamed the Bureau of Sport Fisheries and Wildlife.

1973 Formation of the Wild Turkey Federation.

1974 Bureau of Sport Fisheries and Wildlife is renamed the Bureau of Fish and Wildlife Service again.

1975 Formation of the American Bison Association.

1977 Formation of the Foundation for North American Wild Sheep.

1981 Formation of Quail Unlimited.

1982 Formation of Pheasants Forever.

1983 Formation of the North American Deer Farmers Association and the American Beefalo World Registry.

1984 Formation of the Rocky Mountain Elk Foundation.

1987 Formation of the American Ostrich Association.

1988 Formation of the Mule Deer Foundation.

1990 Game returns to menus and markets but now it is commercially raised.

1992 Formation of the Intertribal Bison Cooperative. Forty-five national tribes are members.

1995 The American Bison Association and the National Buffalo Association merge to form the National Bison Association.

SUPPORTING
AMERICA'S NATIVE GAME

Both nonhunters and hunters can help support wildlife by purchasing stamps or art work, such as limited edition prints, sold by individual state departments of fish and wildlife. The revenues help support research, wetland restoration, and wildlife habitat. Call your state's department of fish and wildlife for more information.

Most of the following nonprofit organizations were founded by and are supported by hunters, but nonhunters can join, too. The money raised goes toward restoring and acquiring wildlife habitat.

Rocky Mountain Elk Foundation
P.O. Box 8249
Missoula, Montana 59807–9942
800–CALL–ELK

Pheasants Forever, Dept. SA
1783 Buerkle Circle
St. Paul, Minnesota 55110
612–773–2000

National Wild Turkey Federation
P.O. Box 530
Edgefield, South Carolina 29824
803–637–3107

Ducks Unlimited, Inc.
National Headquarters
1 Waterfowl Way

Memphis, Tennessee 38120
901–758–3825
http://www.ducks.org

Quail Unlimited
P.O. Box 610
Edgefield, South Carolina 29824–0610
803–637–5731

Foundation for North American Wild Sheep
720 Allen Avenue
Cody, Wyoming 82414
307–527–6261

Mule Deer Foundation
1005 Terminal Way, Suite 140
Reno, Nevada 85902
888–375–DEER

Being a Good Samaritan

If you hit a game animal on the road, report it immediately to the state police. District biologists with the state departments of fish and game are trained as meat inspectors. Any meat that is salvageable is processed for local food banks.

Beyond Fair Chase by Jim Posewitz (Falcon Publishing Co. Inc., Billings, Montana, 1994) is a small paperback on the ethics, traditions, and responsibilities of hunting that all hunters should read. To order contact:

Falcon
48 N. Last Chance Gulch
P.O. Box 1718
Helena, Montana 59601

SHARING THE BOUNTY

Hunters who would like to donate a portion of their game meat to help feed the hungry can do so by having their meat ground and frozen in 1- or 2-pound packages. Many states have programs, such as Hunters Against Hunger, which coordinate the collection of donated game meat from certified meat processors and distribution to local food banks. Call your local food bank—numbers are listed in the *Yellow Pages*—for more information. Or, call the National Rifle Association's Hunters Against Hunger Clearing House hot line (800–492–4868) to find the program nearest you.

MAIL-ORDER SOURCES

In many towns and cities across the country, game is becoming more readily available in grocery stores and meat markets. If you can't find game, look in the *Yellow Pages* under "Meats" or ask your butcher to order it for you. Another alternative is to mail-order it from one of the following suppliers. Many of the companies will send you a catalog or price list upon request. When I mail-order game I buy enough for three or four dinners and store what I do not use in the freezer.

American Beefalo World Registry
3770 121st Avenue
Allegan, Michigan 49010
616–673–4966
616–673–5008
(Call if you need assistance in finding a supplier of beefalo meat near you.)

The American Ostrich Association
3950 Fossil Creek Blvd., Suite 200
Fort Worth, Texas 76137
817–232–1200
e-mail: aoa@flash.net, request Meat Suppliers List or Restaurant & Market List

Broadleaf Venison USA, Inc.
3050 East 11th Street
Los Angeles, California 90023
800–336–3844
Wholesale and mail order
Large and small game, game birds, exotic game

Broken Arrow Ranch
P.O. Box 530
Ingram, Texas 78025
800–962–4263
Wholesale and mail order
Axis venison, fallow venison, Blackbuck antelope, Nilgai antelope (South Texas antelope), wild boar, smoked meats, and sausages

Butterfield's Buffalo Meat
R.R. 3 Box 7
Beloit, Kansas 67420
913–738–2336
Wholesale and mail order
Buffalo

The Chile Shop
109 East Water
Santa Fe, New Mexico 87501
505–983–6080

D'Artagnan Inc.
399 St. Paul Avenue
Jersey City, New Jersey 07306
800–DARTAGNan/327–8246
Wholesale and mail order
Large and small game, game birds, exotic game

Denver Buffalo Company
P.O. Box 480603
Denver, Colorado 80248–0603
800–289–2833
Wholesale and mail order
Buffalo

Durham Meat Company
P.O. Box 26158
San Jose, California 95159
800–233–8742
Wholesale and mail order
Large and small game, game birds, exotic game

Frontier Buffalo Company
395 Southend Avenue
Suite 31 D
New York, New York 10280
888–EAT–BUFF
Wholesale and mail order
Buffalo

Goldmine Natural Food Company
3419 Hancock Street
San Diego, California 92110–4307
800–475–3663
Whole line of organic and macrobiotic foods
Bhutanese red rice and other exotic rices

Hills Foods Ltd.
#109–3650 Bonneville Place
Burnaby, British Columbia
Canada V3N 4T7
604–421–3100
hillsfood@bc.sympatico.ca
Wholesale only
Large and small game, game birds, exotic game

Joie DeVivre
P.O. Box 875
Modesto, California 95353
800–648–8854
Mail order
Duck, smoked duck, rabbit, geese, guinea hens, foie gras

Los Chileros
P.O. Box 6215
Santa Fe, NM 87501
505–471–6967
Chimayo and other chiles

Luhr Jensen & Sons, Inc.
P.O. Box 297
Hood River, Oregon 97031
800–535–1711
Little Chief electric smokers, brine and sausage mixes, wood chips

MacFarlane Pheasant Farm, Inc.
2821 South U.S. Hwy. 51
Janesville, Wisconsin 53546
800–345–8348
Wholesale and mail order
Pheasant, smoked pheasant, and other types of wild game, wild rice, marinades, and sauces

Musicon Farms
157 Scotchtown Road
Goshen, New York 10924
914–294–6378
516–239–8915 (fax)
Wholesale and mail order
Glatt kosher venison

Native Game
12556 WCR 2^1/$_2$
Brighton, Colorado 80601
800–952–6321
Wholesale and mail order
Large and small game, game birds, exotic game

Nicky USA, Inc.
223 S.E. 3rd Avenue
Portland, Oregon 97214
800–469–4162
Wholesale and mail order
Large and small game, game birds, exotic game

Nightbird
358 Shaw Road
South San Francisco, California 94080
650–737–5876
800–225–7457
Wholesale and mail order
Large and small game, game birds, exotic game

Polaricia (Wholesale)/The Game
Exchange (Retail)
P.O. Box 990204
San Francisco, California 94124
800–GAME–USA
Wholesale and retail
Large and small game, game birds, exotic game

Penzey's, Ltd.
P.O. Box 933
Muskego, Wisconsin 53150–0933
414–679–7207
414–679–7878 (fax)
Mail order
Herbs, spices, and seasonings

Prairie Harvest
P.O. Box 1013
Spearfish, South Dakota 57783
800–350–7166
Wholesale and mail order
Large and small game, game birds, exotic game

The Sausage Maker, Inc.
1500 Clinton Street, Bldg. 123
Buffalo, New York 14206
716–824–6510
716–824–6465 (fax)
Wholesale and mail order
Sausage-making supplies

Triple U Enterprises
P.O. Box 995
Pierre, South Dakota 57501
605–567–3624
Wholesale and mail order
Buffalo

Game Sales International
2456 E. 13th Street
P.O. Box 7719
Loveland, CO 80537
800–729–2090
970–667–4090

NUTRITIONAL DATA

Game meat and birds are generally lower in fat and cholesterol than many domestic meats and poultry—for some cooks, the reason for selecting them. This chart compares nutrition among one-serving portions of various varieties and cuts of game.

BIRDS

TYPE	CAL	FAT (G)	%CAL/FAT	CHOLESTEROL (MG)
*Chicken, domestic, breast, no skin	165	4	21	81
*Chicken, domestic, dark meat, with skin	237	18	71	82
*Chicken, domestic, thigh, no skin	119	4	31	83
Dove, domestic, with skin	151	2	15	91
Duck, domestic, with skin	404	39	88	76
Duckling, farm-raised, breast, no skin	132	2	14	153
Duckling, farm-raised, breast, with skin	193	11	51	135
Duckling, farm-raised, leg, no skin	163	5	28	117
Duckling, farm-raised, leg, with skin	206	11	48	113
Duck, wild, breast, no skin	123	4	32	no data
Duck, wild, breast, with skin	211	15	66	80
Duck, wild, mallard	154	2	16	143
Emu, farm-raised, no skin	120	3	23	45
Goose, domestic, no skin	161	7	41	84
Goose, domestic, with skin	371	34	83	80
Goose, wild, Canadian	171	4	28	105
Grouse, wild, sharp-tailed	142	1	6	106
Guinea hen, with skin	156	6	38	53
Ostrich, farm-raised, no skin	107	2	15	61
Pheasant, farm-raised, with skin	151	5	33	49
Pheasant, wild, breast, no skin	134	3	26	49
Pheasant, wild, with skin	181	9	48	no data
Poussin, farm-raised, with skin	166	11	61	51
Quail breast, wild, no skin	123	3	23	no data
Quail, whole, wild, with skin	193	12	58	no data
Squab (pigeon), farm-raised, breast, no skin	144	8	49	no data
Squab (pigeon), farm-raised, with skin	297	24	74	no data
Turkey breast, domestic, with skin	167	8	46	62
Turkey, domestic, dark, no skin	187	7	36	85
Turkey, domestic, lt./dark, no skin	170	5	28	76
Turkey, domestic, light, no skin	114	2	13	62

Sources of information include U.S. Department of Agriculture, Nutritionist III and Nutritionist IV software, research from the University of Wisconsin/Madison, North Dakota State University, Texas A&M University, University of Florida and Louisiana State University, and independent laboratories for game producers, councils, and associations. Data are based on 100-gram (3.6-ounce) raw portions.

* For purposes of comparison

LARGE GAME

TYPE	CAL	FAT (G)	% FAT/CAL	CHOLESTEROL (MG)
Antelope (pronghorn)	114	2	17	95
Bear	161	8	48	no data
*Beef, hamburger, lean	272	18	63	87
Beefalo, all cuts	143	5	32	44
Boar	122	3	26	no data
Buffalo, American	109	2	16	62
Caribou	127	3	25	83
Deer	120	2	19	85
Elk	111	1	12	55
Goat, domestic	109	2	20	57
Moose	102	0.7	7	59
Venison	124	2	14	no data
Venison, dried, salted	142	1	6	no data

Sources of information include U.S. Department of Agriculture, Nutritionist III and Nutritionist IV software, research from the University of Wisconsin/Madison, North Dakota State University, Texas A&M University, University of Florida, Louisiana State University, and independent laboratories for game producers, councils, and associations. Data are based on 100-gram (3.6-ounce) raw portions.

*For purposes of comparison

SMALL/EXOTIC GAME

TYPE	CAL	FAT (G)	% FAT/CAL	CHOLESTEROL (MG)
Alligator	148	3	18	65
Armadillo	174	7	38	73
Beaver	146	5	31	no data
Frog's legs, floured, fried	290	20	63	no data
Hare (jackrabbit)	153	3	20	131
Kangaroo	93	0.5	2	62
Muskrat	162	8	47	no data
Opossum	188	9	43	no data
Rabbit, domestic, with skin	136	6	38	57
Rabbit, wild (cottontail) with no skin	144	2	20	77
Raccoon	217	12	53	no data
Squirrel	120	3	25	83
Turtle	89	0.5	5	50

Sources of information include U.S. Department of Agriculture, Nutritionist III and Nutritionist IV software, research from the University of Wisconsin/Madison, North Dakota State University, Texas A&M University, Stanford Consulting Laboratories, University of Florida, Louisiana State University, and independent laboratories for game producers, councils, and associations. Data are based on 100-gram (3.6-ounce) raw portions.

BIBLIOGRAPHY

Akerman, Joe A., Jr. *Florida Cowman: A History of Florida Cattle Raising.* Kissimmee, Florida: Florida Cattlemen's Association, 1993.

Ambrose, Stephen E. *Undaunted Courage: Meriwether Lewis Thomas Jefferson, and the Opening of the American West.* New York: Touchstone, 1997.

The American Heritage Cookbook. Edited by the American Heritage editors. New York: American Heritage Publishing Co., Inc, 1964.

Andreas, Alfred Theodore. *History of Chicago,* Volume 1. New York: Arno Press, Any Times Company, 1975.

Beard, Yolande S. *The Wappo: a Report, with drawings by the author.* St. Helena, California: Munroe and Francis, 1977.

Benson, Evelyn Abraham, ed. *Penn Family Recipes—Cooking Recipes of William Penn's Wife, Gulielma.* York, Pennsylvania: George Shumway, 1966.

A Boston Housekeeper. *The Cook's Own Book: Being a Complete Culinary Encyclopedia for Cooking Meat, Fish and Fowl, Soup, Gravy, Pastry, Preserves, Essences, During the Last Twenty Years.* Boston: Munroe and Francis, 1832.

Brown, Catherine. *A Year in a Scots Kitchen.* Glasgow, Scotland: Neil Wilson Publishing, 1996.

Callahan, Carol. *Prairie Avenue Cookbook.* Chicago: Chicago Architecture Foundation, 1993.

Catlin, George. *North American Indians.* Edited by Peter Matthiessen. New York: Penguin Books, 1989.

Chamberlain, Andrew B. *Historic Furnishings Report: Indian Trade House.* Harpers Ferry Center, Virginia: National Park Service, 1993.

Cleveland, Bess A. *California Mission Recipes Adapted for Modern Usage.* Rutland, Vermont & Tokyo, Japan: Charles E. Tuttle Company, 1965.

Conrad, Eugene L., comp. and ed. *Game Cookery Recipes Along with Those Sauces Necessary to the Culinary Arts as Prepared at Delmonicos Famous New York Restaurant.* Palmer Lake, Colorado: Filter Press, 1971.

Davidson, D. S. *Family Hunting Territories in Northwestern North America.* New York: Heye Foundation, 1928.

Douglas, David. *Journal Kept by David Douglas During his Travels in North America, 1823–1827.* New York: Antiquarian Press, 1959.

De Graf, Bell. *Mrs. De Graf's Cook Book.* San Francisco, California: H.S. Crocker, Inc., 1922.

Emanuels, George. *California Indians.* Walnut Creek, California: Diablo Books, 1992.

Faulkner, William. *Big Woods.* New York: Random House, 1931.

Fitzgibbon, Theodora. *The Food of the Western World.* New York: Quadrangle/The New York Times Book Co., 1976.

Gilbert, Cabeza de Beca, Fabiola. *The Good Life, New Mexico Traditions and Food.* Santa Fe: Museum of New Mexican Press, 1982.

Hamilton, Archibald. *Plantation Game Trails*. Boston and New York: Houghton Mifflin Company, 1921.

Hansen, David K. *Furnishing Plan for Indian Trade Store/Dispensary*. Vancouver, Washington: National Park Service, Fort Vancouver National Historic Site, 1981.

Hart, Harold H., ed. *Animal Art in the Public Domain*. New York: Hart Publishing Company, 1983.

Haynes, Cynthia. *Raising Turkeys, Ducks, Geese, Pigeons, and Guineas*. Blue Ridge Summit, Pennsylvania: Tab Books Inc., 1987.

Herbst, Sharon Tyler. *Food Lover's Companion*. New York: Barron's, 1990.

Hines, Gustavus. *Life on the Plains; Its History, Condition and Prospects*. Auburn, New York: Derby and Miller, 1851.

Hines, Mary Anne, Gordon Marshall, and William Woys Weaver. *The Larder Invaded: Reflections on Three Centuries of Philadelphia Food and Drink*. Philadelphia: The Winchell Company of Philadelphia, 1987.

Hubalek, Linda K. *Egg Gravy*. Aurora, Colorado: Butterfield Books, 1994.

Hubert, Henry William. *Frank Forester's Field Sports of the United States and British Provinces of North America*, Vol. 1 & 2. New York: Stringer & Townsend, 1849.

Hughes, Mike. *The Broken Arrow Ranch Venison Handbook*, Version 2. 1995.

Kafka, Barbara. *Microwave Gourmet*. New York: William Morrow and Company, Inc., 1987.

Kasper, Lynne Rossetto. *The Splendid Table*. New York: William Morrow and Co., Inc., 1992.

Keegan, Marcia. *Southwest Indian Cookbook*. Santa Fe: Clear Light Publishing, 1987.

Kerckerinck, Josepf. *Deer Farming in North America*. New York: Phanter Press, 1987.

Keyser, Dr. James. *Indian Rock Art of the Columbia Plateau*. Seattle, Washington: University of Washington Press, 1992.

Lavender, David. *Land of Giants: The Drive to the Pacific Northwest 1750–1950*. New York: Doubleday & Company, Inc., 1958.

Leslie, Miss. *Directions for Cookery; Being a System of the Art*. Philadelphia: E.L. Carry & A. Hart, 1837.

Lewis, E. J., M.D. *Hints to Sportsmen, containing notes on Shooting; the Dog, the Gun, the Field and the Kitchen*. Philadelphia: Lea & Blanchard, 1851.

Lewis, Elisha J., M.D. *The American Sportsman: Hints to Sportsmen, Notes on Shooting and the Habits of the Game Birds, and Wild Fowl of America*. Philadelphia: Lippincott, Grambo and Co., 1855.

Lewis, Meriwether, and William Clark. *The History of the Lewis and Clark Expedition*. Volume III. Edited by Elliott Coues. New York: Dover Publications, Inc., 1893.

Maser, Chris. *Forest Primeval*. San Francisco: Sierra Club Books, 1989.

McGee, Harold. *On Food and Cooking*. New York: Charles Scribner's Sons, 1984.

Mathiesen, Johan, ed. *Word of Mouth*, No. 16. Portland, Oregon, July 1977.

Mednick, Christina Singleton. *San Cristóbal*. Santa Fe: Office of Archaeological Studies, 1996.

Moss, Kay, and Kathryn Huffman. *The Backcountry Housewife*, Volume 1. Gastonia, North Carolina: Schiele Museum, 1985.

The New England Cook Book, or Young Housekeeper's Guide. New Haven: Hezekiah Howe & Co., and Herrick & Nayes, 1836.

Packman, Ana Béqué. *Early California Hospitality—The Cooking Customs of Spanish California with Authentic Recipes and Menus of the Period*. Glendale, California: Arthur Clark Company, 1938.

Peterson, Marcus. *The Fur Traders and Fur Bearing Animals*. Buffalo, New York: The Hammond Press, 1914.

Pitcher, Don. *Wyoming Handbook*, 2nd edition. Chico, California: Moon Publications, 1993.

Randall, Henry S. *The Life of Thomas Jefferson*, Volume 1. Philadelphia: J.B. Lippincott Company, 1888.

Roosevelt, Theodore. *The Wilderness Hunter*, Volume 1. Philadelphia: Gribbie and Company, 1903.

Root, Waverly. *Food*. New York: Simon & Schuster, Inc., 1980.

Root, Waverly, and Richard de Rochemont. *Eating in America*. New York: The Echo Press, 1981.

Sanderson, J. M. *The Complete Cook, Plain and Practical Directions for Cooking and Housekeeping*. American Edition. Philadelphia: Lea & Blanchard, 1846.

Schnarwyler, Albert. Eleanor and James Ferguson. *Dining at the Homestead*. Virginia Hotsprings, Incorporated: Hot Springs, Virginia, 1989.

Simmons, Amelia. *American Cookery or the Art of Dressing Viands, Fish, Poultry and Vegetables by an American Ophan.* Conneticutt, 1796.

Skinner, J. S., ed. *American Turf Register and Sporting Magazine.* Volume 2 and 3. Baltimore: J.S. Skinner, 1831.

Skinner, John. *Fish and Wildlife Resources of the San Francisco Bay Area.* San Francisco: Department of Fish and Game, Water Projects Branch No. 1, 1962.

Strong, Emory. *Stone Age in The Great Basin.* Portland, Oregon: Binford & Mort, 1976.

Tannahill, Reay. *Food in History.* New York: Stein and Day Publishers, 1973.

Taylor, Colin F., Ph.D. *The Plains Indians.* London: Salamander Books Limited, 1994.

Thomas, Bryn, and Charles Hibbs, Jr. *Report of Investigations at Kanaka Village, 1980/1981,* Volume 2: *Vancouver Barracks.* Washington. Washington State Department of Transportation, Archaeological and Historical Services, Eastern Washington University.

Thomas, Jack Ward, and Dale E. Toweill, comps. and eds *Elk of North America.* Harrisburg, Pennsylvania: Stackpole Books, 1982.

Velarde, Pablita. *Old Father Story Teller.* Santa Fe: Clear Light Publishers, 1989.

Viola, Herman J., and Carolyn Margolis. *Seeds of Change.* Washington and London: Smithsonian Institution Press, 1991.

Washington, Martha. *Martha Washington's Booke of Cookery,* transcribed by Karen Hess. New York: Columbia University Press, 1981.

Weatherford, Jack. *Indian Givers—How the Indians of the Americas Transformed the World.* New York: Ballantine Books, 1988.

Wood, William. *New England's Prospect.* Boston: The University of Massachusetts Press, 1993. (First published in London, 1634).

ACKNOWLEDGMENTS

To Gary, a hunter whose respect for wildlife and knowledge of the outdoors is an example for all to follow.

To my mother, who shared her passion for cooking with me.

To my children and family, for their love and support.

I wish to express my deep gratitude to Mike Hughes, Rich Flocchini, Ken Durbin, Dr. James Keyser, and Geoff Latham for generously sharing their time and knowledge.

For those who have assisted me along the way, my heartfelt thanks: Harriet Bell, Judith Weber, Barbara Durbin, Ginger Johnston, Robert Shipley, Claude Bigo, Mark Hills, Jupp Kerckerinck-Borg, Heather McPherson, Beverly Cox, Rick Edwards, J. J. Durbin, Chris Durbin, Kathryn Kurtz, Betty and Jim Shenberger, Jeanne Hibler, Jerry and Barbara Boucock, Dottie Trivison, Rob and Judy Kaspar, Zanne Early Stewart, Sheryl Julian, Johan Mathiesen, Kaspar and Nancy Donier, Paula Lambert, Stephan Pyles, Dr. Michael Hooker, Jim Ferguson, the late Senator Terry Sanford, P. T. Morris, Shirley and Aalf Collins, Cheryl and Bill Jamison, Steve Haid, Paula Naughton, Susan Franklin, Crescent Dragonwagon, Zoe and Charles Caywood, Joe White, Marcia Keegan, Katherine Kagel, Lady Fiona and Sir Peter Elworthy, Jim and Anna Guild, Catherine Smith, John Bain, Karen Sehon, Rhonda Braithwaite, Sarah Fritschner, George Rude, Lorinda Moholt, Gerrard Drummond, David Bergen, Jeanne Voltz, Katherin Brown, Toni Allegra, Flo Braker, Fred Millard, Kathleen Curtain, Sandra Oliver, Greg Higgins, Cory Schrieber, Philippe Wagenfuhrer, Rodger Babel, Joseph White, Bill Rowe, Tom Jurgielewicz, Steve Hauff, David Nelson, Mark Henjum, Beverly Cox, Adam Zwerling, Ann Chandonnet, Polly Golden, Burt Culver, Katie Sutton, Tom Douglas, Lynne Loacker, Lynne Rosetto Kasper, Karina McDaniels, John Poister, Thayer Wine, Steven Rarchlen, Katie Hess, Jamey Maddren, and Bob Liner.

I would like to acknowledge the staffs at the following research institutions and libraries for their help:

Bancroft Library
The Charleston Museum
Chicago Historical Society
Coastal Discovery Museum on Hilton Head Island, S.C.
The George Peabody Library of The Johns Hopkins University
Museum of New Mexico
Historical Society of South Carolina
Historical Society of Pennsylvania
Huntington Library Chicago
Jackson Hole Historical Society and Museum
The Library Company of Philadelphia
Library of Congress, Rare Book and Special Collections Division
Plymouth Plantation Foodways Department

Maryland Historical Society
McCracken Research Library/Buffalo Bill Historical Center
National Park Service Fort Vancouver National Historic Site
The Oregon Historical Society
San Francisco Archives
Smithsonian Institution National Anthropological Archives, Bureau of American Ethnology Collection
Stuhr Museum of the Prairie Pioneer
Tennessee State Library and Archives
University of British Columbia Library, Special Collections and University Archives Division
Washington, Special Collections and Preservation Division, Washington State Archives
Wilderness Archives, Special Collections, University of Idaho

PHOTO CREDITS

Washington State Archives, pages ii (negative #2944), 42, 44, 54, 67, 90 (negative #190), 25, 61, 64, 69, 71, 91, 106, 111; The Historical Society of Pennsylvania, pages 13, 265 (negative #Vt 2831); Maryland Historical Society, pages 1, 19, 24, 25, 36, 37, 80, 117, 133, 162, 199; Chicago Historical Society, pages 46, 66 (negative #DN-2433), 112, 115; Smithsonian Institution National Anthropological Archives, Bureau of Ethnology Collection, pages 47 (negative #486), 123 (negative #90-17235), 7 (negative #2978-B); Stuhr Museum of the Praime Pioneer, page 53 (negative #P84-13); Oregon Historical Society, pages 109 (negative #OrHi 8233), 119 (negative #CrHi 26387), 163 (negative #OrHi 37712), 154 (negative #OrHi 4371); Museum of New Mexico, page 125 (negative #152668); Museum of International Folk Art—Museum of New Mexico, page 121; Florida Cattlemen's Association, page 160; Dr. James D. Keyser, pages vi, vii, 31, 197, 203 (and rock art throughout); Collection of the Jackson Hole Historical Society and Museum, pages 136 (negative #3235), 142 (negative #BC 15390), 156 (58.3060), 144 (negative #93.4975.63), 170 (B.C.13.285), 193 (negative #BC.9.175); University of California Bancroft Library, page 140 (X170-I5PQ, No. 6); The Charleston Museum, page 143 (negative #MK 14645A); Jacques Le Moyne, Coastal Discovery Museum, Hilton Head Island, SC, pages 158, 225 (negative #Fla. Coll. 975.901); Library of Congress, page 213 (LC-V5Z62-34794); Special Collections and University Archives Division, University of British Columbia Library, page 241; Jurgielewicz Duck Farms, Long Island, NY, page 205; Gary and Lee Hibler, page 251; The George Peabody Library of the Johns Hopkins University, page 36; *Animal Art in the Public Domain*, pages 95, 129, 149, 173

INDEX

African pheasant. *See* guinea hen
Aioli, Sunshine, for Fried Curried
  Frog's Legs, 176
alligator, 165–66, 298
    Baked Gator Fritters, 174
    Gator Tail with Swamp
      Sauce, 175
antelope, 110
    American (pronghorn), 94,
      108–10, 298
apple(s)
    Brandied, Roast Mallard
      Ducks with, 44
    with Cider-Basted Wild
      Turkey, 87
    Pâté with Shallots and, 208
    Potato, Celeriac, and Apple
      Puree, 273
    Red Cabbage with Fuji
      Apples and Balsamic
      Vinegar, 271
    and Red Currant Sauce, Lady
      Fiona's, 255
    Smoked Duck Salad with
      Jonagold Apples and
      Toasted Hazelnuts, 238
    Spicy Crab Apples in
      Cabernet Sauvignon, 256
armadillo, 166, 298
artichokes
    Chukar Partridge with
      Artichoke Hearts and
      Mushrooms, 63
    Rabbit and Artichoke Pie,
      218
    Roast Squab with Olives
      and, 70

arugula
    Sweet Potato, Arugula, and
      Bacon Hash, 275
    Venison Stew with Radiatore
      and, 149
Asian Pear and Avocado Salad,
  285
asparagus
    Curried Rabbit Soup with,
      190
    Magret with Shiitake
      Mushrooms and, 52
Avocado and Asian Pear Salad,
  285

bacon, 16
    Roast Doves Wrapped in
      Peppered Bacon, 41
    Sautéed Cabbage with
      Apple-Smoked Bacon and
      Wild Rice, 270
    Sweet Potato, Arugula, and
      Bacon Hash, 275
barding, 16
beans, 9
    Baked Wild Goose with
      Gingered Beans, 55
    black, in Taos Rabbit, 184
    Quail with White and Green
      Beans, 81
    Stir-Fried Venison with
      Penne and Beans, 145
bear, 95–96, 298
beaver, 166–67, 298
beef, nutritional data, 298
beefalo, 96, 298. *See also buffalo
  recipes*

berries, 10, 253. *See also specific
  berries*
Bhutanese Red Rice, 279
    Roast Squab in, 72
bighorn sheep, 110–11
birds, 14–17, 297. *See also specific
  birds*
bison. *See* buffalo
blackberries
    in sauce, 254
    in Soused Grouse, 60
black chicken, 17–18
    Stock, 264
black ducks, 18
blueberries
    in sauce, 254
    Smoked Poussin, Papaya,
      and Blueberry Salad,
      239
blue cheese
    Grilled Squab with
      Orecchiette and
      Gorgonzola, 74
    in Loin of Venison Danish-
      Style, 136
boar. *See* wild boar
bobwhite quail, 32. *See also* quail
Bourbon Sauce, Buffalo Rocky
  Mountain Oysters with, 124
brine. *See* wet cure
buffalo, 96–98, 298
    in Anaconda Game Pasties,
      220
    and Beer Pot Roast, 120
    Burgers, with Sautéed
      Onions and Chipotle
      Mayonnaise, 122

Durham Ranch Buffalo
  Tenderloin, 118
Ribeye Burrito, Grilled, 116
Ribs, Grilled Garlic-Herb,
  112
Rocky Mountain Oysters
  with Bourbon Sauce, 124
Steaks, Grilled, 113
T-Bone Steak Smothered
  with Mushrooms and
  Onions, 114
bull fries, 124
burgers. See also sausage
  Buffalo Burgers with
    Sautéed Onions and
    Chipotle Mayonnaise,
    122
  Venison Flips, 157
Burrito, Grilled Buffalo Ribeye,
  116
butter, 9
Butternut Squash Risotto, 277

cabbage
  in Haunch Pie, 215
  Pheasant and Cabbage Pie,
    219
  Red, with Fuji Apples and
    Balsamic Vinegar, 271
  Sautéed, with Apple-
    Smoked Bacon and Wild
    Rice, 270
  Wildwood Fennel Slaw, 287
canvasback duck, 15, 18
caribou, 94, 100–101, 298
Carolina ducks (wood ducks), 18
casings for sausages, 195
Celeriac, Potato, and Apple
  Puree, 273
Cervena venison, 103, 105
chanterelles, 10–11
  in Braised Rabbit with
    Madeira, 188
  Pheasant with Herb
    Dumplings and, 68
charcuterie. See also sausage
  Game Terrine with Roasted
    Shallot Mustard, 210
  Pâté with Apples and
    Shallots, 208
  Potted Game in a Bread
    Bowl, 209

cherries
  Bing Cherry Marmalade,
    259; Smoked Magret
    with, 236
  Braised Rabbit with Bing
    Cherries and Brandy, 179
chicken. See also black chicken;
  poussin
  nutritional data, 297
  pearl. See guinea hen
  Stock, 264
chiles, 9–10. See also chipotle
  chiles
  Chile Sausage, Three-Wave
    Venison, 200
  Chimayo Chile Honey,
    Baked Pears with, 284
Chili
  Oven-Baked Venison, 155
  Venison, with Goat Cheese,
    154
chipotle chiles
  Chipotle Mayonnaise, 260;
    Buffalo Burgers with
    Sautéed Onions and, 122
  Cranberry-Chipotle Sauce,
    Loin of Venison with, 132
chukar partridge, 23. See also
  partridge
  with Artichoke Hearts and
    Mushrooms, 63
  Soused (substitute), 60
  as substitute in Taos Rabbit,
    184
Citrus Salad, Chopped, 286
cold smoking, 228
Col-Vert ducks, 22
Compote, Warm Cranberry-
  Orange, 262
coot, 15
Coriander-Fennel Rub, 247
Crab Apples, Spicy, in Cabernet
  Sauvignon, 256
cranberries
  Cranberry-Chipotle Sauce,
    Loin of Venison with, 132
  in sauce, 254
  Spicy Cranberry-Pear Relish,
    257
  Warm Cranberry-Orange
    Compote, 262
  Wild Rice, Cranberry, and
    Pecan Dressing, 280

curing meat before smoking,
  226–27, 229
Custards, Garlic, on Beds of
  Greens, 282

deer, 94, 101–4, 298. See also
  venison
demi-glace, 253
dove, 18, 297
  Doves Baked in a
    Horseradish Crust, 40
  Roast Doves Wrapped in
    Peppered Bacon, 41
dressings, 266–67
  Lingonberry Stuffing,
    Woodcock with, 89
  Sautéed Cabbage with
    Apple-Smoked Bacon and
    Wild Rice, 270
  Wild Rice, Cranberry, and
    Pecan Dressing, 280
dried fruits, 10
dried mushrooms, 11
dry cure, 226–27, 229
duck, 15, 17, 18–22, 51, 297
  breast, cooking methods, 20,
    22
  breast, in Game Terrine with
    Roasted Shallot Mustard,
    210
  breast, in Potted Game in a
    Bread Bowl, 209
  breast of wild duck, with
    mushrooms (substitute),
    75
  Chinese Smoked Wild Duck,
    230
  Duck Prosciutto with
    Caramelized Pears, 207
  Duck Sausage Raviolis with
    Golden Ginger Plum
    Sauce, 206
  Duck Sausage with Cilantro,
    Ginger, and Coconut
    Milk, 204
  grilled, 22
  Grilled Wild Duck, Ducky's,
    43
  magret, to sauté, 22
  Magret with Asparagus and
    Shiitake Mushrooms, 52
  Muscovy Duck with Sweet
    and Sour Sauce, 50

Pappardelle with Smoked
    Duck and Wild
    Mushrooms, 235
Roast Mallard Ducks with
    Brandied Apples, 44
Roast Muscovy Duck with
    Persimmons and Figs, 48
Roast Pekin Duckling with
    Ducky's Port Sauce, 47
Roast Wild Duck I, 42
Slow-Roasted Duckling with
    Red Currant Sauce, 45
Smoked Duck and Toasted
    Hazelnut Salad, 237
Smoked Duck Hash, 234
Smoked Duck Salad with
    Jonagold Apples and
    Toasted Hazelnuts, 238
smoked, in salad with
    papaya and blueberries
    (substitute), 239
Smoked Magret with Bing
    Cherry Marmalade, 236
Dumplings, Herb, Pheasant with
    Chanterelles and, 68

E. coli, 231
elk, 94, 103, 104–5, 298
    Branding Party Elk Pot, 159
emu, 17, 34, 297
    Grilled Medallions
        (substitute), 86
equipment
    for making sausage, 194,
        195
    for smoking meat, 227–28
Estofado, 152
exotic game. See small and exotic
    game; specific meats

faraona. See guinea hen
fennel
    Coriander-Fennel Rub, 247
    Wildwood Fennel Slaw, 287
Figs, Roast Muscovy Duck with
    Persimmons and, 48
Flumagina, Rabbit Stew with, 180
foie gras, 21
fowl. See birds; specific type of fowl
Fritters, Baked Gator, 174
frog, 167–68, 298
    Fried Curried Frog's Legs,
        176

fruit. See also specific fruits
    about, 10; with duck, 48; in
        sauces, 253
    Grilled Fruit, 283; with chile
        honey, 284

gadwalls, 18
game birds, 14–17, 297. See also
    specific birds
    Braised (Master Recipe), 39
Garlic Custard on a Bed of
    Greens, 282
Garlic-Herb Buffalo Ribs, Grilled,
    112
gator. See alligator
ginger, Saffron-Ginger Rub, 249
goat, 106–7, 298
    Wild Goat Wellington, 161
Goat Cheese, Venison Chili with,
    154
goose, 22–23, 297
    Baked Wild Goose with
        Gingered Beans, 55
    Hunting-Camp Wild Goose
        Breast, 57
    livers, in Pâté with Apples
        and Shallots, 208
    Roast Farm-Raised Goose,
        58
    Roast Wild Goose, 53
    smoked, in hash
        (substitute), 234
    smoked, Pappardelle with
        Wild Mushrooms and
        (substitute), 235
Gorgonzola, Grilled Squab with
    Orecchiette and, 74
grouse, 16, 23–26, 297
    Braised (Master Recipe), 39
    Breast of, with Mushrooms
        (substitute), 75
    Soused Grouse, 60
    as substitute in Taos Rabbit,
        184
guinea fowl. See guinea hen
guinea hen, 17, 26–27, 297
    Braised (Master Recipe), 39
    with Hazelnuts and
        Mustard, 62

hanging
    game birds, 15–16
    large game, 92

hare, 164–65, 169–70, 298
    Braised (Master Recipe),
        39
hash
    Smoked Duck, 234
    Sweet Potato, Arugula, and
        Bacon, 275
Haunch Pie, 215
hazelnuts
    Guinea Hen with Mustard
        and, 62
    Smoked Duck and Toasted
        Hazelnut Salad, 237
    Smoked Duck Salad with
        Jonagold Apples and
        Toasted Hazelnuts, 238
herb(s), 10
    Dumplings, Pheasant with
        Chanterelles and, 68
    Sauce, 258
    Savory Herb and Peppercorn
        Rub, 249
honey, Baked Pears with Chimayo
    Chile Honey, 284
horseradish
    Doves Baked in a
        Horseradish Crust, 40
    Horseradish-Mustard Sauce,
        Pan-Fried Venison Steak
        with, 144
hot smoking, 228
huckleberries
    Loin of Venison with, 141
    in Loin of Venison with
        Mustard-Pepper
        Marinade, 134
    in sauce, 254

ingredients, 8–12

Jam, Sweet Onion, 269
javelina, 108
Jerky, Venison, 231
Juniper-Pepper Rub, 248
    Grilled Wild Boar Chops
        with, 126

kangaroo, 168, 298

large game, 92–94, 298. See also
    specific meats
lentils, 10
    to prepare, 67

Sautéed Pheasant with
Mushrooms and, 66
leprosy, 166
Lingonberry Stuffing, Woodcock
with, 89

magret, 21–22
with Asparagus and Shiitake
Mushrooms, 52
to sauté, 22
in Smoked Duck Salad with
Jonagold Apples and
Toasted Hazelnuts, 238
Smoked, with Bing Cherry
Marmalade, 236
mail-order sources, 294–96
mallards, 15, 18, 22
Chinese Smoked Wild Duck,
230
Roast Mallard Ducks with
Brandied Apples, 44
Roast Wild Duck I, 42
mangoes, grilled, 283
marinades, 242–43. See also rubs
Mustard-Pepper, Loin of
Venison with, 134
Orange, Soy, and Honey, 244
Red Wine, 245
Sherry Vinegar-Herb, 245
White Wine, 246
Marmalade, Bing Cherry, 259;
Smoked Magret with, 236
marsh rabbit. See muskrat
Mayonnaise, Chipotle, 260
Buffalo Burgers with
Sautéed Onions and, 122
mergansers, 15
Mincemeat, 223
Mixed Game Grill with Double
Venison Chop, Quail, and
Rabbit Sausage, 147
moose, wild, 94, 105, 298
moulard duck, 21, 22
mountain goat, wild, 106
muscovy duck, 21, 22
Roast, with Persimmons and
Figs, 48
in Smoked Duck Salad with
Jonagold Apples and
Toasted Hazelnuts, 238
with Sweet and Sour Sauce,
50
mushrooms, 10–11. See also

chanterelles; porcini
mushrooms; shiitake
mushrooms
Breast of Wood Pigeon with,
75
Buffalo T-Bone Steak
Smothered with Onions
and, 114
Chukar Partridge with
Artichoke Hearts and, 63
Pappardelle with Smoked
Duck and Wild
Mushrooms, 235
Sautéed Pheasant with
Lentils and, 66
Venison-Mushroom
Turnovers, 222
Venison Osso Buco with
Rigatoni and, 130
Wild Mushroom Gratin, 268
musk-ox, wild, 107
muskrat, 168–69, 298
mustard
Guinea Hen with Hazelnuts
and, 62
Horseradish-Mustard Sauce,
Pan-Fried Venison Steak
with, 144
Mustard-Pepper Marinade,
Loin of Venison with, 134
Rabbit Tenderloin with
Grainy Mustard, 182
Roasted Shallot Mustard
Sauce, 212 Game Terrine
with, 210

nectarines
grilled, 283
Grilled Quail Salad with
Plums and, 79
New Zealand venison and elk,
102, 103, 105
noodles. See pasta
nutritional data, 297–98
nuts. See also hazelnuts; pecans
to roast, 11

Olives, Roast Squab with
Artichokes and, 70
onions
Buffalo Burgers with
Sautéed Onions and
Chipotle Mayonnaise, 122

Buffalo T-Bone Steak
Smothered with
Mushrooms and Onions,
114
Flumagina, Rabbit Stew
with, 180
Sweet Onion Jam, 269
opossum, 169, 298
orange
in Chopped Citrus Salad,
286
Orange-and-Allspice–Cured
Smoked Rabbit, 233
Orange, Soy, and Honey
Marinade, 244
Warm Cranberry-Orange
Compote, 262
Orecchiette, Grilled Squab with
Gorgonzola and, 74
Orzo Baked with Summer
Vegetables, 278
Osso Buco, Venison, with
Mushrooms and Rigatoni, 130
ostrich, 17, 33–34, 297
Medallions, Grilled, 86
Satay, 85

pan sauces, to make, 252
papaya, Smoked Poussin, Papaya,
and Blueberry Salad, 239
Pappardelle with Smoked Duck
and Wild Mushrooms, 235
paprika, 11–12
partridge, 16, 28. See also
bobwhite quail; ruffed grouse
Braised (Master Recipe), 39
Breast of, with Mushrooms
(substitute), 75
Chukar, with Artichoke
Hearts and Mushrooms,
63
Soused (substitute), 60
as substitute in Taos Rabbit,
184
pasta
Duck Sausage Raviolis with
Golden Ginger Plum
Sauce, 206
Grilled Squab with
Gorgonzola and
Orecchiette, 74
Orzo Baked with Summer
Vegetables, 278

Pappardelle with Smoked Duck and Wild Mushrooms, 235
Stir-Fried Venison with Penne and Beans, 145
Venison Osso Buco with Mushrooms and Rigatoni, 130
Venison Stew with Radiatore and Arugula, 149
Pasties, Anaconda Game, 220
Pastry, Game Pie, 217
Pâté with Apples and Shallots, 208
Peach Chutney Glaze, Grilled Poussin with, 77
Peanut Dipping Sauce, for Ostrich Satay, 85
pearl chicken. See guinea hen
pears. See also Asian pears
  Baked, with Chimayo Chile Honey, 284
  Duck Prosciutto with Caramelized Pears, 207
  Spicy Cranberry-Pear Relish, 257
pecans, Wild Rice, Cranberry, and Pecan Dressing, 280
peccary, wild, 108
Pekin duckling, 20–21, 22
  Roast, with Ducky's Port Sauce, 47
Penne, Stir-Fried Venison with Beans and, 145
pepper, black, 11
  Juniper-Pepper Rub, 248
  Mustard-Pepper Marinade, Loin of Venison with, 134
  Venison Steak with Cracked Pepper and Brandy, 143
peppercorns
  Savory Herb and Peppercorn Rub, 249
  Szechuan and Green Peppercorn Rub, 248
Persimmons, Roast Muscovy Duck with Figs and, 48
pheasant, 16, 17, 29–30, 297
  African. See guinea hen
  and Artichoke Pie (substitute), 218
  Braised (Master Recipe), 39
  and Cabbage Pie, 219

with Chanterelles and Herb Dumplings, 68
to cook older birds, 29
Poached, 65
Sausage, with Cilantro, Ginger, and Coconut Milk (substitute), 204
Sautéed, with Mushrooms and Lentils, 66
smoked, in hash (substitute), 234
smoked, in salad with apples and hazelnuts (substitute), 238
stock, 65
Vietnamese Smoked Pheasant Soup, 240
pies and turnovers, 213–24
  Anaconda Game Pasties, 220
  Game Pie Pastry, 217
  Haunch Pie, 215
  Homemade Mincemeat Pie, 223
  Pheasant and Cabbage Pie, 219
  Rabbit and Artichoke Pie, 218
  Venison-Mushroom Turnovers, 222
pigeon, 30–31, 297. See also dove; squab; wood pigeon
pig, wild. See wild boar
pinnated grouse (prairie chicken), 23, 24, 25. See also grouse
pintade. See guinea hen
pintail, 18
pintelle. See guinea hen
plucking game birds, 16
plums
  grilled, 283
  Grilled Quail Salad with Nectarines and, 79
Polenta, 281
  Quail Roasted in, 84
porcini mushrooms, 10–11
  Ground Porcini Rub, 246
  Stuffed Baked Potatoes with, 274
  Venison Sausage with Wild Rice and, 198
Port Sauce, Ducky's, 261
  grilled wild duck with, 43

Roast Pekin Duckling with, 47
potatoes
  Buttermilk Mashed Potatoes with Garlic Chives, 272
  New Potatoes with Capers and Garlic, 276
  Potato, Celeriac, and Apple Puree, 273
  Quail in Potato Nests with Tomato-Saffron Sauce, 82
  Stuffed Baked Potatoes with Porcini Mushrooms, 274
  Wartime Venison-Potato Sausage, 202
Pot Roast, Buffalo and Beer, 120
Potted Game in a Bread Bowl, 209
poussin, 31, 297
  Grilled, with Peach Chutney Glaze, 77
  smoked, in salad with apples and hazelnuts (substitute), 238
  Smoked Poussin, Papaya, and Blueberry Salad, 239
  with Spinach, 78
  with White and Green Beans (substitute), 81
prairie chicken, 23, 24, 25. See also grouse
pronghorn, 94, 108–10, 298
prosciutto
  Duck, with Caramelized Pears, 207
  Rabbit Loins Stuffed with Prunes and, 178
prunes
  Braised Rabbit with Pinot Noir and, 186
  Rabbit Loins Stuffed with Prosciutto and, 178
ptarmigan, 23, 26. See also grouse

quail, 17, 32–33, 297
  Breast of, with Mushrooms (substitute), 75
  Grilled Quail Salad with Nectarines and Plums, 79
  in Mixed Game Grill, 147
  in Potato Nests with Tomato-Saffron Sauce, 82
  Roasted in Polenta, 84

Roast, Wrapped in Peppered
Bacon (substitute), 41
with White and Green
Beans, 81

rabbit, 164–65, 169–71, 298
and Artichoke Pie, 218
Braised (Master Recipe), 39
Braised, with Bing Cherries
and Brandy, 179
Braised, with Madeira, 188
Braised, with Prunes and
Pinot Noir, 186
Cacciatore, 189
Curried Rabbit Soup with
Asparagus, 190
in Game Terrine with
Roasted Shallot Mustard,
210
livers, in Pâté with Apples
and Shallots, 208
Loins, Stuffed with
Prosciutto and Prunes,
178
Orange-and-Allspice–Cured
Smoked Rabbit, 233
Sausage, in Mixed Game
Grill, 147
Stew, with Flumagina, 180
Taos Rabbit, 184
Tenderloin, with Grainy
Mustard, 182
raccoon, 171, 298
ratites, 33–35. See also emu;
ostrich
rattlesnake, 171–72
Raviolis, Duck Sausage, with
Golden Ginger Plum Sauce,
206
Red Cabbage with Fuji Apples
and Balsamic Vinegar, 271
red currants
Apple and Red Currant
Sauce, Lady Fiona's, 255
Red Currant Sauce, 254;
Slow-Roasted Duckling
with, 45
Red Wine Marinade, 245
relishes
Spicy Crab Apples in
Cabernet Sauvignon, 256
Spicy Cranberry-Pear Relish,
257

Warm Cranberry-Orange
Compote, 262
rhea, 34
rice. See also wild rice
Bhutanese Red Rice, 279;
Roast Squab in, 72
Risotto, Butternut Squash, 277
Rocky Mountain Oysters, Buffalo,
with Bourbon Sauce, 124
Root Vegetables, Pureed, Loin of
Venison or Boar with, 139
rubs, 243
Coriander-Fennel, 247
Ground Porcini, 246
Juniper-Pepper, 248
Saffron-Ginger, 249
Savory Herb and
Peppercorn, 249
Spicy Texas, 247
Szechuan and Green
Peppercorn, 248
ruffed grouse, 23, 24. See also
grouse

saffron
Saffron-Ginger Rub, 249
Tomato-Saffron Sauce, Quail
in Potato Nests with, 82
sage hen (sage grouse), 23, 25.
See also grouse
salad(s)
Avocado and Asian Pear, 285
Chopped Citrus, 286
Grilled Quail, with
Nectarines and Plums, 79
Smoked Duck and Toasted
Hazelnut, 237
Smoked Duck, with
Jonagold Apples and
Toasted Hazelnuts, 238
Smoked Magret with Bing
Cherry Marmalade, 236
Smoked Poussin, Papaya,
and Blueberry, 239
Wildwood Fennel Slaw, 287
Salsa, Tomatillo, 117
salt, 11
and curing meat, 226–27
Satay, Ostrich, 85
sauce(s), 252–53. See also relishes
Apple and Red Currant,
Lady Fiona's, 255
Bing Cherry Marmalade,

259; Smoked Magret
with, 236
Bourbon, Buffalo Rocky
Mountain Oysters with,
124
Chipotle Mayonnaise, 260;
Buffalo Burgers with
Sautéed Onions and, 122
Cranberry-Chipotle, Loin of
Venison with, 132
Flumagina, Rabbit Stew
with, 180
Golden Ginger Plum, Duck
Sausage Raviolis with,
206
Herb, 258
Peanut Dipping Sauce, for
Ostrich Satay, 85
Port, Ducky's, 261; grilled
wild duck with, 43; Roast
Pekin Duckling with, 47
Red Currant, 254; Slow-
Roasted Duckling with,
45
Roasted Shallot Mustard,
212; Game Terrine with,
210
Sunshine Aioli, for Fried
Curried Frog's Legs, 176
Swamp Sauce, Gator Tail
with, 175
Sweet and Sour, Muscovy
Duck with, 50
Tomato-Saffron, Quail in
Potato Nests with, 82
sausage, 194–95
Duck, with Cilantro, Ginger,
and Coconut Milk, 204; in
Raviolis with Golden
Ginger Plum Sauce, 206
German-Style Venison, 196
Rabbit, in Mixed Game Grill,
147
Three-Wave Venison Chile,
200
Venison, with Wild Rice and
Porcini Mushrooms, 198
Wartime Venison-Potato,
202
scaup, 18
Scottish game, 17, 26, 30, 101–2,
169
shallots, Roasted Shallot

Mustard, 212; Game Terrine with, 210
sharp-tailed grouse, 24, 25, 60. *See also* grouse
sheep, wild, 110–11
Sherry Vinegar-Herb Marinade, 245
shiitake mushrooms, 10–11
    in Anaconda Game Pasties, 220
    Buffalo T-Bone Steak Smothered with Mushrooms and Onions, 114
    Magret with Asparagus and, 52
    in Pappardelle with Smoked Duck and Wild Mushrooms, 235
shovelers, 18
side dishes, 266–67. *See also* relishes; salads
    Baked Pears with Chimayo Chile Honey, 284
    Bhutanese Red Rice, 279
    Buttermilk Mashed Potatoes with Garlic Chives, 272
    Butternut Squash Risotto, 277
    Garlic Custards on Beds of Greens, 282
    Grilled Fruit, 283; with chile honey, 284
    New Potatoes with Capers and Garlic, 276
    Orzo Baked with Summer Vegetables, 278
    Polenta, 281
    Potato, Celeriac, and Apple Puree, 273
    Red Cabbage with Fuji Apples and Balsamic Vinegar, 271
    Sautéed Cabbage with Apple-Smoked Bacon and Wild Rice, 270
    Stuffed Baked Potatoes with Porcini Mushrooms, 274
    Sweet Onion Jam, 269
    Sweet Potato, Arugula, and Bacon Hash, 275
    Wild Mushroom Gratin, 268

Wild Rice, Cranberry, and Pecan Dressing, 280
skinning game birds, 16
small and exotic game, 164–65, 298. *See also specific meats*
smoked game, 225–40
    about smoking methods, 226–29
    Chinese Smoked Wild Duck, 230
    Orange-and-Allspice–Cured Smoked Rabbit, 233
    Pappardelle with Smoked Duck and Wild Mushrooms, 235
    in Potted Game in a Bread Bowl, 209
    Smoked Duck and Toasted Hazelnut Salad, 237
    Smoked Duck Hash, 234
    Smoked Duck Salad with Jonagold Apples and Toasted Hazelnuts, 238
    Smoked Magret with Bing Cherry Marmalade, 236
    Smoked Poussin, Papaya, and Blueberry Salad, 239
    Venison Jerky, 231
    Vietnamese Smoked Pheasant Soup, 240
smoking game, equipment and techniques for, 226–29
snipe, wild, 35
soup
    Curried Rabbit, with Asparagus, 190
    Thai Green Curry Turtle, 192
    Vietnamese Smoked Pheasant, 240
spice rubs. *See* rubs
spices, 11–12
spinach
    in Branding Party Elk Pot, 159
    doves with polenta and, 40
    Poussin with, 78
    salad, with grilled quail, nectarines and plums, 79
squab, 17, 18, 30–31. *See also* dove; pigeon
    Breast of, with Mushrooms (substitute), 75

Grilled, Chinese-Style, 73
Grilled, with Gorgonzola and Orecchiette, 74
Roast, in Bhutanese Red Rice, 72
Roast, with Artichokes and Olives, 70
squash, Butternut Squash Risotto, 277
squirrel, 172, 298
steaks
    Buffalo, Grilled, 113
    Buffalo T-Bone, Smothered with Mushrooms and Onions, 114
    to sauté, 93
    Venison, Pan-Fried, with Horseradish-Mustard Sauce, 144
    Venison, with Cracked Pepper and Brandy, 143
stew(s)
    Branding Party Elk Pot, 159
    Estofado, 152
    Rabbit, with Flumagina, 180
    Venison, with Radiatore and Arugula, 149
    Wild Boar, 128
stock, 12
    Black Chicken, 264
    Chicken, 264
    Game (venison), 263
    Pheasant, 65
stuffing(s), 266–67
    Lingonberry, Woodcock with, 89
    Sautéed Cabbage with Apple-Smoked Bacon and Wild Rice, 270
    Wild Rice, Cranberry, and Pecan Dressing, 280
Sunshine Aioli, for Fried Curried Frog's Legs, 176
Swamp Sauce, Gator Tail with, 175
Sweet and Sour Sauce, Muscovy Duck with, 50
Sweet Potato, Arugula, and Bacon Hash, 275
Szechuan and Green Peppercorn Rub, 248

Taos Rabbit, 184

teal, 18
Terrine, Game, with Roasted
    Shallot Mustard, 210
Thai Green Curry Turtle Soup,
    192
Tomatillo Salsa, 117
Tomato-Saffron Sauce, Quail in
    Potato Nests with, 82
trichinosis, 94
tularemia, 170
turkey, 35–37, 297
    Cider-Basted Wild Turkey,
    87
    wild, to roast, 36
Turnovers, Venison-Mushroom,
    222
turtle, 172–73, 298
    Thai Green Curry Turtle
    Soup, 192

vegetables. *See also specific*
    vegetables
    Loin of Venison or Boar with
    Pureed Root Vegetables,
    139
    Orzo Baked with Summer
    Vegetables, 278
venison, 101–4, 298. *See also* deer
    in Anaconda Game Pasties,
    220
    Branding Party Elk Pot, 159
    Chili, Oven-Baked, 155
    Chili, with Goat Cheese, 154
    Chop, in Mixed Game Grill,
    147
    Chops, Grilled, 146
    Estofado, 152
    Flips, 157
    Game Stock, 263
    Haunch Pie, 215
    Jerky, 231

Kebabs, Grilled, 151
Loin of, Danish-Style, 136
Loin of, Grilled, in Pancetta,
    138
Loin of, with Cranberry-
    Chipotle Sauce, 132
Loin of, with Huckleberries,
    141
Loin of, with Mustard-
    Pepper Marinade, 134
Loin of, with Pureed Root
    Vegetables, 139
in Mincemeat, 225
Osso Buco with Mushrooms
    and Rigatoni, 130
to roast, 103–4
sausage, about, 195; in
    Venison-Mushroom
    Turnovers, 222
Sausage, German-Style, 196
Sausage, Three-Wave Chile,
    200
Sausage, Wartime Venison-
    Potato, 202
Sausage, with Wild Rice and
    Porcini Mushrooms, 198
steak, to cook, 103
Steak, Pan-Fried, with
    Horseradish-Mustard
    Sauce, 144
Steak, with Cracked Pepper
    and Brandy, 143
Stew, with Raclatore and
    Arugula, 149
Stir-Fried, with Penne and
    Beans, 145
Venison-Mushroom
    Turnovers, 222
Wellington (substitute), 161
Vietnamese Smoked Pheasant
    Soup, 240

wet cure, 227, 229
white Pekin ducks, 20–21, 22
White Wine Marinade, 246
widgeon, 15, 18
wild boar, 98–100, 298
    Chops, Grilled, with
    Juniper-Pepper Rub, 126
    Loin of, with Pureed Root
    Vegetables (substitute),
    139
    Roast Leg of, 127
    Stew, 128
wildlife organizations, 292–93
wild mushrooms, 10–11. *See also*
    chanterelles; porcini
    mushrooms; shiitake
    mushrooms
    Pappardelle with Smoked
    Duck and, 235
    Wild Mushroom Gratin, 268
wild rice
    Sautéed Cabbage with
    Apple-Smoked Bacon and,
    270
    Venison Sausage with
    Porcini Mushrooms and,
    198
    Wild Rice, Cranberry, and
    Pecan Dressing, 280
wines to accompany game, 12
woodcock, 37
    with Lingonberry Stuffing,
    89
wood ducks (Carolina ducks), 18
wood for smoking game, 228
wood pigeon, 31
    Breast of, with Mushrooms,
    75

HUNTING AND FARMING

". . . . . and all of a sudden I thought about how maybe planting and working and then harvesting oats and cotton and beans and hay wasn't jest something me and Mister Ernest done three hundred and fifty-one days to fill in the time until we could come back hunting again, but it was something we had to do, and do honest and good during the three hundred and fifty-one days, to have the right to come back into the big woods and hunt for the other fourteen; and the fourteen days that old buck run in front of dogs wasn't jest something to fill his time until the three hundred and fifty-one when he didn't have to, but the running and the risking in front of guns and dogs was something he had to do for fourteen days to have the right not to be bothered for the other three hundred and fifty-one. And so the hunting and the farming wasn't two different things atall—they was jest the other side of each other."

Big Woods by William Faulkner